Doing Foreign Language

Doing Foreign Language

Bringing Concordia Language Villages into Language Classrooms

Heidi E. Hamilton

Georgetown University

Cori Crane

University of Illinois at Urbana–Champaign

Abigail Bartoshesky

Southern Methodist University

PEARSON

Merrill
Prentice Hall

Upper Saddle River, New Jersey
Columbus, Ohio

Library of Congress Cataloging in Publication Data

Hamilton, Heidi Ehernberger.
    Doing foreign language : bringing Concordia Language Villages into language
classrooms / Heidi E. Hamilton, Cori Crane, Abigail Bartoshesky.
       p. cm.
    Includes bibliographical references and index.
    ISBN 0-13-113968-1
    1. Language and languages—Study and teaching—United States. 2. Language
camps—United States. 3. Concordia Language Villages (Moorhead, Minn.) I. Crane, Cori.
II. Bartoshesky, Abigail. III. Title.

P57.U7H36 2005
18'.0071'273—dc24   2004048652

Vice President and Executive Publisher: Jeffery W. Johnston
Executive Editor: Debra A. Stollenwerk
Editorial Assistant: Mary Morrill
Production Editor: Kris Roach
Production Coordination: WordCrafters Editorial Services, Inc.
Design Coordinator: Diane C. Lorenzo
Cover Designer: Jeff Vanik
Cover image: John Borge
Production Manager: Pamela D. Bennett
Director of Marketing: Ann Castel Davis
Marketing Manager: Darcy Betts Prybella
Marketing Coordinator: Tyra Poole

This book was set in Palatino by Carlisle Communications, Ltd. It was printed and bound by Banta Book Group. The cover was printed by
Phoenix Color Corp.

Photo Credits: All photos by John Borge.

Pearson Prentice Hall™ is a trademark of Pearson Education, Inc.
Pearson® is a registered trademark of Pearson plc
Prentice Hall® is a registered trademark of Pearson Education, Inc.
Merrill® is a registered trademark of Pearson Education, Inc.

Pearson Education Ltd.   Pearson Education Australia Pty. Limited
Pearson Education Singapore Pte. Ltd.   Pearson Education North Asia Ltd.
Pearson Education Canada, Ltd.   Pearson Educación de Mexico, S.A. de C.V.
Pearson Education—Japan   Pearson Education Malaysia Pte. Ltd.

10 9 8 7 6 5 4 3 2 1
ISBN: 0-13-113968-1

Foreword

The National Capital Language Resource Center (NCLRC) is funded by the United States Department of Education's Title VI with the mission of "improving the teaching and learning of foreign languages in the United States." The NCLRC believes that our support for the development of this book can, indeed, help accomplish this mission.

Anyone who has had the good fortune to visit a Concordia Language Village has surely fallen under the spell of its magical atmosphere of the language and culture of . . . the French-speaking world . . . the German-speaking world . . . the Spanish- or Japanese- or Russian- or Korean- or Finnish-speaking world! Or they may have been enticed by the wide variety of experiences available in the Norwegian, Swedish, Danish, Chinese, or Italian Villages. Even non-native English speakers can immerse themselves in the American way of life in the English as a Second Language Village. Each of the Villages transports its temporary inhabitants into an authentic linguistic and cultural experience.

As a visitor to Concordia Language Villages, I was entranced and I kept asking myself, "How can this magical experience be bottled for the foreign language classroom?" In this book, the authors have accomplished just that: they have bottled the magic for foreign language teachers to use and adapt in their own classrooms.

The activities suggested in this book are Standards-based and learner-centered. Each activity is correlated with two or more of the ACTFL Standards, covering all of the 5 Cs (Communication, Cultures, Connections, Comparisons, and Communities). The interests and needs of students are the focus of each activity, and students are encouraged to reflect on their own learning. This experiential and personal approach to teaching and learning another language is embodied in its title: *Doing Foreign Language*. We all know that engaging in meaningful communicative activities is the best possible way to develop proficiency in a new language. As a foreign language teacher, you will find in this book a treasure trove of ideas that will bring the magic of Concordia Language Villages into your classroom.

Anna Uhl Chamot, Ph.D.
Co-Director
National Capital Language Resource Center
Washington, DC
and
Professor of Secondary Education
ESL and Foreign Language Education
Graduate School of Education and Human Development
The George Washington University

Preface

INTRODUCTION

Doing Foreign Language: Bringing Concordia Language Villages into Language Classrooms introduces readers to the active and engaging language learning philosophy and practices of Concordia Language Villages, the oldest and most extensive live-in summer language camp program for elementary and secondary students in the United States. (Readers unfamiliar with Concordia Language Villages are encouraged to read the section entitled Background on pages xi-xii.) This text is organized around six principles that guide Concordia Language Villages curriculum and programming: Giving Learners Courage, Learner Investment, Linguistic and Cultural Authenticity, Creating a Need to Communicate, Experiencing the Language, and Learning within Extended Projects. Each principle is illuminated by representative best practices from the Villages that are ready to be brought to life within more traditional language classrooms.

Doing Foreign Language is intended for preservice and in-service language educators—including ESL educators—who teach or aspire to teach modern foreign languages to elementary and/or secondary students. Through its activities, teachers can offer their students authentic, invigorating, and challenging ways to make progress toward all *National Foreign Language Standards* as identified by the American Council on the Teaching of Foreign Languages (ACTFL). These interconnected opportunities for language use serve as natural *active* extensions of classroom textbooks, motivating teachers and students to *do* foreign language together in a wide variety of contexts. Throughout the book, verbal and visual images and guiding questions encourage readers to make connections between Concordia Language Villages principles and practices and the 5 C's (Communication, Cultures, Connections, Comparisons, and Communities) that form the backbone of the ACTFL *National Foreign Language Standards*—as well as to envision a range of relevant learning theories and methodologies *in action*.

ORGANIZATION OF THE BOOK

Chapter 1, Building a Language Learning Community, describes Concordia Language Villages, outlines the goals and principles that guide its curriculum and programming, and clarifies the connections between the practices of Concordia Language Villages and the ACTFL 5 Cs (Communication, Cultures, Connections, Comparisons, and Communities) mentioned above. Each of the following six chapters explores one of the six guiding principles in greater depth and illustrates it with ready-to-implement classroom activities. Readers with limited time—or those who are primarily interested in understanding the philosophical underpinnings of Concordia Language Villages—can focus their attention on Chapters 1 and 8, along with the brief introductions and It's Your Turn! sections of Chapters 2 through 7.

Chapter 2, Giving Learners Courage, and Chapter 3, Learner Investment, offer teachers and their students long-term programs that set the tone of the classroom as an open, welcoming, comfortable place that both encourages and rewards active participation by all students. Activities outlined in Chapters 4 through 7 provide students with opportunities to develop their use of the target language within rich, intriguing contexts. As they move through the activities in Chapter 4, Linguistic and Cultural Authenticity, students are encouraged to reflect on similarities and differences between cultural products and practices in their target and home cultures. Activities in Chapter 5, Creating a Need to Communicate, gently prod students into using the target language by feeling a real need to communicate. Chapter 6, Experiencing the Language, offers activities that help students draw on all of their senses—not just those of sight and hearing—to experience the target language more holistically. Chapter 7, Learning within Extended Projects, offers students opportunities to accomplish entire projects with their classmates through the systematic use of the target language. The final chapter, Bringing the Principles to Life in Your Classroom, encourages readers to envision a fertile classroom environment that will allow Concordia Language Villages principles to flourish, activities such as those presented in the book to be successful, and ideas for new activities to grow.

FEATURES

Each activities-based chapter (Chapters 2–7) comprises the following features:

- Introduction to the guiding principle highlighted in the chapter
- Four extension activities that illuminate the highlighted principle in action
- **In the Villages** feature describes the essence of the activity as it is typically enacted within one or more Concordia Language Villages programs
- **In the Classroom** feature describes one way the Village activity might be adapted to a foreign language classroom
- **Objectives** list expected learning objectives as related to the ACTFL 5 C's
- **Language Functions in Focus** feature identifies language functions that are practiced in the activity
- **Preparation and Materials** section lists necessary materials and suggests how teachers may prepare for the activity
- **Generating Interest** section describes how teachers may generate interest for the activity among their students by using materials, guiding questions, brainstorming, and demonstrations
- **Presentation and Practice** section describes the body of the activity, focusing on the presentation and practice of both language and content related to the activity
- **Expansion** explains (1) how teachers and students can develop the activity further; (2) how students can apply concepts to other aspects of language learning; and (3) how students can apply concepts to other academic disciplines and real-life situations
- **Adaptation** identifies how the activity can be modified to suit differences across learners, including proficiency level and age; differences in numbers of students in the class; differences in type of school facility and equipment and/or in amount of available time
- **Options for Evaluation** provide several options for evaluating products and processes related to the activity, including Expectations Rubrics, Student Journal Questions, and Portfolio Entries
- **Customizing This Activity for Your Classroom** section prompts teachers to personalize the activity to their own circumstances by considering issues related to choice of content, learner diversity, practical matters and classroom management
- **It's Your Turn!** section pulls together themes that cut across the activities in the chapter. These sections include: Discussion Questions to help teachers visualize the chapter's philosophy and content at work in their classrooms, For Further Reading, and Helpful Web Sites.

AUDIENCE

This book was written with two primary audiences in mind. One is second language educators—including ESL educators—who teach elementary and secondary students. We are hopeful that new and experienced teachers alike who are looking for ways to give their students courage to use the target language will find the principles and activity ideas helpful. Using the activities in our book, these teachers can offer their students important opportunities to explore the target language in interconnected ways within rich, intriguing contexts that range from the arts and humanities to the social and natural sciences. As they allow for extensive practice of the interpersonal, interpretive and presentational modes which are foundational to the success of any language learner, these activities add refreshing breadth and depth to students' learning experiences.

The other primary audience of *Doing Foreign Language* is preservice education students who aspire to work in elementary or secondary language education. Questions in It's Your Turn! sections and end-of-chapter suggested readings can be integrated seamlessly into college and graduate school discussions, as these provide initial sites for exploring connections to learning theories and methodologies currently prominent in the fields of second language acquisition and foreign language pedagogy. For example, readers can view task-based learning, form-focused instruction, and content-based language instruction in action, as they read through the book's practical on-the-ground illustrations. Within the teaching methods classroom, the extended activities themselves can be used to inform teacher preparation assignments, such as lesson planning, creating thematic units, and in-class teaching demonstrations. Teachers in practicum and student teaching situations may also find them helpful in the production and presentation of detailed lesson plans.

BACKGROUND

Concordia Language Villages (http://www.concordialanguagevillages.org)
Since its founding in 1961 with one Village and seventy-five participants, Concordia Language Villages in northern Minnesota has blossomed into the oldest and most extensive live-in summer language camp program for elementary and secondary students in the United States. Each year 9,500 young people, ages 7–18, from all 50 of the United States plus 25 other countries, participate in internationally acclaimed 1-week, 2-week, and 4-week language and cultural immersion programs that surround learners with the sights, sounds, smells, tastes, and textures of the target language and culture. Over its 44 years of existence, more than 130,000 language learners have participated in Village experiences in the following thirteen languages: German, French, Spanish, Italian, Russian, Japanese, Chinese, Korean, Norwegian, Swedish, Finnish, Danish, and English as a Second Language.

These camp programs take place within actual Villages where participants live everyday life in the target language, typically engaging in a range of culturally authentic activities, including sports, arts and crafts, cooking, nature programs, singing, dancing, theater, banking, and shopping. Several times each day, villagers meet with a small group of peers at their language level to focus specifically on language forms and functions that are subsequently practiced in ongoing daily activities. For some participants, the Village experience supplements or complements their academic-year language instruction. It provides others with the opportunity to learn a language not taught in school, or to pursue the language of their heritage. And, although villagers may not become fluent users of the target language after one, two, or four weeks in the program, the goal of Concordia Language Villages is that each villager will leave the experience wanting to learn more of the language and more about other cultures for years to come. And most of them do, as evidenced by the fact that more than half of the villagers return for additional opportunities to live life in the language—many for 5 to 10 more years!

The programs of Concordia Language Villages have attracted financial support from a variety of national and international sources, ranging from corporations such as IBM and General Mills to foundations such as Kresge and Freeman to the German federal government. Some of these grants have supported facilities; others have funded tuition scholarships. Still others have supported curriculum development and research.

INCEPTION OF *DOING FOREIGN LANGUAGE*

Doing Foreign Language is the product of such outside funding, being sparked by collaboration between Concordia Language Villages and two Title VI Language Resource Centers funded by the United States Department of Education: the National Capital Language Resource Center (NCLRC) of Georgetown University, The George Washington University, and the Center for Applied Linguistics in Washington, DC, and the National Language Resource Center housed at the Center for Advanced Research on Language Acquistion (CARLA) at the University of Minnesota in Minneapolis. As part of the 1999–2002 funding cycle, the NCLRC supported a project entitled "Best Practices: Adapting Concordia Language Villages Practices to Formal Educational Settings" that led directly to this book. CARLA funded a complementary study during the same time period entitled "Language Learning in a Non-School Environment" which, although published elsewhere, provided important insights to contextualize the work reported here. The challenge put to us by both collaborations was straightforward: to figure out what made the Villages in the woods of northern Minnesota "tick" and to capture this in such a way that it could be used within more traditional foreign language classrooms in elementary and secondary schools across the country.

ABOUT THE AUTHORS

I was energized to take on this challenge, as I had personally experienced the effectiveness of Concordia Language Villages almost three decades earlier. It was the summer of 1971 when I first set foot on Concordia Language Villages soil. I had arrived at the German Language Village *Waldsee* for a 2-week program after my sophomore year in high school. And, although I had been learning German for six years in school, when I arrived at *Waldsee* I found I wasn't actually able to *speak* the language, but only to manipulate pieces of it into their proper places if given enough time. My brief experience living life in German that summer somehow clicked a switch in my brain. The language started making sense to me. I understood it now as something that *real* people spoke to communicate *real* ideas and feelings with each other. I began to overcome my inhibitions to speak and the pieces began to fall directly into place.

That summer started me on what would become an adventure of more than 30 years. Over the course of those many years, as Concordia Language Villages was steadily expanding in breadth and depth, I was spending my summers teaching German at *Waldsee* and my academic years preparing for my position as professor of linguistics at Georgetown University, where I specialize in sociolinguistics and discourse analysis today. As I was learning more and more about how language worked, I began to view the Language Villages in a new, more analytical, light. As I learned how to investigate conversations, I used these approaches and tools to understand more systematically what was happening in verbal interactions around me. And as I learned about sociolinguistic variation across speech events and contexts, I started to understand more completely how the Villages were able to help learners extend and deepen their abilities and performance in their non-native language. As I continued to learn from and teach others along the way, my mind was increasingly occupied with attempts to figure out just how life in the Villages works to help learners make a *foreign* language into *their own*.

In this process of carrying out the NCLRC and CARLA projects, I was joined by my co-authors, Cori Crane and Abigail Bartoshesky. At the time they carried out their work in Minnesota, both were doctoral students in language education: Cori within the German Department at Georgetown University writing her Ph.D. dissertation on "Expanding the L2 Learner Profile: Evaluative Choices in Advanced L2 Writing in Three Genres" and Abby within the Teacher Preparation and Special Education Department at The George Washington University writing her Ed.D. dissertation on "Cyber Resources for Language Education: Accessing and Using Web-Based Target Language Materials." My long-term understanding of the Concordia Language Villages experience was enhanced by the freshness of perspective and sound background in second language theories and methodologies brought in by Cori and Abby.

AIMS OF THIS BOOK

The book you hold in your hands is our attempt to capture the organic shaping of the Concordia Language Villages learning community, as practices that caught and held the attention of learners survived and those that stifled imagination and excitement for learning were tossed to the side. Over the years, the ebb and flow of Village staff members brought new ideas in and washed old ones away. The principles we identify today as guiding Concordia Language Villages can be seen as the result of real-life "testing" of a range of educational theories, methods, strategies, and practices brought into the community with staff members trained to implement them. Some ideas took hold immediately; others failed. Most were adapted to the concept of living life in a Village, where language is used at work and at play—and not confined to specific periods of instruction. Those ideas that could be integrated into the constellations of cultural practices represented within each individual Village and stood up robustly against the rigorous time pressures of an intensive summer program are still standing.

In *Doing Foreign Language*, we hope to extend the reach of Concordia Language Villages first by identifying its best practices and then by articulating ways in which they can be brought to life within more traditional foreign language classrooms. We hope the reader will find our perspective useful, thought-provoking, and invigorating.

Acknowledgments

Our thinking was shaped by discussions with Dr. Andrew D. Cohen, University of Minnesota; Dr. Heidi Byrnes, Georgetown University; and Dr. Jeff Connor-Linton, Georgetown University, all of whom traveled to northern Minnesota to visit the Villages, carried out extensive discussions with staff and villagers, and shared their views about how the Villages work. We thank all of them for enriching our understanding of the Village experience.

Within the National Capital Language Resource Center, vital support was given by co-directors Dr. James E. Alatis of Georgetown University and Dr. Anna Uhl Chamot of The George Washington University. (In fact, we owe the idea for the title of the book to Anna who said, after being immersed in Concordia Language Villages programming for a couple of days, "You aren't just *teaching* foreign languages, you're *doing* them!") Upon our return to Washington, DC, from northern Minnesota in the fall of 2001, the Associate Director of the NCLRC, Dr. Catharine Keatley, was instrumental in helping us conceptualize the book, giving us important tips for focusing our work and staying on track.

Our work has also benefited from the Federal Republic of Germany's interest in Concordia Language Villages German curriculum. Germany's ERP Transatlantic Program has been a critical source of support for our efforts to make *Waldsee's* innovative teaching methods accessible to teachers of German and other languages. This particular focus on one language has helped us identify common principles guiding best teaching practices across the Villages.

Within Concordia Language Villages, we are grateful for and continue to be amazed by the creative contributions and support of Village deans and administrators. We especially would like to thank Daniel S. Hamilton, Laurie Iudin-Nelson, François Fouquerel, Tove Dahl, and Ross King. Research assistants Stuart Gorman, Nathan Garth, and Anne Skoe Fouquerel kept meticulous and insightful field notes, carried out extensive videotaping, conducted exciting interviews and focus groups, and engaged us in constructive discussions of their experiences. Conversations with Lisa Graefe, Jon Berndt Olsen, Blake Peters, Tara Fortune and Paul Magnusen—and many other counselors and teachers too numerous to mention—were foundational to our work. Donna Clementi, Dean of the Concordia Language Villages Teachers Seminar, has been an inspiration in her pathbreaking work to bring classroom teachers into meaningful conversations with Village staff and participants. We owe a great deal to discussions of this material with her—and with her seminar participants. John Borge's masterful photographs of the Villages bring our words to life; we thank him for his central contribution to this book. *Merci beaucoup* to Christine Schulze, Executive Director of Concordia Language Villages, for her unwavering support of our work, and to her able office staff at Concordia College in Moorhead, Minnesota, especially Denise Phillippe, Martin Graefe, Alex Loehrer, and Sheila Koser. And, finally, a huge thank-you goes to the counselors, teachers, villagers, and parents of villagers of Concordia Language Villages for their energy and cooperative spirit as we undertook this study. We couldn't have done this without all of you!

Our book benefited in numerous ways from the careful reading and insightful comments by the following text reviewers: Frank B. Brooks, Florida State University; Denis Cloonan Cortez, Northeastern Illinois University; Don Hones, University of Wisconsin, Oshkosh; Susan Lara, University of Texas of the Permian Basin; Phyllis A. Mithen, Saint Louis University; Denise M. Overfield, University of West Georgia; and Frank Tang, New York University. Also of tremendous help were my research assistant at Georgetown, Jen McFadden, and NCLRC research assistant Alisa Belanger. A special thank-you to Debbie Stollenwerk at Merrill/Prentice Hall for her enthusiastic and helpful conversations as well as Kris Roach and Mary Morrill for their editorial and other assistance.

On a personal note, loving gratitude goes to my parents, Claire and Jerry Ehernberger, who knew the power of Concordia Language Villages before I did. Thank you for continuing to encourage me to live life to the fullest there—and everywhere else I have been. Finally, thank you, Dan, for sharing your boundless vision of what language learning can be, and to our children, Siri and Sean, for sharing your "growing up time" by spending each summer with us at the place where the birch trees, loons, and lakes are at one with the sounds of the world's languages. (HH)

I would like to thank my parents, Frank and Terry Crane, for showing me the value of exploring other languages at an early age and encouraging me to develop my curiosities about the world in years beyond. (CC)

I am grateful to my parents, Lou and Pat Bartoshesky, for teaching me to view the world as a community and encouraging me to explore new languages and cultures. (AB)

Brief Contents

Contents

Note: Every effort has been made to provide accurate and current Internet information in this book. However, the Internet and information posted on it are constantly changing, so it is inevitable that some of the Internet addresses listed in this textbook will change.

1

Building a Language Learning Community

If you've picked up this book, you're most certainly a dedicated teacher who is constantly on the lookout for ways to energize your classroom, invigorate your students, and keep them excited about learning. The concept of *doing* foreign language may have piqued your interest. Perhaps you are already familiar with Concordia Language Villages, whose practices are highlighted in this book, and you're intrigued to discover what contributes to the Villages' long-standing success. Maybe you're ready to surprise your students with something new. Whatever your motivation, we welcome you to sit down, relax, and spend some time with us!

This first chapter introduces you to Concordia Language Villages, outlines the goals and principles guiding its curriculum and programming, and ties these to the 5 Cs (communication, cultures, connections, comparisons, and communities) that form the backbone of the Standards for Foreign Language Learning published by the American Council on the Teaching of Foreign Languages (ACTFL). The following six chapters then explore these guiding principles in greater depth, illustrating each with representative effective activities that are ready for you to use. You'll think about setting the tone of your classroom with motivational and student-centered programs such as Language Masters or the Superstar Obstacle Course. You'll learn how to create a Living Map or a Sensory Path with your students. Descriptions of projects such as the International Film Festival or the World

Cup Soccer Tournament await you. The final chapter of the book helps you bring these principles to life as you work to enhance the language learning community in your own school. So what are we waiting for? Let's get started!

About Concordia Language Villages

Concordia Language Villages, based in Minnesota, is the oldest and most extensive live-in summer language camp program for elementary and secondary students in the United States. Since 1961, Concordia Language Villages has worked to create a safe, positive, and caring environment that motivates participants to use the language they're learning, explore other cultures, better understand themselves and relate to others, and become responsible citizens in our global community. Currently, programs with annual total enrollments of over 9,500 young people, ages 7 to 18, are offered in the following 13 languages: German, French, Spanish, Italian, Russian, Japanese, Chinese, Korean, Norwegian, Swedish, Finnish, Danish, and English as a Second Language.

These camp programs take place within actual villages where participants live everyday life in the target language, typically engaging in a wide variety of activities, including sports, arts and crafts, cooking, interactive nature programs, singing, dancing, theater, banking, and shopping. Several times each day, villagers meet with a small group of peers at their language level (usually six to eight learners) and a counselor to focus specifically on language forms and functions that are subsequently practiced in ongoing daily activities.

Participants choose from among 1-, 2-, and 4-week language and cultural immersion programs that surround participants with the sights, sounds, smells, tastes, and textures of the target language and culture. The youngest villagers can select a 1-week introductory experience. The basic 2-week program, for young people of all ages, focuses primarily on oral language with a secondary focus on literacy skills. High school students have the option of choosing the more intensive 4-week program that offers 180 hours of instruction and focuses on both oral and written language. Successful completion of this program carries with it the recommendation of a 1-year high school language credit.

For some participants, the village experience supplements or complements their academic-year language instruction. It provides others with the opportunity to learn a language not taught in school or to pursue the language of their heritage. And, although villagers may not become fluent users of the target language after 1, 2, or 4 weeks in the program, the goal of Concordia Language Villages is that each villager will leave the experience wanting to learn more of the language and more about other cultures for years to come. And most of them do, as evidenced by the fact that more than half of the villagers return the next year for another chance to live life in the language.

As I write this chapter, I have just completed my 29th summer as a staff member with Concordia Language Villages. These many years on staff were preceded by two summers as a 2-week villager at Waldsee, Concordia's German language program. What I experienced as a high school student 30 years ago was pivotal for me—the foreign language I had been learning in school had been transformed from an interesting intellectual exercise (akin to cracking a secret code) to a living language used for real purposes by a community of people I cared about and wanted to be like. I was hooked! As one villager exclaimed just this past summer, "Waldsee isn't a place—it's a way of life!"

During those many summers, I have had numerous opportunities to talk with teachers, both those who have in-depth experience living in the villages as well as those who are spending just a few hours visiting. Almost always, one of their first reactions is to comment on the high level of energy and enthusiasm evident among the counselors and villagers. Most mention a palpable sense of belonging that pervades the villages, along with the extensive opportunities that students have for hands-on, real-life language use. It's easy to get caught up in the sea of smiles and spirited shouts as children race each other to the beach or sing at the top of their lungs in the dining hall.

But viewing such activities can bring on a bittersweet feeling in some visitors. Yes, it's invigorating to see kids having so much fun learning, but sometimes a realization sets in that the programs of Concordia Language Villages are different from most school-based learning situations in fundamental ways relating to time, space, and participants.

First, Concordia Language Villages has its learners 24 hours a day, 7 days a week. Villagers interact with a range of other villagers and counselors throughout the day, from wake-up routines in their cabins through breakfast with a different group of friends, large group singing sessions, small language groups, soccer games, stained glass activities, nature hikes, working on a newspaper, and on and on. Repetition is pervasive, but it is almost invisible to the learners as they hear the same songs, phrases, and vocabulary from different people in different activities at different times of the day.

Second, each village is made up of many different kinds of buildings and spaces. These spaces include dining halls, residential buildings, activity areas, classrooms, stores, cafes, banks, health centers, offices, soccer fields, marketplaces, beaches, nature trails, and campfire circles. When a teacher wants to practice requests, she doesn't have to set up a role play in her classroom; she can take her learning group to the store. When another teacher wants to practice prepositions, he doesn't have to draw objects and arrows on the blackboard; he can take his group to the ropes course or on a canoeing trip.

Finally, the participants. Concordia Language Villages operates with a very favorable villager-to-staff ratio, usually 6 to 1 or so, and virtually all the staff members are native speakers or near-native speakers of the target language, with a substantial amount of experience living outside the United States. The teachers and counselors are united by their interest in languages and language learning, of course, but that's not all. They share a love of children and understand that they're working to shape the future by listening to these young participants' views. They share a love of the outdoors and understand how critical it is to provide children with opportunities to get to know and love their natural environments. They share a love of creative play and understand that fun can be a huge motivator and community builder. They share the belief that language learning is inextricably linked to insights into other ways of living and experiencing life; they understand that these insights can very naturally develop into a healthy curiosity about issues affecting the world as a whole. The teachers and counselors recognize their vital role in helping children think about a wide range of sensitive issues, including the environment, human rights, literacy, health, and war and peace.

At this point you may be thinking about the fact that you don't have 24 hours a day with your students, but only 45 or 50 minutes; that you don't have a whole village to teach within, but usually only a single room; and that you don't have 6 students in your class, but 20 or 30. If so, you're certainly not alone. But that's no reason to close this book and reach for another one that seems to be more in tune with your teaching conditions. Yes, it's true that some of these differences present challenges. But most of these challenges are not insurmountable. In fact, that's what this book is all about. Experienced teachers have helped us take what is good about the philosophies and practices of Concordia Language Villages and figure out just what *can* be used, as is or in a slightly altered form, in more traditional language classrooms.

The main secret behind the success of Concordia Language Villages is the building of a community based on love of learning and respect for all learners. Every individual in the community comes with his or her own strengths and weaknesses, interests and experiences. By building on existing strengths, interests, and experiences and by offering participants safe opportunities to experience new things and to practice in their areas of weakness, we not only make those individuals stronger and more interesting, but we also build the entire larger community.

In the rest of this chapter, we'll identify the goals and principles that guide the teaching practices within the communities of Concordia Language Villages. We encourage you to take some time to think about which of these goals and principles already guide your teaching. In your experience, how effective are the resulting practices? Are any of the goals or principles on our list new to you? Can you imagine how following them might influence your teaching? What challenges do you foresee? What potential benefits? Which goals and principles might be most effective in building the kind of community that embraces language learning in your classroom and school?

GOALS OF CONCORDIA LANGUAGE VILLAGES

As is probably clear from the previous discussion, the programs of Concordia Language Villages have several goals, only one of which relates *exclusively* to the learning of the target language. These goals are the following:

1. Safeguarding the personal health and safety of every participant
2. Building and maintaining a community that encourages tolerance of and respect for others
3. Providing varied opportunities for participants to learn and practice the target language
4. Providing varied opportunities for participants to learn about cultural norms and directly experience cultural practices related to the target language studied
5. Providing varied opportunities for participants to explore issues of relevance to the world at large (for example, environment, war and peace, justice, literacy, health, and human rights)
6. Providing opportunities for participants to learn and practice skills *using the target language* from among the wide range represented by staff members (for example, woodcarving, calligraphy, dancing, canoeing, sewing, fencing, soccer, and baking)

Virtually all programming strives to fulfill several of these goals simultaneously; that is, within a safe and respectful environment, participants use the target language to experience relevant cultural practices, explore global issues, and/or learn and practice new skills. For example, learners in the photograph on page 4 are using the German language not only to learn how to canoe safely and efficiently, but also to investigate environmental issues in their local lake.

GUIDING PRINCIPLES OF CONCORDIA LANGUAGE VILLAGES

Observations of and participation in village life; discussion with teachers, counselors, and learners; and analyses of written staff questionnaires have led us to identify the following six principles that guide Concordia Language Villages' practices in the fulfillment of the goals just articulated. Practices related to curriculum and programming

1. Should give learners courage to participate and use the language
2. Should be learner centered so that learners become invested in their own learning
3. Should take place in linguistically and culturally authentic surroundings
4. Should take place out of a real need to interact and communicate
5. Should be experiential and hands-on, involving multiple senses and drawing on multiple intelligences
6. Should be embedded within extended projects

Each of the following six chapters illuminates one of these principles, providing first an introduction to the principle and then four extensive activities that are ready to be used in your classroom. At the end of each chapter you'll find a section called It's Your Turn, which highlights common threads running throughout the chapter's activities. Following this synthesis, we pose questions to help you envision how best to put the chapter's principle into practice, given your own personality, interests, and teaching circumstances. As a preview, we touch now on a few points that will be made in upcoming chapter discussions.

1. Practices related to curriculum and programming should give learners courage to participate and use the language.

- Frame learning as opportunities to grab, not as work to be done.
- Emphasize what learners *can* and *may* do, not what they *can't do* or *aren't allowed* to do.
- Use rewards instead of punishments wherever possible. Provide many different external motivations to use the target language to bolster learners' own internal motivations to do so.

- Point out errors very delicately. Model the correct form and functions. Be careful to balance accuracy with motivation. Don't let inhibition replace the joy of expression.
- Frame your instruction as play with occasional serious moments, rather than as work with occasional playful moments. Does instruction have to be serious? Can learners be bored when they're laughing?
- Use old language in new contexts. Encourage learners to be creative with what they already know. Write a skit using lines from songs. Cut titles out of old magazines and combine them to make a poem. Repetition doesn't have to be tedious; it can be virtually invisible and still be highly effective.

2. Practices related to curriculum and programming should be learner centered so that learners become invested in their own learning.

- Ask learners *what* they'd like to learn and *how* they like to learn. Have them help to design the areas to be covered in your course. Try to make the topics relevant to each learner in your class.
- Respect all learners for what they bring to the classroom in terms of different ways of thinking, different life experiences, and different areas of interest.
- Put learners into positions of leadership. Have them teach what they know or love best.
- Encourage learners to explore new interests, to try on a new identity, to stretch. Give them new responsibilities. Nudge them out of their comfort zone.

- Bring learners of different language levels together occasionally. Use more advanced students as peer teachers to encourage beginning language students.
- Encourage group work. Have these groups teach each other. Step back and gently guide what unfolds.

3. Practices related to curriculum and programming should take place in linguistically and culturally authentic surroundings.

- Use the target language continuously, switching into English only as a last resort. Speak more slowly; simplify; use gestures, facial expressions, visual aids, and props. Have learners use other learners as resources or interpreters. Encourage active listening on the part of learners.

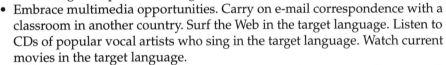

- Allow learners to (over)hear you speaking with other native (or near-native) speakers. Expose them to different paces of the language, different levels of formality, and different social and regional dialects.
- Expose learners to unexpected everyday cultural differences. Pepperoni pizza has peppers on it, not sausage?! Popcorn with sugar, not salt?!
- Embrace multimedia opportunities. Carry on e-mail correspondence with a classroom in another country. Surf the Web in the target language. Listen to CDs of popular vocal artists who sing in the target language. Watch current movies in the target language.
- Use authentic everyday written materials to complement more literary and expository texts. Read subway maps, restaurant menus, TV guides, concert schedules, classified ads, and travel brochures.

4. Practices related to curriculum and programming should take place out of a real need to interact and communicate.

- Frequently regroup learners as they carry out their activities. This regrouping will lead to natural communication as real information gaps emerge in the interaction. Learners will need to talk with each other to find out what the other groups know.
- Put learners into situations where they need to use different kinds of language, such as formal requests in a store, commands during a game, descriptions around an arts and crafts table, aesthetic language at a magnetic poetry wall, or persuasive prose at a model United Nations meeting.

- Make sure that learners need to use the target language every day. Identify natural "service encounters" or "gatekeeping" times when they are with you. When do they need supplies? When do they need to ask your permission to leave the room? Make sure learners know what they need to know in the target language to accomplish these everyday routines.

5. Practices related to curriculum and programming should be experiential and hands-on, involving multiple senses and drawing on multiple intelligences.

- Keep learners on the edge of their seats. Don't always let them know what's coming. Uncertainty can be a great motivator and does wonderful things to combat boredom. Just be careful not to tip the scale toward anxiety.

- Let learners experience something before they even know what they're experiencing. Start them on an activity before they know why they're doing it. Let them figure out the "why" together and discuss it with you.
- Use all of the learners' senses. Think about not only what they can see and hear, but what they can feel, taste, and smell.
- Have learners learn by doing, using their entire bodies to learn. Get them up out of their seats. Get them away from the chalkboard and the computer screens. Get them outside and moving around. Go to the playground to practice prepositions (*around* the slide, *down* the pole, *up* the ladder, *between* the swings). Go to the local park to work on nature poems.
- Sing! Dance! Play sports! Do art! Act!

6. Practices related to curriculum and programming should be embedded within extended projects.

- Have learners work in groups on a multifaceted project that depends for its success on the actions of more than one group. Put learners in charge of conceptualizing the entire project, making many of the decisions, planning the individual steps, and working through the consequences. A national film festival with student-produced films, a jury process, and a public awards ceremony is an illustration of one such project.
- Think up projects that the class can work on to benefit other individuals and groups in the school or surrounding communities. Examples include designing and building a nature trail, a community art project, or compiling a book based on life story interviews with native speakers in the community.
- Think up projects that your class can work on with other classes—either other foreign language classes or other departments in the school. What about a model United Nations? An international film festival? A World Cup soccer tournament?

CONCORDIA LANGUAGE VILLAGES AND THE NATIONAL STANDARDS FOR FOREIGN LANGUAGE LEARNING

At this juncture, you may be wondering how the Concordia Language Villages' goals and guiding principles just discussed relate to the well-known 5 Cs that form the backbone of the Standards for Foreign Language Learning published in 1996 by the American Council on the Teaching of Foreign Languages (ACTFL). As you probably know, in the ACTFL report of the National Standards in Foreign Language Education Project, 11 standards were developed within five goal areas, the famous 5 Cs: communication, cultures, connections, comparisons, and communities. The members of the task force were very clear in saying that these 11 national standards did not describe the current status of foreign language education in the United States, but were rather put forward as a gauge by which to measure future progress—a kind of yardstick that reflects the best institutional practice within foreign language education.

So, I'll use this gauge to comment briefly on some ways in which the practices of Concordia Language Villages work to help foreign language learners accomplish these goals. Included in my discussion are references to aspects of some of the 24 activities that make up the heart of this book. This discussion is meant to clarify the connections between the practices of Concordia Language Villages and the National Foreign Language Standards and to assist you in deciding which of our activities might be the most helpful to you as you put together your lesson plans.

Communication

The first three national standards support the goal of communicating in languages other than English.

Standard 1.1   Students Engage in Conversations, Provide and Obtain Information, Express Feelings and Emotions, and Exchange Opinions

Because Concordia Language Villages are set up as actual villages, with learners interacting with each other and with staff in a variety of ways over the days they spend there, it will come as no surprise that learners gain a great deal of practice related to standard 1.1. They engage in conversations with a wide range of partners over the course of each day—while cleaning their cabins, eating breakfast in the dining hall, and making plans for afternoon activities. They provide and obtain information at the bank, express feelings and emotions after seeing a foreign film, and exchange opinions regarding the best song to dance to.

Standard 1.2 Students Understand and Interpret Written and Spoken Language on a Variety of Topics

Standard 1.2 focuses primarily on one-way listening and reading comprehension. In Concordia Language Villages, learners have a number of opportunities to practice listening comprehension: they listen to goodnight stories in their cabins, short cultural presentations by staff or other villagers, announcements in the dining hall, and game rule descriptions at the beginning of evening programs.

Reading comprehension is incorporated to a slightly lesser extent into village programming. Notable exceptions include the reading of comic books, newspapers, magazines, and short stories, either within instruction periods or during free time in the cafe or library, as well as the many foreign language posters, signs, and other authentic texts such as train schedules and menus located around each village. (In addition to the basic 2-week summer program, Concordia Language Villages offers intensive 4-week programs that allow high school students to accomplish the equivalent of a typical 1-year high school or 1-semester college course. These 180-hour programs obviously include a heavier focus on reading comprehension than does the 2-week program.)

Standard 1.3 Students Present Information, Concepts, and Ideas to an Audience of Listeners or Readers on a Variety of Topics

Standard 1.3 focuses on the formal presentation of information, concepts, and ideas in spoken and written form and highlights one-way speaking and writing for the most part. In the language villages, learners have opportunities to work in small groups on meal presentations or news and weather programs. Some also keep daily journals, write short pieces for the village newspaper, or create travel brochures or reports on lake water quality for class projects.

Illustrations of These Standards in Upcoming Activities Your students will have opportunities to engage in conversations on the telephone (Activity 5.3), obtain information during a school tour (Activity 5.1), express feelings and emotions in a discussion about student rights and responsibilities (Activity 3.4), and exchange opinions about student-made videos during a film festival (Activity 7.4). They will work hard to understand oral presentations by visiting native-speaker experts (Activity 4.4) or write-ups of the soccer tournament results (Activity 7.2) in the class newspaper (Activity 7.1).

Cultures

The next two national standards are in the service of gaining knowledge and understanding of other cultures.

Standard 2.1 Students Demonstrate an Understanding of the Relationship between the Practices and Perspectives of the Culture Studied

Again, because the Concordia Language Villages program operates within actual villages in which learners come to experience daily life in the foreign language, it should not be surprising that this standard is greatly emphasized within village programming. Learners encounter cultural practices at every turn during each day, from the way eating utensils are used in the dining hall, to the way friends are greeted along the paths, to the way audiences express their appreciation following a concert or play. The fact that the majority of staff members are either native speakers who live these cultural practices daily or are nonnative speakers who have lived for an extended time in the target culture helps to intensify the authenticity of these practices for the learners. Learners learn "what to do when and where" within the target culture.

Standard 2.2   Students Demonstrate an Understanding of the Relationship between the Products and Perspectives of the Culture Studied

This standard focuses both on the tangible (painting, literature, chopsticks) and the intangible (dance, system of education) products of the target culture. Over the years, individual villages have acquired more and more of the tangible products that help to construct the sensory authenticity of the villages: the sights of authentic mailboxes and street signs, the sounds of authentic musical instruments, the tastes and smells of authentic spices, the touch of authentic fabrics. The intangible products enter into learners' consciousness through sports, art, and dance activities, as well as through extended simulations focused on educational or political systems.

Illustrations of These Standards in Upcoming Activities   Your students will be exposed to the cultural products and practices related to eating out in the target culture (Activity 5.2) beginning with how to (or whether to) reserve a table, how to interact with the servers, how to read the menu, and how to pay the bill. Related activities encourage students to think about newspapers (Activity 7.1) and films (Activity 7.4) as cultural products and to investigate the cultural practices surrounding gardening (Activity 7.3) and dancing (Activity 6.2).

Connections

The following two national standards focus on the connections between foreign language learning and other disciplines.

Standard 3.1   Students Reinforce and Further Their Knowledge of Other Disciplines through the Foreign Language

This standard highlights the importance of learning across disciplines, that is, of connecting information, approaches, and perspectives learned in one area with those in others. Underpinning this standard is the important distinction between learning a language for its own sake and using that language in an endeavor to learn about other content areas. The approach used in the villages is multifaceted; several times each day, learners meet in small groups to focus on the language itself. The rest of the day, however, is filled with opportunities to use the target language in order to learn other things: geography, history, martial arts, dancing, baking, canoeing, pottery.

Standard 3.2   Students Acquire Information and Recognize the Distinctive Viewpoints That Are Available Only through the Foreign Language and Its Cultures

This standard focuses on language learning as providing a "new window on the world." A great deal of programming within the language villages is directed specifically toward the attainment of this standard. Through discussions with target-language-speaking staff, learners have numerous opportunities to learn about viewpoints not usually represented within their own home and school communities. These viewpoints often relate to current political events or global environmental issues, but may just as well have to do with more local issues, such as popular music and literature, or even how much and what kind of homework is most beneficial for students. A crucial source of this kind of exchange of perspectives comes through debriefing phases following a variety of simulations offered in the villages. The point of this standard is to emphasize that learners of a foreign language can use the language to gain access to engaging, alternative viewpoints that they otherwise might not have been exposed to.

Illustrations of These Standards in Upcoming Activities   Your students will be encouraged to use their foreign language to learn more about modes of inquiry in the natural sciences through participation in the sensory path (Activity 6.1) and the gardening activity (Activity 7.3). They may be exposed to art history in the Space and Time Museum (Activity 4.1) or to soccer through the World Cup Tournament (Activity 7.2). They may gain "new windows on the world" through engaging in discussions with guest experts (Activity 4.4), viewing and discussing foreign films (Activity 7.4), or participating in a cross-cultural simulation (Activity 6.4).

Comparisons

The next two national standards highlight the importance of the role of comparison and contrast in the development of insight into the nature of both language and culture.

Standard 4.1   Students Demonstrate Understanding of the Nature of Language through Comparisons of the Language Studied and Their Own

This standard focuses on the impact that learning a new language has on students' own abilities to examine and understand their first language. They develop hypotheses about the structure and use of languages and can use these to learn new languages later in life. Because the vast majority of learners in Concordia Language Villages speak English as their first language, these kinds of discussions take place naturally at many places and times throughout the village. Upon learning that German nouns can be one of three genders, an English-only speaker may be surprised that there are feminine or masculine nouns at all. But a learner who already knows French may only be surprised that it's possible for nouns to be of neuter gender, in addition to the possibility of being feminine or masculine. The fact that many participants are learning their second or third foreign language in the Language Villages encourages them to compare and contrast the language of their village with other languages they are learning as well.

Standard 4.2   Students Recognize That Cultures Use Different Patterns of Interaction and Can Apply This Knowledge to Their Own Culture

Here, too, it is absolutely natural within the language village environment for learners to be confronted with an unexpected cultural product or practice and to wonder for a moment about what they are experiencing. This element of surprise encourages the learners to reflect on what they have come to take for granted within their own lives. They begin to understand that what seems logical to them is merely logical because it is all they have known until now. Because learners come to the villages from a wide variety of geographic, social, and cultural backgrounds, these cultural comparisons and contrasts do not take place solely between U.S. American culture and cultures related to the language learned in the village; comparisons are also made between the city or suburban life that many learners are used to and the life in the wooded environment of northern Minnesota.

Illustrations of These Standards in Upcoming Activities   Your students will have opportunities to compare and contrast cultural products and practices—and the language forms and functions that go along with them—through the activities that focus on dancing (Activity 6.2), films (Activity 7.4), soccer (Activity 7.2), telephoning (Activity 5.3), and eating out (Activity 5.2). Through the e-mates activity (Activity 5.4), students can even use their foreign language to learn about life in an entirely different geographic location (for example, Indonesia or New Zealand) by setting up correspondence with students learning their foreign language in that location.

Communities

The final two national standards identify the importance of the use of the foreign language to enable active participation within multilingual communities both at home and around the world.

Standard 5.1   Students Use the Language Both within and beyond the School Setting

This standard focuses on the role that knowledge of a foreign language can play in allowing a learner to participate within a community, either within the educational institution itself or outside it. Because Concordia Language Villages are actual villages, it happens quite naturally that the language of village life is fundamental to the creation of a community feeling. The target language is literally the single common denominator among all the participants. The fact that learners and staff come together from around the globe with the primary purpose of encouraging language learning and use makes it easy to build a community around the learning itself. Many learners take their first supported steps in the language within the village and then go on to use the language in future educational or professional opportunities, either within the United States or abroad.

Standard 5.2   Students Show Evidence of Becoming Lifelong Learners by Using the Language for Personal Enjoyment and Enrichment

This standard highlights the importance of getting off to a positive start when learning a foreign language. It is much easier to take what one has learned about a language, recognize the ways in which it provides access to new information and entertainment sources, and be motivated to put it into practice over a lifetime, if one has developed a love for the language and culture within a community of people who share this passion. And it is easier still when one is having fun with and in the language—through skits, games, chants, and songs! It is this type of community that the language villages aspire to offer—not only to young learners of the language, but to their teachers as well. The fact that the majority of staff and villagers return again and again for this kind of language–learning experience indicates the beginning of a commitment on the part of many participants to be lifelong learners of other languages.

Illustrations of These Standards in Upcoming Activities   Your students will be motivated to reach for the stars, using what they know of the target language to the greatest extent possible, through the Language Masters program (Activity 2.1) and the Superstar Obstacle Course (Activity 2.2). These programs help develop a lifelong appreciation of the language and of what it means to be a second-language speaker. Beyond these ongoing programs, they will use their foreign language to help build communities—within the classroom, across classrooms within the school, and by reaching out to local community members. Within the classroom, learners can work together to develop Students' Rights and Responsibilities (Activity 3.4) that will help guide their learning environment. They can also draw on their relative strengths and interests as they teach their peers in the Students as Experts program (Activity 3.2). Across classrooms within the school, students can work together on a foreign language newspaper (Activity 7.1), a film festival (Activity 7.4), or a World Cup soccer tournament (Activity 7.2). More advanced students are encouraged to help students in lower-level language classes through the Student Mentors program (Activity 2.3) or the School Tour (Activity 5.1). Finally, students can reach out to interested community members through the Visiting Experts program (Activity 4.4) or by inviting them to take a tour through the Space and Time Museum (Activity 4.1) or to enjoy an awards ceremony of the film festival (Activity 7.4).

ON TO THE ACTIVITIES

Now that you've had a chance to familiarize yourself with Concordia Language Villages and to connect the goals and principles of the villages with the National Foreign Language Standards, let's move on to the heart of the book: the activities that illustrate the Concordia Language Villages guiding principles we've just discussed. Each of the next six chapters introduces one of these principles and then illuminates it through four extensive activities. At the end of each chapter you'll find a section called It's Your Turn! that pulls together common themes and poses questions to help you visualize the chapter's philosophy and content at work in your own classroom. Following these questions, we list several publications and Web sites that may help you explore in greater depth issues related to the guiding principle and activities highlighted in that chapter.

Each activity follows the format outlined in the following text.

In the Villages

This section describes the essence of the activity as it is typically enacted within one or more Concordia Language Villages programs. All these sections are accompanied by a relevant photograph of life in the villages.

In the Classroom

This section briefly introduces one way the village activity might be adapted to a more traditional foreign language classroom situation.

Objectives

This section lists expected learning objectives as related specifically to the relevant 5 Cs of the Standards for Foreign Language Learning published by the American Council on the Teaching of Foreign Languages: communication, cultures, connections, comparisons, and communities. All activities list objectives for communication and at least two of the other four areas.

Language Functions in Focus

This section identifies the language functions that will be practiced in this activity.

Preparation and Materials

This section suggests how you may prepare for this activity and lists necessary materials.

Generating Interest

This section describes how you may generate interest for this activity among your students by using materials, guiding questions, brainstorming, and demonstrations.

Presentation and Practice

This section describes the body of the activity by focusing on the presentation and practice of both language and content related to the activity. In more elaborate activities, this section may contain several stages. In most of these cases, it is possible to simplify the activity by focusing on only one stage.

Expansion

This section explains how (1) you and your students can develop the activity further, (2) students can apply the concepts to other aspects of language learning, and (3) students can apply the concepts to other academic disciplines and real-life situations.

Adaptation

This section identifies how the sample lesson can be modified to suit differences among learners, including proficiency level and age; differences in numbers of students in the class; differences in the type of school facility and equipment; and/or differences in the amount of available time.

Options for Evaluation

This section provides several options for evaluating the products and processes related to the activity. *Expectations rubrics* are meant to evaluate students' progress toward meeting the expected learning objectives of the activity. The rubrics presented are meant to serve as a starting point for your own rubric design. We expect that individual teachers will wish to put differing degrees of emphasis on various parts of the described activity. *Student journal questions* are meant to be used in classes that encourage learners to write regularly in the target language in journals. These sample prompts can help learners follow up on aspects of the activity; reflect on what they have learned linguistically, culturally, and in terms of content; and apply this new knowledge to other domains. *Portfolio entries* are meant to help you and your students identify products from the activity that can be added to a student portfolio as evidence of a given student's language-learning process and progress. In addition to these three options for evaluation, occasionally suggestions are given for self-assessment or performance-based assessment. (Go the end of this chapter for a list of useful resources on evaluation options.)

Customizing This Activity for Your Classroom

This section consists of a set of questions to help you personalize the activity. After reading the activity, but before you actually implement it, these questions will encourage you to imagine how your students and your classroom will look and sound during the activity. In thinking through the answers to these questions, you will be prompted to consider issues related to the following topics:

- ■ Choice of content (related to your own training, experiences, background, and interests)
- ■ Learner diversity (related to proficiency levels, age, needs and interests, and background of learners)
- ■ Participant contributions (related to roles, assignments, and division of labor)
- ■ Practical matters (related to time, financial, and physical resources; interaction with students' families, community members, fellow teachers, and school administrators; and the physical layout of the classroom and school)
- ■ Classroom management

The activities in the following six chapters are meant to illustrate the principles that guide the curriculum and programming practices within Concordia Language Villages. As you read through the following list, you'll notice that the 24 activities fall into two basic categories. The first 8 activities, under the headings Giving Learners Courage and Learner Investment, help to set the tone of your classroom as welcoming, supportive, and challenging from the very first days of the year. They describe programs that can be set up and used for as long as you work with your students, sometimes stretching over years of involvement. The other 16 activities, under the headings of Linguistic and Cultural Authenticity, Creating a Need to Communicate, Experiencing the Language, and Learning within Extended Projects, are more self-contained, independent units that can be used in virtually any order you'd like, at any point over the course of the year. These activities offer your students important opportunities to explore the target language in interconnected ways within rich, intriguing contexts that range from the arts and humanities to the social and natural sciences. As they allow for extensive practice of the interpersonal, interpretive, and presentational modes that are foundational to the success of any language learner, they add refreshing breadth and depth to the learning experiences of your students.

Setting the Tone
Giving Learners Courage
2.1 Language Masters
2.2 Superstar Obstacle Course
2.3 Student Mentors
2.4 Bob, the Imaginary Fly
Learner Investment
3.1 Discovering Student Interests
3.2 Students as Experts
3.3 Creative Bulletin Boards
3.4 Students' Rights and Responsibilities

Taking Off!
Linguistic and Cultural Authenticity
4.1 Space and Time Museum
4.2 Living Maps
4.3 Culinary Explorations
4.4 Visiting Experts
Creating a Need to Communicate
5.1 School Tour
5.2 Eating Out
5.3 Telephoning
5.4 E-mates
Experiencing the Language
6.1 Sensory Path
6.2 Dancing
6.3 Tracing Bodies
6.4 Simulations
Learning within Extended Projects
7.1 Newspaper
7.2 World Cup Soccer
7.3 Gardening
7.4 Film Festival

As you read through these activities, you may find yourself thinking, "Oh, but I don't even like art history. How could I ever pull off the Space and Time Museum?" or "I'm not athletic at all. I couldn't ever put on a World Cup Soccer Tournament." That's why we've included the Expansion and Adaptation sections in all activities. These are the sections to read if you think you might be interested in incorporating the activity into your classroom life, but something in the way the activity is described turns you off. The Expansion section will help you and your students get even more out of the activities by helping you to extend the described activity to more in-depth explorations and creative alternatives. The Adaptation sections will help you adapt the activity to different language levels, age ranges, or a shorter amount of time.

And remember the most important feature of the activities: They're adaptable—and meant to be adapted—in ways far beyond what we could ever predict. So take the heart of the activity and mold it to your own circumstances and fascinations. These slight alterations will most certainly lead to greater success of the activities within your classroom. We've found in the villages that teachers are often more engaging when they're talking about people, places, and ideas that interest them. Even the learners notice this and mention it to us in our talks with them.

"Teach what you're passionate about" is what we hear learners say. So if you don't like dancing but love karate, adapt the dancing activity to karate. If you don't have time to produce films with your students, produce commercials instead. You get the idea! Now run with it!

For Further Reading

Celce-Murcia, M., & Olshtain, E. (2000). *Discourse and context in language teaching*. New York: Cambridge University Press.

Hall, J. K. (2001). *Methods for teaching foreign languages: Creating a community of learners in the classroom*. Upper Saddle River, NJ: Prentice Hall.

Hamilton, H. E. (2005). Repair of teenagers' spoken German in a summer immersion program. In D. Boxer and A. D. Cohen (Eds.), *Studying speaking to inform second language learning* (pp. 88–114). Tonawanda, NY: Multilingual Matters Ltd.

Hamilton, H. E., & Cohen, A. D. (2004). Creating a playworld: Motivating learners to take chances in a second language. In J. M. Frodeson and C. A. Holten (Eds.), *The power of context in language learning and teaching*. Festschrift in Honor of Marianne Celce-Murcia. Boston: Heinle & Heinle.

Klee, C. A., Lynch, A., & Tarone, E. (1998). *Research and practice in immersion education: Looking back and looking ahead*. Selected Conference Proceedings. Minneapolis: University of Minnesota.

National Standards in Foreign Language Education Project. (1996). *Standards for foreign language learning: Preparing for the 21st century*. Yonkers, NY: American Council on the Teaching of Foreign Languages.

National Standards in Foreign Language Education Project. (1999). *Standards for foreign language learning in the 21st century*. Yonkers, NY: American Council on the Teaching of Foreign Languages (this revised version includes sections devoted to standards for the following languages: Chinese, Classics, French, German, Italian, Japanese, Portuguese, Russian, and Spanish).

Helpful Web Sites

To learn more about Concordia Language Villages, visit http://www.concordialanguagevillages.org

To learn more about the Standards for Foreign Language Learning published in 1996 by the American Council on the Teaching of Foreign Languages (ACTFL), go to http://www.actfl.org. Click on Proficiency Guidelines and then select Standards for Foreign Language Learning: Executive Summary under publications.

Resources on Evaluation Options

Rubrics: For help in creating your own materials to evaluate your students' progress and performance, visit http://www.rubistar.4teachers.org and http://www.school.discovery.com/schrockguide/assess.html, and follow other leads from there.

Student Journals: see G. B. Cobine, *Effective use of student journal writing* (1995). ERIC Digest online at http://www.ericfacility.net/ericdigests/ed378587.html

Portfolios: See E. A. Hebert, *The power of portfolios: What children can teach us about learning and assessment* (2001). San Francisco: Jossey-Bass.

PART 1

Setting the Tone

Chapters 2 and 3, Giving Learners Courage and Learner Investment, offer you and your students long-term programs that set the tone of your classroom as an open, welcoming, comfortable place that both encourages and rewards active participation by all students. Over the first days and weeks of the academic year, learners contribute to a healthy classroom culture through Discovering Student Interests (Activity 3.1) and Students' Rights and Responsibilities (Activity 3.4). They are empowered to take responsibility for their own learning in Students as Experts (Activity 3.2) and Creative Bulletin Boards (Activity 3.3). They spread their wings on the Superstar Obstacle Course (Activity 2.2). They gain valuable confidence in themselves as learners of the target language through the Language Masters (Activity 2.1) and Student Mentors (Activity 2.3) programs. The quirkiness of your new teaching assistant, Bob, the Imaginary Fly (Activity 2.4), will make them smile—and capture their attention.

To be sure, some of these programs involve a healthy amount of risk taking for both you and your students. But once you've embarked on them, you and your students will find that the activities that form the basis of your time together are being shaped by your own personalities and passions. By putting your personal stamp on what you're teaching and learning, you and your students will come to own the activities. You'll be invested in them. And this ownership and investment will buoy you up and go a long way toward ensuring success throughout the year.

So we encourage you to take some time to read through the long-term learning programs proposed in these two chapters. We hope you'll take the plunge and start your year off with one or more of these ideas. Once they're in place, the proverbial snowball will begin to roll. Whatever initial tentativeness there may be on the part of some of your students will be overcome in time. As some students come forward to participate in the programs, others will see that their learning and excitement are being propelled forward through their own efforts. These programs will continue to gather momentum until they are seen simply as "the way things work around here." And things will only become easier the next year—and the next and the next.

chapter
2

Giving Learners Courage

We'll start our journey right here, at the heart of the Concordia Language Village philosophy—giving students courage. Courage to take the plunge into a new way of speaking, a new way of being. Courage to make "funny" sounds. Courage to take on a new identity. Courage not to be perfect. And what could be more critical to success?

It's hard to speak another language. It's embarrassing to pick the wrong words. It's humiliating to have to repeat and repeat and repeat, all just because your pronunciation of the "r" is so bad the teacher can't understand what you're trying to say. It's annoying to have to try to remember all the prefixes and suffixes and word orders when all you want to do is get an idea across. It's frustrating not to be able to be as funny as you are when you can speak English.

These inherent challenges in learning a foreign language can be demoralizing to some learners, but actually seem to invigorate and energize others. As teachers, we need to figure out a way to support the internal motivations of some of our students while providing external incentives for the others and to set the tone for students to have courage to step over their inhibitions and get on with living in the new language.

The activities outlined in this chapter are designed to provide support to learners as they make tentative steps forward. They are meant to en-courage, in the sense of giving courage, learners to continue to use the target language even in the face of these challenges.

Activity 2.1

LANGUAGE MASTERS

In the Villages

Some villages have programs that encourage villagers to speak the target language the entire day, from breakfast through dinner time. Villagers who choose to participate simply pick up a "name tag" (typically a small, round piece of wood hanging on a string) labeled Sprachmeister or Super Français at the beginning of the day and try their best to speak only the target language, even if this means speaking little. Although not all villagers participate, we've found it's an effective and supportive way to offer motivated students a systematic way to practice the language. Eventually, positive peer pressure comes into play with entire groups of friends participating together in the program.

In the Classroom

In the Language Master program, students are encouraged to use the target language on a voluntary basis throughout the entire language class period. Participating students pick up a Language Master nametag or a desk sign from a designated place in your room and begin speaking the target language. If all goes as expected, they'll be true to their language pledge even when you're not monitoring them specifically. The program becomes invaluable when the Language Masters are integrated into small groups at work in your class. When learners speak willingly to other learners in the target language, now *that's* a great way to offset a high student–teacher ratio in the classroom!

Objectives

- ■ **Communication**
  - • Students will be able to use language related to the classroom environment.
  - • Students will be able to use language functions in a variety of meaningful contexts.
- ■ **Cultures**
  - • Students will be able to identify famous individuals (real or fictional) found in the target culture (expansion activity).
- ■ **Communities**
  - • Students will develop courage and interest in speaking in the target language outside planned class activities.

Language Functions in Focus

- ■ Asking for information
- ■ Attracting someone's attention
- ■ Expressing opinions
- ■ Giving commands
- ■ Giving directions
- ■ Giving reasons
- ■ Greeting
- ■ Narrating
- ■ Reporting
- ■ Suggesting
- ■ Taking leave

Preparation and Materials

- ■ Index cards or small pieces of poster board (for name tags, one for each student in your class)
- ■ Yarn or twine (for name tags)
- ■ Poster board (for desk signs, one for each student in your class)
- ■ Three pieces of poster-sized paper (for lists of Language Masters, Frequently Asked Questions, and Useful Expressions)
- ■ Small rewards (e.g., stickers, candy, key chains, or target-language comic books)

First, decide what to call a Language Master in your target language. Of course, you can just translate the words more or less directly, but it may be more fun for you and your students to come up with a term together. Think about superheroes in your target culture—or funky cartoon characters. Perhaps even a well-known historical or literary figure. If you're having trouble coming up with an idea, or just can't decide which one to choose, think about having a naming contest among your language students.

Next, decide whether to use name tags or desk signs to display participation, and consider the choice of material. At the Villages, villagers and counselors wear tags made of small, round wood blocks with holes for string to go through (see the photograph on page 23). While not everyone has the luxury of a lumberyard nearby, there are more accessible and less expensive alternatives. You can laminate index cards or small pieces of poster board. Use a hole puncher to make two holes for the string to go through. Desk signs can be made with pieces of folded poster board.

Make one poster entitled Language Masters in the target language to display students' participation. Every time a student completes a lesson without resorting to the use of English, write his or her name on the poster for all to see. Each additional time thereafter can be noted with a gold star or other symbol.

Make a second poster entitled Frequently Asked Questions in the target language (see sample questions and answers in the following section, Generating Interest).

A third poster, entitled Useful Expressions, will be made together with your students following the related discussion described in the next section.

Generating Interest

To build up your students' courage for the project, you'll first want to address some of their trepidations. Start by talking about the difficulty of communicating in a place where no one else speaks English. Ask your students if they have stories to share about having to speak in these survival situations.

Next, tell your students about the Language Master program. Let them know what the purpose of the program is. Make sure they know that you don't expect them to be able to speak accurately all the time in the target language, but that you are convinced that trying to do so will help them become more comfortable with and fluent in the language. Demonstrate what is appropriate and inappropriate language behavior while wearing the name tag. It may be effective to decide as a group what the exact performance goals of the program are (see Activity 3.4, Students' Rights and Responsibilities). For example, depending on the language level of your students, you may decide it makes sense to allow minor slip-ups by Language Masters, especially at the beginning of the year.

Frequently Asked Questions

A poster (in the target language) including the following questions and answers can provide the class with more specific information.

1. What is a Language Master?
   Someone who speaks [insert name of target language here] for the entire class period.
2. What do I need to do to become a Language Master?
   Simply pick up a name tag at the beginning of the class period. Speak [insert name of the target language here] for the entire class period. Try as hard as you can not to speak English. At the end of the period, place the tag back on its hook and you can speak whatever language you would like.
3. What happens if I speak English?
   Quietly place the name tag back on the hook from where you picked it up at the beginning of the class. Since you can try to be a Language Master any or every day during the school year, you can try it again the next day.

4. What happens if I speak [insert name of target language here] for the entire class period?

   Your name is added to the Language Masters poster. If you are a Language Master five times, you become a Language Monster and receive [insert reward here, such as Gummi bears, sticker, or pencil].

Maintaining interest among your students is obviously paramount to the success of this activity. This means not only keeping the program positive for the students, but also making sure the students have enough of the relevant language tools to enable them to stay in the target language. Brainstorm with your students beforehand as to what kinds of language expressions they might need to use if they decide to undertake the challenge. Some of these might be the following:

"How do you say X in [insert name of the target language here]?"
"I have a question."
"Could you repeat that, please?"
"May I go to the restroom?"

You and/or your students could write the collected expressions on a poster for students to refer to when necessary.

Presentation and Practice

At the beginning of each class period, interested students simply pick up a name tag or desk sign from a designated place in the classroom and place it around their neck or on their desk. They try to speak the target language exclusively throughout the class period.

If you hear a Language Master speaking English during class, you may choose to remind him or her gently of the language oath. If that same Language Master speaks English again, he or she returns the tag or sign to its original place in the room. Students making it to the end of the class period without uttering a word of English are Language Masters for that day. Depending on the age and motivation of your students, you may wish to institute a brief ritual at the end of each period in which you ask the Language Masters to stand up or otherwise identify themselves. Before leaving class that day, participating Language Masters return the tags and signs so that they can be used by other classes. Upon returning to class the next day, they will find their names up on the Language Masters poster.

Expansion

Have Language Masters work together to brainstorm ideas for future feats and creative ways to recognize students' motivation and performance.

Have each of your students be responsible for creating one name tag or desk sign that portrays a famous individual or character from the target language culture. Students can find pictures of these personalities on the Internet or in old magazines and newspapers and then write a brief paragraph about the individual chosen to be placed on the reverse side of the tag or sign.

To encourage continued participation, institute a Language Monster (or Groovy Gabber) for those students who attain the honor of Language Master five or more times. Language Monsters could receive a special reward, such as a monthly in-class pizza lunch or extra credit points.

Adaptation

Culturally appropriate neckwear (such as Mardi Gras beads for French classes), stickers, or pin-on buttons can be used in lieu of name tags or desk signs.

If you don't have your own room to display the award winners poster, bring an official Language Masters logbook in a three-ring binder to class with you. Students can sign their name in it at the end of class.

To motivate participation among older students, you can adapt this activity to make it more teamlike by offering a visible goal at the end, such as a pizza or ice cream party. The rules might be as follows: every participant who successfully speaks in the target language for the duration of class gets a point. But the points go up exponentially with participation of more than one student, so that two students earn 3 points, three students earn 5, and so on. After a while, the class should see how much easier it is to reach their goals with the help of their classmates, rather than individually. (You can even have the students practice their math skills in the target language by calculating the points at the end of the period.) If your students are seated at common tables or in rows, you could have tables or rows compete against each other for the greatest levels of participation in the program.

Options for Evaluation

Individual Self-assessment	
	Student's Answer
My first time as Language Master, I was successful at . . . I had problems with . . . I felt . . . My goal for next time is . . .	
My second time as Language Master, I was successful at . . . I got better at . . . I still had problems with . . . I felt . . . My goal for next time is . . .	

Student Journal Questions

Recording thoughts on the experience of being a Language Master in a journal can be prompted by questions that record development over time. The following prompts can be reformatted to serve as a record sheet for students to fill out over the year or grading period and can be included in the learner's portfolio.

Think about the time(s) you were a Language Master:

1. What was difficult? What was easy? Explain your answer. If you were a Language Master more than once, what was easier the second time (or subsequent times)? What was still a challenge?

2. Did you set any goals for yourself? What were they? Were you able to accomplish them?

3. What did you learn from the experience? You can answer this in terms of specific language features or vocabulary that you were able to practice. You can also talk about your confidence and comfort levels.

4. What advice would you give another student who wanted to try to be a Language Master, but was worried about not knowing enough of the language?

Portfolio Entries

1. Include a journal response comparing a student's first experience as a Language Master with subsequent experiences.

2. Include a digital or Polaroid photograph of the Language Master poster containing the students' names to serve as an important reminder of the number of classmates who participated in the overall program.

3. Some students may wish to make a replica of the Language Master name tag or desk sign to include in the portfolio along with the journal response and photo.

Customizing This Activity for Your Classroom

1. Imagine introducing and implementing a Language Master opportunity in your classes. How would you encourage your students to participate?

2. Identify additional useful language expressions that your Language Masters might need in order to succeed.

3. Some students will be enthusiastic participants. How might you motivate some of your students who seem less likely candidates?

4. What are some classroom benefits you could offer as a reward instead of prizes?

5. How can you encourage learners to challenge each other into participating?

6. How might Language Master pairs or trios make staying on task easier?

7. After considering these questions, how do you envision this activity with your students?

Activity 2.2   SUPERSTAR OBSTACLE COURSE

In the Villages

Recognizing community involvement at the villages is as fundamental to the success of the villagers' experiences as is the language learning aspect. The two work together on many levels. At some Villages, a set of Herculean tasks (a list of various activities carried out by the villagers on an individual basis over 2 to 4 weeks) has been used to encourage villagers to explore new ways of using the target language. On the Superstar Obstacle Course, villagers contribute directly to the village community by, for example, coteaching a song or dance, writing an article for the village newspaper, or creating a poster identifying local plants and animals. Positive peer pressure typically emerges, and friends work together toward their common goals. The idea behind this program is to encourage students to practice the target language in a range of learning contexts. Upon completing all of the tasks along the course, a villager becomes a Superstar!

In the Classroom

On the Superstar Obstacle Course in your classroom, learners have the opportunity to participate in and complete a number of exciting and rewarding activities across a wide variety of domains—sports, arts, literature, music, dance, etc.—all in the target language. The tasks are designed to enhance the language-learning community and to open the door to new areas for participating students. The activities can be aimed at different learning styles and intelligences so that students can choose activities that match their personal interests, expertise, and talents, as well as those that introduce them to new areas.

The tasks are represented graphically in the classroom with a map of the course. Participating students have a personal booklet or sheet that describes the task options and provides room for feedback and/or a signature from you as each project is completed.

Objectives
- **Communication**
  - Students will be able to use a variety of task-specific language abilities (depending on the tasks chosen).
- **Connections**
  - Students will develop knowledge about cross-disciplinary content through the target language.
- **Communities**
  - Students will be equipped with skills to take responsibility for their own learning.

Language Functions in Focus
- Expressing opinions
- Reporting
- Suggesting

Preparation and Materials
- Two pieces of poster board (for the Superstar Obstacle Course map and the Superstar Obstacle Course activities poster)
- Colored markers
- Index cards

First, decide whether the Superstar Obstacle Course will be an integral part of your course and require the participation of all your students or whether you will be offering it as an extra credit option to challenge motivated students. This decision will influence how you create your materials and present the program.

Next, decide what to call the Superstar Obstacle Course in your target language. For example, think about famous geographic sites in regions where your target language is spoken. Name the course after a well-known mountain and have your students get closer to its summit as they accomplish projects along the way. Name the course after an important river and have your students travel from town to town as they make their way from the river's source to the ocean. Consider naming the course after a long-distance race held within your target culture.

Based on your chosen theme, create a Superstar Obstacle Course map on poster board that will keep track of the tasks your students complete. For example, if your students will be climbing a mountain, leave spaces for the names of participating students along the bottom of the poster and identify six or eight resting places along their paths to the top. If your students will be running a race, leave spaces for their names along the left side of the poster and draw squiggly lines across the poster to suggest their route.

Finally, come up with a list of activities your students could do to enhance your class. Create a Superstar Obstacle Course Activities poster that lists activities that can be completed individually, in pairs, or in small groups. Here are some ideas you might include:

> Tape yourself interviewing a native speaker (Activity 4.4).
> Prepare authentic food and provide the recipe and a short description of your experience (Activity 4.3).
> Work as the editor of your class newspaper (Activity 7.1).
> Help to teach soccer to your classmates, or even coach your team (Activity 7.2).
> Work as a peer teacher for a beginning language student and have yourself videotaped doing so (Activity 2.3).
> Create a bulletin board for your classroom (Activity 3.3).
> Teach a song or dance from the target culture (Activity 6.2).
> Create collages, posters (for movies, rock bands, learning languages, or others), or target language travel brochures.
> Find and summarize or review a newspaper or magazine article on a particular topic that the class has studied or is now studying.
> Create a poem or story that involves characters or a setting from school or takes place in the target culture.
> Read and report on short stories, poems, and legends in the target language or about the target culture.

As an alternative to this list, you may wish to allow students to come up with their own tasks that fall within predesignated categories. These categories may be the ACTFL 5 Cs; the interpersonal, interpretive, and presentational modes of communication; or even different disciplines, such as art, music, literature, history, or sports.

Generating Interest

Hang up the Superstar Obstacle Course Activities poster and map in your classroom. Introduce the program to your students. Highlight the program's overall purpose—to have students use the target language to accomplish activities in a variety of contexts—and describe the theme of the course map (for example, climbing a mountain, traveling along a river, or running a race). If you've decided to have all of your students participate in the program, let them know the nuts and bolts: How many activities will each student need to complete? How much time do they have for each activity? Can students work in pairs or small groups on the activities? How will the activities be graded? If you've decided to use this program to provide students with extra credit options, explain how this will work. How many extra credit points will they receive for each activity?

Presentation and Practice

Have your students talk about the listed activities in medium-sized groups to identify those that seem particularly interesting and those that seem less so. Encourage them to brainstorm specific ideas for their favorite activities. Invite students to come up with additional ideas to add to the list you have posted. Help them find partners with similar interests. (This might mean matching with several different partners depending on how many activities you ask them to do.)

Recommend this activity as an excellent way for students to practice language-learning skills that are giving them trouble. For example, if a student thinks her pronunciation needs work, suggest that she set up conversations with a native speaker. If a student thinks he doesn't write well, have him write a report on a topic that interests him.

Once each participating student has decided which activity to start off with and who any collaborators might be, fill in student names on the course map poster. Review activity deadlines and provide regular opportunities in class for students to keep you updated on their progress.

Chart your students' progress on the Obstacle Course map in your classroom. As they begin each activity, have students write a brief description of their task along with the start date on an index card. Post this card at the first station of the obstacle course. The friendly competition to complete the course has begun! When each activity has been completed, have participating students give a brief oral report with any relevant props to the class or turn in a brief written report to you. Students can then add the completion date to their posted index card. To mark the start of the second activity, students post a second descriptive index card at the second station on the course map. And off they go!

When one student or group of students has reached the end of the obstacle course, mark the accomplishment with a celebration! Review all the amazing tasks that all participating students have completed since the day the competition began. Then teach a cheer in the target language and congratulate everyone!

Expansion

Organize an open house for parents and friends to display the students' accomplishments. For this event, have each participating student choose one of his or her activities to represent visually on a poster. Make sure students include descriptions of different stages of the activity, as well as their own thoughts as to what they learned. At the open house, students can provide explanations to their visitors.

Share the obstacle course idea with other teachers in your department. For extra credit, older language learners can help younger students complete obstacle course tasks.

If you have your students write up descriptions of their tasks, keep them for next year's class. This will save you time in introducing the projects and will provide you with a standard from which to work. Even more useful for your future students is to have current students create a list of "how to" instructions or just general advice for accomplishing different activities.

Adaptation

Arrange and design the activities carefully according to language and interest levels. Make some of the projects easy-to-reach extensions of topics already covered in class, while making others totally new for students. This will give everyone the opportunity to participate, as well as to explore new interests.

Although this activity is meant to encourage individual or small-group work in the target language, you can easily adapt it to suit a more teamlike environment. If your classroom is arranged by group tables or rows of desks, you can instigate a bit of friendly competition by encouraging tables or rows to compete against each other. At the end of the process, give each team one grade that represents their project quality and teamwork.

If you'd like to carry out this idea on a nongraded basis, you can do the obstacle course with one team made up of the entire class. When all of the activities on the list have been completed by individuals or groups, celebrate with a party or other reward. Highlight students' successes on the map described previously to encourage the class to work together.

Options for Evaluation

Individual Self-assessment

Self-assessment is suggested for each activity completed on the obstacle course. During the semester and again at the end, provide students with opportunities for self-evaluation and reflection through class discussions or reflective essays. Sample prompts include the following:

	Student's Answer
I learned the following words, grammar points, or language functions through the project or activity . . .	
I learned about the following topics through my project or activity . . .	
The part I liked best about my project or activity was . . .	

Student Journal Questions

1. Which activities were your favorite? Your least favorite? Why?
2. Which activities were the easiest? The most difficult? Why?
3. In which activities did you learn the most [Spanish/Chinese/French]? Why do you think that was the case?
4. What advice would you give a classmate who wanted to try the obstacle course?

Portfolio Entries

1. Include a pictorial map of students' activities (for example, on a trail through Candy Land) in which they write down the activity, the date it was carried out, and a one-sentence description of the activity.
2. Include a completed individual self-assessment rubric, as just outlined, following each individual activity. Students can draw pictures of the activity if they'd like. The pages can be collected and transformed into a book with a cover page.

Customizing This Activity for Your Classroom

1. Picture presenting this activity to your students. What questions can you anticipate?
2. How could you include cross-disciplinary activities such as science experiments, geometry designs, and social studies projects in the obstacle course?
3. Think about how you could elicit support for this activity from parents and other faculty.
4. Long-term projects like the obstacle course require self-discipline. How can you help learners to manage their learning, set incremental deadlines, and monitor their progress?
5. Think about more activity ideas to include in your obstacle course.
6. Ask a senior teacher what innovative and enjoyable activities they think would interest the learners in your school.
7. Now imagine the course again. Has your image changed? How did you decide to resolve some of the issues that arose?

Activity 2.3   STUDENT MENTORS

In the Villages

Peer teacher is one of the many roles that villagers may take on during their stay at Concordia Language Villages. Coteaching lower language levels allows villagers to speak the target language with their peers, to become knowledgeable about particular aspects of the target language, and to reflect on how languages are learned. Of course, at the heart of this are the social interactions with others and the role of expert that learners are encouraged to play. Peer mentoring also serves as a motivating experience for younger learners of the target language, who look up to the older villagers.

In the Classroom

In this beyond-the-classroom Student Mentors program, pairs of advanced learners of the target language develop materials and activities under your guidance to help younger or lower-level language students practice aspects of the target language being taught in their classes. Activities including language games and songs are integrated into 20- to 30-minute beyond-the-classroom practice sessions offered weekly, biweekly, or monthly after school, or even by the students acting as teaching assistants in classes of younger, beginner, and intermediate language learners.

Objectives
- **Communication**
  - Students will be able to model and teach the target language to younger students.
- **Connections**
  - Students will reflect on how to teach a foreign language.
- **Communities**
  - Students will develop leadership skills.
  - Students will be able to develop younger learners' interest in the target language.

Language Functions in Focus
- Attracting someone's attention
- Describing procedures

- Evaluating
- Expressing opinions
- Giving directions
- Greeting
- Introducing oneself
- Presenting information
- Suggesting
- Taking leave

Preparation and Materials

Identification of Student Mentors

This would also be an ideal internship opportunity for college language majors. School districts may be able to arrange for local college students to get credit for mentoring younger learners.

Because of the great deal of planning and responsibility involved in student mentoring, we recommend this program for older, mature, and motivated high school students who have advanced language proficiency. Through conversations with other teachers and observing and reflecting on your classes, identify students who might be willing and able participants in a mentoring program. Set up an informal meeting to describe the program and to discuss both the extrinsic and intrinsic benefits of participation. Benefits may include recommendation letters for future job and school applications, extra credit for language classes, and the satisfaction that comes from being a role model for younger students and experiencing their successes. If your school system requires volunteer-service credit hours of their students for graduation, find out if student mentoring might be recognized as such.

Identification of Students to be Mentored

If you teach the same target language at several language levels, this decision can be as easy as having some or all of your advanced language students working as mentors for your beginners. If you teach only advanced language students, you should discuss the possibility of starting this program with one or more faculty members who teach lower-level language classes in your language. If you teach only beginning students and would be interested in having this kind of mentoring program for your students, you could approach one or more faculty members who teach upper-level language classes to discuss the possibility of coordinating this effort.

Identification of Topics for the Student-Run Beyond-the-Classroom Practice Sessions

If you teach the beginning level of your target language, all you need to do is to look over the topics you are planning to cover beginning in 6 weeks and extending over the course of the year. (It's good to leave a 4- to 6-week period at the beginning of the semester to give the student mentors adequate time for preparation and training.) Make a list of topics that often cause trouble for beginners and on which your students could benefit from extra practice with their student mentors. If you do not teach beginners, ask the teacher(s) of this level to make up such a list.

Preparation of a Training Workshop

If you are teaching a small group of very advanced students, you may decide to incorporate this program into your course curriculum. In this case, the training workshop could be conducted fully in the target language during class time.

Once you have a group of student mentors, it's important to offer them some training before the actual mentoring begins. Create a hands-on workshop for your students that could be offered after school. Enlist help from your school counselor and any other expert teachers (particularly other foreign language teachers) who you think could provide insight on working with younger students. Think about which portions of the training should be conducted in English and which can be done in the target language.

Workshop activities could include the following:

1. Student brainstorming of effective and ineffective learning experiences they've had
2. Student reflection on their first experiences learning the target language

3. Modeling effective and ineffective teaching with another teacher
4. Student identification of aspects of the target language they would like to be responsible for coteaching
5. Designing effective games and other hands-on materials for language teaching

Materials for Language Games and Other Hands-on Activities to Be Used in Practice Sessions

- Dice
- Spinners from used board games (such as Life)
- Markers from board games
- Poster board
- Construction paper
- Index cards
- Post-It notes
- Colored markers and crayons
- Adhesive tape and glue
- Balls of various types
- Dominoes
- Variety of hats and caps
- Variety of small stuffed animals

Generating Interest

After you've identified all the relevant participants in this program—student mentors, students to be mentored, and any other teachers who need to be involved—then you're ready to start the mentor training. This can be run as either an after-school activity (if student mentors will come from a variety of classes) or an in-class activity (if student mentors are all from the same class). Depending on the interest level of the participants, these 20- to 30-minute practice sessions can be offered weekly, biweekly or monthly. If another teacher will be involved (either as the teacher of the mentors or of the beginning students), it would be very helpful to have that teacher involved in this session.

First Training Workshop for Student Mentors

1. Describe the student mentoring program, taking care to outline the responsibilities of the mentors (for example, taking part in regular mentor meetings, working with a partner or two to design and create teaching activities, and designing and conducting one or more 20- to 30-minute beyond-the-classroom practice sessions for younger and lower-level language students) and to characterize the sessions the students will be leading.

2. Have students come up with illustrations of effective and ineffective learning experiences they have had (no naming of names!). Encourage students to keep this discussion in mind when they mentor.

3. Have your students think about their first experiences learning the target language. What did they find easiest to learn? What did they find the most interesting? The most enjoyable? What did they find confusing or especially hard to learn? How did they eventually get over these difficulties? Following this identification, the teacher of the beginning students should provide his or her understanding of the students' areas of strength and weakness.

4. Model one brief, exaggerated (and even comical) "good" language-learning activity and one "bad" one with another teacher. Discuss with the student mentors what made these activities effective or ineffective. Show your students how effective and fun it is to integrate games and songs into the lesson.

5. Hand out copies of a written set of possible topics for mentoring sessions, based on both the beginning language course syllabus and the beginners'

strengths, weaknesses, and interests. Talk through each topic, giving clear examples of what the goals will be for a session and identifying one or two possible activities to be used in the mentoring session. Ask the prospective mentors to think about the topics on the list that they feel most confident and interested in teaching. Ask each potential mentor to talk with other participating students after the training workshop to identify one or two other students with whom he or she would be comfortable working.

6. Ask potential mentors to think very carefully about their decision to become a student mentor. Give them a deadline by which you would like to hear from them about their decision. Ask them to submit a list of possible teaching topics and student partners if they decide to go forward with the mentoring program.

Presentation and Practice

Once you have heard from all potential mentors, look over the students' suggestions of topics and possible collaborators to ensure that you agree with them. Coordinate the mentoring topics with the beginner course syllabus. Be sure to leave enough time for student mentors to prepare and practice their practice session activities. It would make sense to schedule the first session a minimum of 4 weeks after your second meeting with the mentors.

Set up a calendar of dates on which beyond-the-classroom practice sessions could be held. Depending on the number of interested mentors, these sessions could be held weekly, biweekly, or monthly. Determine time and room availability. Type up this information and make copies for all mentors.

Second Meeting of Student Mentors

Set up a second informal meeting with the student mentors to talk about the proposed mentoring pairs or threesomes, session topics, and timetables. Make sure that each student mentor knows with whom he or she will be coteaching, what his or her topics are, the dates on which the practice sessions will be held, and how long the sessions will be. Remind the mentors that they will not be responsible for first-time teaching of their topics. Lower-level language students participating in student-run sessions will already have worked on these topics in class; they will be coming to gain additional confidence through activity-based practice with the mentors. Hand out copies of your calendar of the student-run sessions to reinforce this information.

Make clear your expectation that the students should work together to come up with possible teaching activities for their practice sessions. Let the students know what materials are available (and at what time) for the creation of these activities. Share some language activities that you have found to be successful in your classroom by modeling them right then and there. Have the student mentors play the role of younger, less proficient students as you lead the activities. This brief modeling will go a long way toward clarifying your expectations of the student mentors.

End the workshop with a brainstorming session on the students' specific topics. If another teacher or two could be available to help with the brainstorming, even better! Schedule a third meeting within 2 weeks or so for the students to try their activities with you and the other student mentors.

If you haven't yet decided what you'd like to call the beyond-the-classroom Student Mentors program, enlist the help of your student mentors. If you have time at this session, do some brainstorming right now. Otherwise, encourage your students to contact you with any ideas they have before the next meeting.

Third Meeting of Student Mentors

Set up a third meeting to give student mentors (especially those responsible for the first two or three sessions) the opportunity to try their language activity sessions with you and the other mentors. Each mentoring pair or threesome should have

To get the ball rolling on effective and appropriate language games, have students think about adapting childhood favorites such as Simon Says; 20 Questions; Charades; Spud; Red Light, Green Light; or Memory. In some cases, it will be obvious how to integrate the target language. In other cases, students will need to be creative in adding a language component to games that don't have them. If you are familiar with children's games and songs from the target culture, describe these to the mentors and encourage them to figure out how to turn these into language-learning activities.

After the first group of mentors is trained and has experience, these mentors can assist with subsequent training sessions. Follow a train-the-trainer model. This means that the time commitment on your part will gradually lessen as student mentors attain trainer levels. Ultimately, this student mentoring program should save you and your colleagues time as students help other students to learn. Simultaneously, the number and types of opportunities for language use among the students should increase.

approximately 10 minutes to introduce and practice their activities. Begin with the student-run sessions that come up first on the calendar so there will be adequate time to address them. You and the mentors playing the role of the beginners should give feedback, emphasizing first the qualities of each activity they liked best and then offering constructive ideas for improvement. If you think that a particular activity needs serious improvement, call the relevant student mentors in for a separate conference with you at a later time.

Advertising the Beyond-the-Classroom Mentoring Program

If you feel they are making sufficient progress, ask the student mentors to begin to advertise the peer mentoring program. Several options are possible, depending on your school situation:

1. Student mentors can hold an orientation meeting to which lower-level language classes come with their teachers to find out about the mentoring program. The student mentors should be encouraged to put together a funny skit to invite the visiting students to participate and to emphasize the fun, learning-by-doing model that will be used in the practice sessions.
2. Student mentors can visit lower-level language classes with a brief presentation of the program.
3. Student mentors can make posters to advertise the practice sessions. Be sure to have students include the target language topics, the time, the location, and some indication of the activities that will be offered.

First Student-Run Beyond-the-Classroom Practice Session

Suggest that the student mentors come up with a good warm-up activity for each practice session. One idea revolves around a secret bag containing small objects. Students participating in the session first try to guess what's in the bag simply by looking at it. Then they pass it around and feel it for additional clues. Once the objects have been identified, they can serve as a spark for role-plays or skits—or even for grammar or vocabulary practice.

When the time has come for the first student mentors to offer the first practice session, make sure it has been advertised sufficiently in the appropriate classes. Teachers of those classes may be able to give extra credit for student participation in the practice session or offer some other type of incentive. Encourage all student mentors to attend the first session in order to give the presenting mentors psychological support. You should be at the session to introduce the student mentors and to monitor things as they go along. Following the session, be sure to give the presenters some positive feedback. Negative feedback should probably wait until the next day. It's hard to get up in front of a group and teach, after all!

Subsequent Mentor Meetings

Depending on the number of student mentors, the number of student-run practice sessions, and the amount of time in between them—and how effective the practice sessions are!—you will want to schedule regular meetings of the mentors. These meetings serve at least two purposes: (1) They allow student mentors the opportunity to try out new activities that will be part of upcoming practice sessions and (2) they allow for valuable discussion of the mentors' experiences. Mentors should be encouraged to reflect on what worked well and what could be improved upon. You can help them with challenges ranging from classroom management to specific language questions.

Some benefits that your mentors will gain from this process may not be completely obvious to them along the way. Be sure to provide them with ample opportunities for self-evaluation and reflection through their mentor meetings or reflective teaching journals following each student-run practice session. They will almost certainly be surprised by all that they have taught and learned!

Expansion

After the program has been up and running and the mentors are becoming more comfortable in their roles, suggest that the students allow you to videotape a student-run practice session. You can then view the tape in a subsequent meeting with all the mentors and use it as a springboard to provide general feedback to the entire group.

Invite the mentors along on field trips for the younger classes. Bus rides are great for learning songs, riddles, and games. Have older students teach their younger counterparts such songs, riddles, and games from the target language culture or have them make up their own using the target language.

If your school has a tradition of offering peer-to-peer tutoring during lunch hour or after school, ask your student mentors if they would like to take turns staffing a tutoring table on a regular basis. This is a good way to extend the mentors' reach without any additional preparation on their part.

Ask your mentors if they'd like to sit at target-language-only tables during lunch in the cafeteria. Depending on interest levels among students, these language tables could be offered once a week or even once a month. Invite anyone who is interested in practicing the target language to join in the informal lunchtime conversation!

Adaptation

You can transform the mentor-run practice sessions into a class event. As a class, your more senior students can perform a song, skit, cooking lesson, or commercial to a class of younger students or one of lower proficiency. Coordinate the content and language to fit the goals of the established curriculum before the class embarks on its lesson plan.

If you're unable to have your students work with language classes in your high school, consider getting in touch with your local elementary school colleagues. Not only is this sure to be fun for your older students, but it's also a great way to promote the benefits of language learning to learners at a young age. Have your older students create a first-day lesson plan involving the target language, with plenty of games, songs, and action built in.

Options for Evaluation

Expectations Rubric

The following rubric can be used either as a self-assessment tool or as a way for mentors to gain feedback from their supervising teacher.

	Agree				Disagree
You developed and used appropriate materials to communicate the content matter of the lesson clearly and effectively to the participating students.	5	4	3	2	1
You feel comfortable modeling and teaching language points to other learners.	5	4	3	2	1
You reflected on your teaching, including the identification of problems and attempts to find solutions for them.	5	4	3	2	1
You have taken on a leadership role in language education.	5	4	3	2	1
You feel ready to help younger learners develop an interest in language learning.	5	4	3	2	1

Student Journal Questions

1. What did you think would be the greatest challenges in student mentoring? What did you think would be relatively easy?
2. Were you able to accomplish all the goals that you and your teaching partner(s) outlined for the practice session?
3. What were the dynamics of the practice session like? Did the students participate actively? What did you and your partner(s) do to encourage students to speak more?
4. Did you run into any problems while teaching that you weren't expecting?
5. What parts of the practice session do you think went really well? Why did you think they were successful?
6. Was it easy to stick to your lesson plan?
7. What three tips would you pass on to a student in next year's class who wanted to be a student mentor?

Portfolio Entries

1. Include the student's practice session plan and related teaching journal entry.
2. Include materials related to a teaching activity the student created.
3. Include a videotape of the student's practice session.

Customizing This Activity for Your Classroom

1. Think about how this program would work in your department. What implementation problems could you face?
2. Why is positive peer pressure so important for giving learners courage?
3. How could native speakers from your community help you manage a peer mentoring program in your school?
4. Identify some internal and external rewards you can offer your peer mentors.
5. Reflect on how peer mentoring builds a language-learning community.
6. Brainstorm field trip and extracurricular activities that student mentors and beginning language students might take part in together.
7. As you visualize peer mentoring at your school, think about how it could enhance your school's language program.

Activity 2.4   BOB, THE IMAGINARY FLY

In the Villages

Imagination is one of the most valuable resources that counselors draw on at Concordia Language Villages. Whether it comes clad in humor, pure silliness, or unadulterated creativity, the villagers respond consistently in a positive manner to this move away from the real world.

Using his imagination, one of our counselors developed an "imaginary fly" to help him introduce and practice relevant vocabulary and language functions. "Bob," as he was lovingly called, became such a staple in the lessons that the villagers soon included their newfound friend in other activities and stories and asked for him when he wasn't around.

In the Classroom

Make-believe characters, like the imaginary friends of our childhood, can act as old and trusted companions in the classroom and are a great way to focus the class's attention on particular language forms and functions. With a little preparation and some courage on your part, Bob, the Imaginary Fly, can come to life in your classroom. You'll gain a target-language-speaking teaching assistant and your students will gain a friend!

Objectives
- **Communication**
  - Students will be able to use specific language forms and functions related to the goals of particular units.
- **Communities**
  - Students will become more motivated to participate in classroom activities due to a fun learning environment.

Language Functions in Focus
- Describing places
- Expressing opinions
- Giving reasons
- Narrating

Preparation and Materials

No materials are necessary for this activity (that's the point!). If you prefer, however, you can use some type of physical object to represent Bob. Roll up a scrap of paper or find a small plastic insect in a toy store.

It's time to get into character! Practice the hand shape you will use to represent Bob by cupping your hand and pinching your forefinger and thumb together to pick him up. Or, if you have decided to use a small object to represent him, practice picking up the object and carrying it around. Decide on a distinctive voice quality to use when you are speaking as Bob. A high pitch may work best to capture the attention of your students.

Generating Interest

Start off by introducing your class to Bob, your fragile target-language-speaking friend, and explaining that he has decided to help you with teaching. Now's the time to ham it up! Physically, show Bob to your students, using the hand shapes and motions you've practiced or pulling out the small piece of crumpled paper or other small object that represents him. During these initial introductions, you may want to embellish Bob's teaching and language background as necessary to drive home that Bob is no ordinary fly. Don't forget to use your special voice quality when you are speaking as Bob. The students will quickly try to catch you speaking as yourself with a high pitch or as Bob with your normal voice. They'll be paying attention and you'll all have a lot of fun learning with Bob's help!

Presentation and Practice

Before having Bob appear and reappear, make sure to give him ample introduction. You may wish to provide a short story or particular scenario to get your students' attention. Explain to the class, for example, that Bob likes to fly everywhere, is very curious, and hence sees and experiences everything. As things constantly happen to Bob, and Bob is always on the go, you and your students may want to trace Bob's tracks. This is a great way to introduce and practice prepositions of location and direction, verbs of direction, and/or tense differences. Ask the students questions like these:

> Where did he go? Where is he now?
> Does anyone see Bob?
> Does anyone know where he's gone?

Elaborate these questions with colorful comments about Bob's character and/or behavior to keep students' interest in the activity:

> Oh, no! We lost him again.
> This is so typical of him to go off flying without telling us where he's going.

After possible answers are offered by the students, you might find Bob leaning against your pencil or taking a nap in your empty coffee cup. Show him to the students and if you accidentally drop him, carefully pick him up by his wing and return him to safety in your cupped hand.

In addition to practicing language related to location and direction, you can also have students practice a number of other language features, such as causality. Maybe Bob is having a particularly rough day (it's raining, his fly friends have moved away, and such) and is flying into everything, or he is particularly quiet. Have students guess why Bob is behaving the way he is. Lead students with ap-

The more dramatic you are about Bob, the better. The students will be encouraged to take your lead, giving him a "voice" and practicing language that they might otherwise be hesitant to produce. They'll most likely pay greater attention to what you are saying when you're speaking as Bob or using him as a conversational partner.

propriate language forms if they have not yet been introduced. Possible responses could be these:

Bob is quiet, because he misses his mom.
. . . because he's reading.
. . . because he's sad.
Why is he sad? . . . Because he lost his left shoe.

Follow up with a worksheet. If your lesson focuses on the use of prepositions, the sheet could recount all the places that Bob has traveled, with gaps in place of the prepositions. If you focus on causality, you can create a story about Bob with students filling in the appropriate blanks.

Once you have introduced Bob to the class, you can develop the story line of Bob's life by divulging information about his past, his family, the love(s) of his life—whatever aspects of his life may seem appropriate for a given lesson. Use him to warm up the class, spark interest, and introduce new projects.

Expansion

As a follow-up activity, have students write about Bob's experiences in the classroom. Encourage them to use the vocabulary and language structures practiced in class. Here are some ideas:

- After not seeing Bob for a few days, students write a missing person's police report. This can include the last place Bob was seen, a description of Bob, and maybe even a picture of him.
- Students write about class from Bob's perspective, a fly on the wall. How does he interpret the class goings-on? What insights does he have to offer?
- The class helps Bob, who has just been evicted from his home, to find a new one by using the newspaper classified ads.

Adaptation

Bob's invisibility makes him easy to tote all over. A variation of this activity could involve using a homemade finger or hand puppet or a character from the target language culture.

Not sure how Bob will fare with the older crowd? Invite a scary or intriguing ghost based on a cultural icon from the target language culture to your classroom. Tell a ghoulish story to introduce him or her.

Options for Evaluation
Teacher's Self-assessment

Expectations Rubric					
	Agree				**Disagree**
My students learned how to use the targeted language form or language function correctly by the end of the lesson.	5	4	3	2	1
My students participated actively in the oral portion of the activity.	5	4	3	2	1
My students' motivation seemed to improve when I used Bob.	5	4	3	2	1

Student Journal Questions

1. Write a pen pal letter from Bob to your classmates. Have him describe his family in the letter. Does he have any brothers and sisters? What do his mother and father do? What are Bob's favorite activities? What kinds of music does he like? Does he do any sports? What was his favorite vacation? What does he want to do when he grows up?
2. Imagine that your teacher lets Bob visit you for the weekend. How would you introduce him to your family and friends? What would you show him first in your house? Where would you take him in your neighborhood? What would you eat? What would you do for fun?

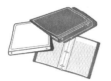

Portfolio Entries

1. Include a written text based on one of the ideas presented in the Expansion section. Artistically inclined students may wish to illustrate the text. You may be surprised to see how your students imagine Bob's appearance!
2. Include a list of five facts about Bob, as discussed in class. This can be either a group or individual project.

Customizing This Activity for Your Classroom

1. Imagine yourself role playing, communicating with learners, and modeling language constructions through Bob the Fly (or your version of an imaginary friend).
2. Think about the reasons why Bob keeps learners on task and encourages them to participate.
3. How could Bob help heritage learners?
4. Give examples of how Bob could assist in presenting language constructions, language functions, and vocabulary.
5. How could Bob help learners practice speaking in the target language?
6. Could students use their own versions of Bob the Fly? How might using an imaginary friend make speaking easier?
7. Think of a personality and name for your fly (or mosquito or ladybug). Now imagine the activity again.

IT'S YOUR TURN!

It's hard to learn anything without making mistakes along the way. It's nearly impossible to get it right on the very first try. All of the activities in this chapter open up opportunities for learners of a new language to summon up the courage to try something new, even though these attempts may come with a heavy dose of mistakes. In taking on the challenges presented in these activities, your learners can propel themselves on to higher levels of language use.

In implementing the first three of these programs (Language Masters, Superstar Obstacle Course, and Student Mentors), you will be providing the motivated risk takers in your class with opportunities for further growth and development. As Language Masters, they'll push themselves to try their hardest to get through the entire class period without speaking any English. On the Superstar Obstacle Course, they'll break outside their comfort zones to use the target language to experience something new. As Student Mentors, they'll grow into leadership roles and gain the self-confidence it takes to teach someone else what one has learned perhaps not all that long ago.

If all goes as expected, there will be a trickle-down effect among your students. Students who were somewhat reluctant at first to try out these programs will see their friends taking on the challenge, having fun, and succeeding at it—and might just give it a try themselves!

The goal underlying all of these programs, including your use of Bob the Imaginary Fly as a classroom assistant, is to create a learning environment that's comfortable for all learners. Your students will know they can check their anxieties and inhibitions about speaking another language at the classroom door, step inside your classroom, and relax. Yes, there are indeed times when perfection is possible—and even demanded. But alternating these times with times when learners can feel comfortable enough to take risks—to undertake the all-important activity of making mistakes and learning from them—will make all the difference in the world in getting students to sign on as lifelong learners of the language.

Discussion Questions

1. A key to helping learners summon the courage to take risks is to find out what makes them anxious in the first place. Making mistakes in front of the class? Getting a bad grade? Fear of seeming silly in front of their friends?

Identify some of the obstacles to learning the target language that you've observed among your students. What are the classroom manifestations of these? How can you customize the activities in this chapter to accommodate these challenges?

2. Think about what motivates your students to use the target language. Do some have friends or family who speak the language? Do others just want to add another A to their report cards? Do still others have plans to go to school abroad or to work in the future with the language? How might you use these differing motivations to customize the activities in this chapter?

3. The first three of these activities (Language Masters, Superstar Obstacle Course, and Student Mentors) rely on a good deal of student initiative. How might you monitor your students' progress? How can you check to see that students are continuing to be motivated to overcome their personal roadblocks? How often do you need to check in with them?

4. You may be wondering if you can summon up your own courage to dive in and try the Bob, the Imaginary Fly activity, especially if the inherent playfulness of this activity presents a side of you that you normally don't show to your students. Think about adapting this activity to your personality or teaching style. How can you keep the advantages of the activity while toning down the quirkiness?

5. Participation in these activities will almost certainly lead to higher levels of learner self-confidence. How can you capitalize on this? How can you continue to develop this self-confidence and keep students excited and open to language growth opportunities? How can you integrate this excitement back into the classroom?

For Further Reading

Brown, H. D. (2000). *Principles of language learning and teaching.* (4th ed.). Upper Saddle River, NJ: Pearson Education.

Cook, G. (2000). *Language play, language learning.* New York: Oxford University Press.

Dornyei, Z. (2001). *Motivational strategies in the language classroom.* New York: Cambridge University Press.

Lefevre, D. N. (2002). *Best new games: 77 games and 7 trust activities for all ages and abilities.* Champaign, IL: Human Kinetics.

Helpful Web Sites

The Web has endless examples of successful peer tutoring and mentoring programs, such as the Cross-Age and Peer Tutoring program outlined in the ERIC Clearinghouse digest on Reading, English, and Communication Digest 78: http://reading.indiana.edu/ieo/digests/d78.html

Valuable resources are available to language teachers through 14 federally funded Language Resources Centers. Start your exploration through the joint Web site at http://www.ed.gov/help/site/expsearch/language.html

Share ideas for encouraging learners with other language teachers on the FLTEACH listserv: http://www.cortland.edu/flteach/flteach-res.html. The FLTEACH Web site also includes a variety of links to language teaching and learning resources.

chapter

3

Learner Investment

We all know that you can't force a student to learn. All the talking in the world—all the theatrics at the front of the classroom—won't sink in if a student doesn't want to learn or simply doesn't care. Awakening the interest, that's the key. But what can we do to create an environment in which students will be invested in their own learning?

Activity 3.1	Discovering Student Interests
Activity 3.2	Students as Experts
Activity 3.3	Creative Bulletin Boards
Activity 3.4	Students' Rights and Responsibilities

In response to this challenge, many speak of *student-centered* education, but the term seems to mean different things to different people. In the villages, student-centered works on at least three distinct, but related levels: content, management, and personal growth. First, students are asked what they're interested in learning about and how they'd like to learn it. What kinds of expertise, language related or

otherwise, do the students have? Second, students are frequently put into positions of leadership within the villages. Students share areas of expertise with their classmates and sometimes teach younger students.

Finally, students aren't allowed to get complacent, learning only about areas with which they're already familiar. They're often nudged out of their comfort zone and encouraged to try new things, all with the goal of personal growth in mind.

The activities in this chapter will help you get students involved in the entire process of learning, from the very beginning to the very end. The more your students' thinking has been integrated into the design of the classroom—how it looks, what topics are discussed, and even the rules that govern it—the more likely they will open their minds and their attitudes to learning with you. And isn't that the whole point?

Activity 3.1   DISCOVERING STUDENT INTERESTS

In the Villages

Informal needs and interest assessments are used regularly in the villages to determine what the villagers need or want to learn about. During the time outside of small language groups, learners choose which activities they'd like to participate in. Even within the more structured language sessions, learner input is often gathered to help teachers and counselors decide which aspects of the target culture to cover and which forms and functions of the language to focus on. Allowing villagers to influence their learning environment has proven to be an effective way to getting their attention and keeping them engaged.

In the Classroom

In this activity, you will use questionnaires and student discussions at a variety of times throughout the year to give your students a say in their learning. Early in the semester, you'll brainstorm functional language topics and cultural themes and tie these to your instructional plans. As the year progresses, you'll discover which of your teaching strategies and methods your students find most helpful. Through periodic student self-assessments and reflections on learning, both you and your students will gain insights into the crucial interconnections between teaching and learning.

Objectives
- **Communication**
  - Students will be able to express likes, dislikes, interests, needs, and learning preferences in the target language.
- **Connections, Cultures**
  - Students will pursue their favorite topics and personal interests in the target language and culture.
- **Communities**
  - Students will develop a sense of community spirit by having a voice in the course curriculum and instruction.

Language Functions in Focus
- Evaluating
- Expressing opinions
- Suggesting

Preparation and Materials

Think about your plans for the course. What are your overall learning objectives for the students as related to the 5 Cs (communication, cultures, connections, comparisons and communities)? Where in your curriculum, semester, or year timetable is there some flexibility? What options could be given to the students? Might they be able to suggest cultural topics to pursue or vote on their favorites from a set of topics you present? Might they be able to choose from among different types of homework or from among different types of evaluation? Use these answers to prepare for the classroom discussion outlined next.

Following this discussion, be prepared to create a student interest questionnaire (as illustrated in the Presentation and Practice section) to distribute to all your students.

Create three forms to be completed by your students at various points throughout the course (see the Presentation and Practice section for details):

- Form 1:   Feedback on teaching strategies and methods (Figure 3.3)
- Form 2:   Learner self-assessment (Figure 3.4)
- Form 3:   Reflection on learning(Figure 3.5)

Generating Interest

Start off the project with a class discussion in which students come up with ideas for activities they would like to do throughout the year. Throw out some exciting suggestions, like a film festival (Activity 7.4) or a class newspaper (Activity 7.1), to get the ball rolling!

Compile your students' contributions into one list to gain a more complete view of all of their interests and wishes (see Figure 3.1). Hand out this list to your students in questionnaire form. Remember that some of your less vocal students may not voice their ideas during a public brainstorming session. To hear from all your students, you'll need this written version.

Presentation and Practice

Early in the Semester

Distribute your questionnaire to assess your students' likes and dislikes based on the brainstorming discussion. Add topics that did not come up during the discus-

FIGURE 3.1   *Sample Student Interest Questionnaires*

> Now it's time to think about what YOU want to DO in the target language! Circle everything you'd like to learn how to do or practice this year. Can you think of other situations?
>
> Order off a restaurant menu
>
> Buy something in a shop
>
> Write a letter or e-mail
>
> Make a phone call
>
> Read travel brochures
>
> Make travel arrangements
>
> Talk about your family and your interests
>
> Describe your city
>
> Tell a story
>
> Understand a movie
>
> Understand a TV show
>
> Invite someone out
>
> Other ideas:

> Thanks, everyone, for the terrific ideas! To give me a better idea of how our class can incorporate YOUR interests, please circle the topics you would most like to learn about this year. If you can think of any more ideas, add them to the list. Make sure to give specific ideas for the topics, if you have them:
>
> Food
>
> Music
>
> Cinema and TV
>
> History
>
> Politics and government
>
> Sports
>
> Poetry
>
> Other ideas:

FIGURE 3.2 *Sample Student Survey Results*

Your Survey Results

Topics	Percentage for This Topic	Plans for This Year
Food	100	We'll have our own cooking show.
Music	90	We're going to listen to French rap music.
Cinema and TV	100	We'll watch one of the most popular French movies from last year.
History	70	We'll look at works of art that portray the French Revolution.
Politics and government	50	We'll learn about several important politicians in French-speaking countries.
Sports	60	We'll play soccer against the Spanish class.
Poetry	55	We'll read and write poetry in French.

sion, but that you find interesting and important. You may wish to design separate questionnaires focusing on different types of classroom objectives (communication, cultures, connections, comparisons, and communities).

Once your students have completed the questionnaires and you've tallied up the votes, compare your students' feedback with your own plans for the class. Are there any matches? Can you incorporate some of the new ideas into your syllabus without much trouble? Will some ideas have to wait a year or two? Share the survey results with your students a day or so after they've turned them in. Display the information on an overhead transparency or give it out as a handout, as shown in Figure 3.2. It's important to show the students that their feedback is being considered in a thoughtful manner.

Periodically throughout the Year

Throughout the year, have regular check-in discussions to track how students feel about the class and their own learning. You may find it helpful to use questionnaires to guide the discussion. (See the sample questionnaires in Figures 3.3 through 3.5 for ideas, which you can expand or adapt as necessary.) In small groups or individually (depending on the topic you're asking about and the trust level among your students), ask the class to address such topics as teaching pedagogy, areas of learner

FIGURE 3.3 *Sample Teaching Strategies and Methods Questionnaire*

FORM 1:   Feedback on Teaching Strategies and Methods

Which of these helps you most in class?

Seeing constructions on the board

Practicing pronunciation

Listening to native speakers

Doing grammar exercises

Working in groups

Practicing conversations

Playing language games

Watching target language films

Reading short literary pieces

Writing reflection pieces

FIGURE 3.4   *Sample Learner Self-Assessment*

If you've designed your curriculum around interpersonal, presentational, and interpretive modes, simply incorporate these into Form 2: Learner Self-assessment. Think about using the following categories: interpersonal speaking and listening (conversation) and reading and writing (e-mail and letter correspondence); presentational speaking (giving an oral report) and writing (a project description on a class bulletin board); and interpretive listening (listening to an oral report) and reading (reading a project description or other more extended texts in class).

FORM 2:   Learner Self-assessment

Pronunciation

I think that pronouncing words in the target language is:

Easy

Fairly easy

Somewhat difficult

Difficult

Here's a word I think is hard to pronounce:

Here's a word I think is easy to pronounce:

Here's a word I think sounds funny!

Reading

I think that reading the target language is:

Easy

Fairly easy

Somewhat difficult

Difficult

Insert names of texts:

I liked reading _____ because:

I didn't like reading _____ because:

(continued)

FIGURE 3.4   *continued*

Writing

I think that writing in the target language is:

Easy

Fairly easy

Somewhat difficult

Difficult

Insert names of writing assignments:

I liked writing _____ because:

I didn't like writing _____ because:

Understanding Spoken Language

I think that understanding the spoken target language is:

Easy

Fairly easy

Somewhat difficult

Difficult

The easiest part about understanding spoken language is _____ .

The hardest part about understanding spoken language is _____ .

Speaking

I think that making myself understood when I speak the target language is:

Easy

Fairly easy

Somewhat difficult

Difficult

The easiest part about speaking is _____ .

The hardest part about speaking is _____ .

FIGURE 3.5 *Sample Student Reflection Form*

FORM 3: Reflection on Learning

Since the last time I completed this form,

My favorite activity in class was:

My least favorite activity in class was:

Two things I'm proud of:

1.

2.

Two things I could have done better:

1.

2.

I would like to improve in the following area between now and the next time I complete this form:

_____   _____
Name of student   Date of reflection

difficulty, learner progress, and goal setting. Collect the questionnaires and use their contents to make necessary or helpful changes in your curriculum and teaching style. Be sure to save the students' self-assessments and reflections on their learning and return them to the students when it's time to revisit this activity. Seeing what they wrote the last time will serve as important benchmarks for students and help them see how they are progressing and where they need to redouble their efforts.

Expansion

Have students identify material from other disciplines that would be interesting to learn about in the target language. For example, you can encourage them to learn more about the range of target culture views on health care or the environment. A class discussion on the topic might lead to e-mail or letter correspondence with native-speaker students of the target language or with your e-mates (see Activity 5.4).

Have advanced students write up a proposal of what they want to learn. This can be in a signed-petition form, lending itself well to small-group work. You may wish to provide a template for this genre and review grammatical structures that are likely to be used in persuasive prose before students embark on their own write-ups.

For extra credit, encourage students to research and report in the target language on a topic of their choice, such as a sports or entertainment icon, historical figure, holiday, or geographic region. See Superstar Obstacle Course (Activity 2.2) for more ideas.

Adaptation

We encourage you to adapt the ideas in this activity to your own interests, curricula, and teaching materials. For example, if you are going to study Tokyo, consider offering your students choices about which aspects of the city they'd like most to explore. If you are planning to focus on past tense, think of a range of possible contexts for the lesson (for example, elementary school years, family vacations, or political history) and let your students choose from among them.

Although the topics and activity choices may vary among age groups, student choice is important for everyone. You can limit choices to the areas you are willing and able to offer by providing explicit examples of the available options.

Options for Evaluation

Expectations Rubric					
	Agree				Disagree
You expressed your likes and dislikes in the target language regarding topics to be explored in class.	5	4	3	2	1
You identified which teaching methods are helping you the most to learn the target language.	5	4	3	2	1
You identified your relative strengths and weaknesses in the target language.	5	4	3	2	1
You reflected on what you have done well and not so well in class so far and have set specific goals for yourself for the near future.	5	4	3	2	1

Student Journal Questions

The questionnaires given in this activity already serve as good opportunities to record individual students' needs, interests, and development. At the end of the year, you can have students write a reflective piece that explores their development as language learners over time. As they address the following questions, encourage your students to draw on their past written reflections:

1. Were you able to learn everything that you decided you wanted to at the beginning of the year? What topics do you look forward to learning more about in future language courses?
2. How do you think you have improved over the semester in terms of speaking, reading, writing, and listening? How have your abilities in these four areas changed from the start of the semester? What do you attribute this to? (Alternatively, how do you think you have improved over the semester in terms of interpersonal, presentational, and interpretive modes?)
3. What activities helped you learn the most? Why do you think this is so?
4. What were your favorite and least favorite parts of the class? Why?
5. What do you think about having the opportunity to tell your teacher about your interests and goals in learning the target language? Do you think it made a difference in your learning? Do you think future students should have the chance to make suggestions and give feedback on class the way you were able to this semester or year?

Portfolio Entries

1. Include copies of Forms 1 to 3 (Figures 3.3 through 3.5) that were completed by students over the course of the year. Answers to the journal questions above can serve as the final piece.
2. For beginning learners, include the survey-results handout, followed by a short written response to journal question 1.

Customizing This Activity for Your Classroom

1. Before collecting your students' ideas, take a little time to think about your own. What kinds of responses do you expect your students to give in terms of their specific interests and needs? If you've done the activity already, in which ways did your students' responses differ from your original expectations? What do you attribute this to?
2. Think about a language class you participated in in years past. Did your instructor encourage the development of learner autonomy by giving you choice in the syllabus and room for feedback on the course? How did you view this as a student? How do you see such opportunities for feedback now?
3. What do you think about giving students a voice in their own learning? Do you believe there are limits? Are there certain contextual variables, such as age, proficiency level, and gender, that might influence your answer?
4. Can you think of any challenges to giving the students this much say in the classroom?
5. Can you think of additional ways to foster students' voices in their learning beyond this activity?
6. If you've conducted this activity already, what have you learned from your students' insights? How did their self-assessments measure up against your assessments of their language learning?

Activity 3.2   STUDENTS AS EXPERTS

In the Villages

Concordia Language Villages' counselors occasionally allow learners to take on the role of teacher. Some villagers work as peer teachers, perform meal presentations in the dining hall, edit the village newspaper, or even act as counselors for an entire day. This flipping of expert and novice roles seems to energize learners and increases their involvement in the learning process. It seems that being a leader—even for a brief while—brings out the best in language learners!

In the Classroom

In this activity, your students as experts will have a choice: Either they can use the target language to teach their fellow students something the experts are already good at, such as playing the drums or doing a magic trick, or they can *become* experts on a language or cultural topic of their choosing and then teach that topic to the class. Either way, learners become directly involved in the curriculum and solidify their own target language presentational abilities—and they help you out in the process!

Objectives
- ■ **Communication**
  - • Students will be able to present an area of interest and/or expertise to their peers.
- ■ **Connections**
  - • Students will develop knowledge in an area of their interest through the target language.
- ■ **Communities**
  - • Students will develop autonomy in the learning process.
    Students will understand how their individual contributions serve to develop the larger classroom community.

Language Functions in Focus
- ■ Describing procedures and processes
- ■ Presenting information
- ■ Reporting
- ■ Suggesting

Preparation and Materials

You won't need any special materials for this activity. Just grab a piece of paper and pencil for the initial brainstorming exercise to get you thinking about what it means to be an expert. Look up the word *expert* in several dictionaries and write down the definitions. Then think about yourself and friends, colleagues, and family members. What are your areas of expertise? What makes you feel like an expert in a particular area? What makes you think that another individual is an expert in his or her area?

Now decide what you'd like to call this activity in your target language. Designate a bulletin board in your classroom to display audience responses to the Students as Experts projects. Decorate the board with a sign announcing the program.

Next, it's time to come up with a set of topics you'd like your students, as experts, to present on in class. Look over the language and content topics that you plan to cover during the entire course. Which of these areas could be expanded with a student presentation—and how? Presentation options can be arranged according to particular themes, such as holidays, geography, or everyday culture, or according to language topics. If you'd like to highlight the diversity of the French-speaking world, for example, have one group of students present on the geography of North Africa and another on the geography of Provence. If you'd like to have students learn about various aspects of everyday culture, have different groups present on current music, television series, school systems, and food.

An alternative is to allow your learners to present their own chosen interests outside the target language and culture, such as astronomy, making friendship bracelets, even taking apart a motor! Just make sure that they realize they'll be teaching their hobby to their friends *in the target language*. This is a good way to get some of your less enthusiastic learners to take on a more active role in class.

Once you've decided on the approach you'd like to take, create a sign-up list with the topics and a set of possible presentation dates.

Make a handout outlining the criteria for successful student presentations. See the Presentation and Practice section for details and some guidelines.

Create a worksheet to help your students prepare for their presentations. See the Presentation and Practice section for one model (Figure 3.6).

Generating Interest

With your students, brainstorm possible definitions of the word *expert*. Probe further by asking such questions as these: Can *everyone* be an expert in something? How do we get to be experts in an area? How can we tell when others are experts?

Then ask your students about their individual interests and hobbies. What do they think they're good at? These areas *don't* have to have anything to do with the target language and culture. Some will be good at skiing; others will be good at photography. Be ready to share with them your own special area of skill and/or knowledge, whether it be in ballet, baseball, or baking.

Now begin to make the connection to your course. Ask students which aspects of the target language or culture they would like to learn more about, maybe even to become expert in.

Presentation and Practice

After talking about your students' responses, it's time to introduce the Students as Experts program. Explain to the students that each week pairs of student experts will teach their fellow class members something. They can either teach something they're *already* good at (but in the target language, of course!), or they can spend some time becoming an expert in an area related to the target language and/or culture and *then* teach it to the others.

Before you ask your students to commit to a topic, go over the criteria for the short presentations. Here are some guidelines you can use.

---

1. You will have 10 to 15 minutes to present with your partner on your area of expertise.
2. Leading up to your presentation, list four to eight vocabulary words or phrases on the board that are important for your audience's understanding of your presentation. Go over these briefly.
3. In your presentation, you should
   A. Introduce your topic.
   B. Give three to five different facts about your topic that you think your audience will find interesting.
   C. Conclude by talking about the significance of the topic.
4. Use pictures, music, and other props to liven up your presentation.
5. Part of your grade depends on the level of preparation you give to the project. Two weeks before your presentation, you'll have a planning meeting with me. Bring an outline of your presentation with you. (You'll get an advance organizer from me to help you organize this information.)

After sharing the criteria, you may wish to model a presentation for the class so that students understand the expectations.

FIGURE 3.6 *Worksheet Model*

Student names:

Our topic is:

We chose this topic because:

Important vocabulary words or phrases (4 to 8) for this topic are:

Interesting facts (3 to 5) about this topic are:

We will include the following pictures, music, or other props:

The significance of this topic is:

Now it's time to bring out the sign-up list you created previously. Add any suitable new ideas that surfaced in your discussion with your students. Have your students sign up with partners for a topic that interests them. (If you have a large number of students and topics, you may want to ask students to turn in a sheet with their top three choices for both topic and partner. In this way you'll be able to make sure that each student gets one top choice and gets to work with a friend.)

Once the students have chosen their topics, emphasize the importance of preparation for this presentation. Distribute a worksheet (modeled on Figure 3.6) to help the students organize their ideas for their talks.

Two weeks prior to the presentation date, each pair should meet with you. They'll bring an outline of their presentation (based on the worksheet) to discuss their progress. Give the students feedback on language and content and help them to structure their information.

On the day of a presentation, introduce the "experts." As they are presenting, take a Polaroid or digital photograph of the experts at work and ask students who are listening to take notes on what they are learning. The audience members will use their notes to write a brief response to the experts, in which they highlight their favorite part of the presentation. Once you've collected all the comments, post them along with the photograph of the experts on the Students as Experts bulletin board.

Provide students with an opportunity for self-evaluation by opening a class discussion the following class period or having students write an essay or journal entry about their experiences as presenting experts.

At the end of the school year or semester, review the range of material that was presented as part of this activity and brainstorm new topics to be used with the next class.

Expansion

Use presentations by the student experts as part of the Generating Interest phase of other activities in this book. For example, students presenting on the topic of dance could prepare their classmates with background information related to the dance they'll be learning as part of Dancing (Activity 6.2). Other students with an interest in gardening could prepare their classmates with valuable information leading to long-term Gardening activity (Activity 7.3). The interconnections across activities in this book are virtually limitless. Encouraging these connections will both strengthen the activities and increase your students' investment in them.

Tie each Students as Experts presentation directly to the Creative Bulletin Boards activity (Activity 3.3). In this way you can emphasize the presentational mode through both writing and speaking.

Work with other teachers of your target language to give your students opportunities to present their topics to other classes.

Adaptation

Have students work in larger groups or teach smaller parts of a lesson to work around time constraints.

Have younger or less advanced learners come up with an activity to review previous material or things already discussed in class to refresh the class and to give speaking practice.

Create templates in the target language to help beginning students gather information and prepare their presentations. Scaffolding the assignment in this way will provide these students with valuable models for future projects.

Options for Evaluation

Expectations Rubric					
	Agree				Disagree
Your preparation for the presentation was well-developed and organized.	5	4	3	2	1
Your presentation included the following: An introduction to the topic Three to five different facts about your topic that you think your audience would find interesting A conclusion in which you identify the significance of your topic	5	4	3	2	1
Your presentation displayed independence and self-initiative in learning.	5	4	3	2	1

Student Journal Questions

1. Why did you choose the particular topic for your presentation?
2. What was the biggest challenge in this activity?
3. What did you learn about your topic?
4. What did you learn about your fellow classmates' topics?
5. How do you think you did in presenting your topic? What advice would you give to next year's students for presenting in front of a class?
6. What sorts of topics would you want to become an expert in next year?
7. What topics would you suggest for next year's class? Why would you choose these topics?

Portfolio Entries

1. Include the worksheet that was used to prepare the presentation.
2. Have student presenters include copies of the audience's responses to their presentation.
3. Have intermediate and advance students write a short report of their presentation based on the advance organizer and their presentation.
4. Have beginning students as a class write a list of tips for next year's students. A group list of presentation topics can also be created.

Customizing This Activity for Your Classroom

1. Think back on your own language-learning experiences. Did you ever give an in-class presentation? What was the topic? How did it go? What did you learn? How did it contribute to your overall language-learning experience?
2. This activity may involve considerable in- and out-of-class time for preparation and presentation. How could it be conducted to fit into an already full curriculum?
3. What kinds of topics or themes associated with the target language or culture do you think younger learners would be interested in presenting? What about older learners? Why?

4. Think about sources of information for this project. How might you direct your students toward relevant information for their projects?
5. What areas would you view as potential challenges in this activity? How could you overcome them?
6. How can other disciplines be brought into this activity? Are there resources at your school that you could tap into for ideas?

Activity 3.3   CREATIVE BULLETIN BOARDS

In the Villages

At Concordia Language Villages, learners have important opportunities to make creative presentations in the target language in front of large groups of villagers and staff. These learners are encouraged to interweave cultural themes of the day, selected language forms and functions, songs, and even in-jokes in these presentations. Illustrations include ethnic food presentations in the dining hall before each mealtime, live radio shows, moonlit theatrical performances, and introductions of village-wide evening programs.

In the Classroom

One way to bring the presentational opportunities of Concordia Language Villages into the classroom is through this Creative Bulletin Boards program. By having your students design bulletin boards, they can help to create a welcoming classroom environment, gain expertise on particular thematic units in the curriculum, exercise their creative spirit, and take responsibility to help others to learn. Ideally, this program should be introduced at the beginning of the year and continued throughout the entire school year or semester.

Objectives
■ **Communication**
  • Students will review and develop language forms and vocabulary of a particular unit in a more intensive way.
  • Students will develop a deeper understanding of unit themes and language content.

- **Cultures**
  - Students will be able to extend unit knowledge through exploration of the target culture.
- **Communities**
  - Students will build confidence and investment in language learning through the development of autonomy and expertise.
  - Students will work together as a team to reach a common goal.

Language Functions in Focus

- presenting information
- suggesting

Preparation and Materials

- One large bulletin board
- Colored construction paper
- Scissors
- Tape
- Stapler
- Colored markers or crayons
- Other materials to be used to decorate the bulletin board

You may decide to combine the visual focus of this bulletin board activity with the oral presentation focus in the Students as Experts program (Activity 3.2). In that case, you could come up with one cover term for both programs.

Decide what you will call this program in your target language.

Come up with a list of possible bulletin board topics. Decide how often you would like the bulletin board design to change (once a week? once a month?). The size of your class and the frequency of board changes will influence the size of student groups working on each board.

Make a handout outlining the guidelines and evaluation criteria for the creative bulletin board. See the Generating Interest section for one model (Figure 3.7).

Design the first bulletin board yourself as a model for your students to follow in subsequent weeks and months.

Generating Interest

Introduce this activity to your students. Show them the bulletin board you designed as a model. As you describe the activity, highlight the information in Figure 3.7. Connect this information to relevant parts of your bulletin board. Be sure to outline how you plan to evaluate their work.

Presentation and Practice

Split the class into groups of four to six students. Hand out a list of units you plan to include in your course. Have students write down ideas for bulletin board content and design that are sparked by the topics on the list.

Have each small group turn in a sheet listing two or three topics that interest them. Look over these lists to align the selected topics with your syllabus and school calendar. Hand out a sheet listing the groups and topics assigned to them, along with the dates on which each group is responsible for the bulletin board.

Two weeks before each due date, have the responsible group turn in a proposal to you. This can be in the form of a sketch of their ideas with labeled items, along with materials they plan to use. You may wish to ask students to list their individual responsibilities to ensure that the work is distributed fairly among group members. Refer the students to Figure 3.7 for specific information and evaluation criteria. If your students are stuck on how to frame the information, suggest cartoon strips, stories, diagrams, maps, game boards, or even more interactive texts like those found in a pop-up book.

Give the students quick feedback so that they can begin putting together their ideas in time for the unit. Pay special attention to the language and/or cultural information to be presented.

FIGURE 3.7 *Guidelines for Activity 3.3*

The purpose of this program is to give you the opportunity to work with a small group of students in the design of a classroom bulletin board. In this way, you can learn with others about a particular cultural or language theme in our curriculum, let your creative juices flow, and ultimately use your knowledge and creativity to share with other students in the class what you've learned. Keep this in mind as you both choose the information you want to highlight and design the bulletin board.

Be as creative as you'd like, but make sure to include the language forms and functions (or cultural information) introduced and practiced in our unit.

I will act as your editor. Turn in a proposal to me 2 weeks before the unit begins (you'll see the schedule attached to this sheet) so that I can give you feedback on the language and/or cultural content. In your proposal, include a sketch of how your bulletin board will look and a list of materials you plan to use. Be sure to highlight the ways in which you will present the major language and/or cultural information.

Your bulletin board will be graded according to the following criteria:

Presentation of Information on the Bulletin Board

Q: Is the information organized and presented effectively so that the class can refer to the bulletin board in class?

Language Use

Q: Does the language on the board represent the language highlighted in the unit?

Cultural Content

Q: Do the vocabulary and information given show knowledge of the cultural topic?

Oral Presentation

Q: Did your group present the main points on your board clearly and effectively to the class members?

Teamwork

Q: Did everyone participate equally?

Negotiate a time when the students can gather to assemble their bulletin board. Can they come in before school? Stay after school? Come in during lunch? Think about allowing several days between the dismantling of the previous bulletin board and the unveiling of the new one. This will allow students to carry out their work during a designated period of class time. No matter how the board is assembled, make sure the students cover their work-in-progress with a large sheet of butcher block paper so that the unveiling will be a surprise!

On the day of the unveiling, call up the presenting students to the front of class. Perhaps you can think of a ritual to be chanted or sung as the bulletin board is being unveiled. Once the bulletin board is in full view, give the presenters 5 to 10 minutes to describe the main points on the board. Encourage them to be especially creative in their oral presentation. Perhaps they would like to dress like some of the figures on the board. Maybe they would like to become verbs or adjectives (or whatever is highlighted on the board). The crazier the presentation is, the more attention they'll get from class members—and the more the class members will want to go up to the board after class and look carefully at the information and images on it.

While you are teaching related information in your unit, refer to the information on the bulletin board, especially to point out variations and extensions of the language and/or cultural information presented. This recognition will send a message to your presenting students that their work is useful and meaningful, both to you and to the class.

Expansion

Create contests for the most creative, most helpful, and funniest bulletin boards and have the students vote.

Set specific parameters around the project, such as including classmates' names, photos, and brief biographical information on the board or hiding a "Where's Waldo"-like character or object.

Make this activity a part of Activity 2.2 (Superstar Obstacle Course) and tie this activity to Activity 3.2 (Students as Experts). In this way you can emphasize the presentational mode through both speaking and writing.

Adaptation

If you do not have a bulletin board to work with, try using flip-chart-sized paper. Take a few minutes before class to hang up these sheets for the class to see during the lesson. Keep them up during the entire unit and refer to them periodically.

Younger learners may need more guidance and structure than older students on this project. Provide these students with precut images or figures for them to place on the bulletin board.

Or try this variation with your youngest students: Every culture has mythical, folk, and cartoon characters that appeal to children. Copy a page from a coloring book of the target culture (or from a target culture Web site) onto a transparency. Trace the enlarged image from the overhead projector onto a big piece of white paper hung on the bulletin board. Have students color and label different parts of the picture.

Options for Evaluation

Expectations Rubric					
	Agree				Disagree
Your bulletin board contained the following: Clear presentation of the material Language use highlighted in the unit Knowledge of the topic in the unit	5	4	3	2	1
Your group presented the information from the bulletin board effectively.	5	4	3	2	1
You contributed to the team effort to complete the bulletin board and help in the presentation.	5	4	3	2	1

Student Journal Questions
1. What did you learn from the bulletin board project?
2. What did your fellow classmates learn from your bulletin board?
3. What part of the bulletin board are you most proud of? Why?
4. Did any questions or problems come up with your group? How did you deal with them?
5. If you had to do your bulletin board over again, what would you do differently?

Portfolio Entries
1. Include the proposal that was used in preparation for the project and presented to you for feedback.
2. Take a photo of the students during their presentation of the finished bulletin board. Make photocopies of this picture to include in each participating student's portfolio. If you would like students to focus on the development of the project, rather than merely the product, you can take pictures of their bulletin board at various stages. Under each photo to be included in the portfolio, have students write a few sentences to capture the process of their work.

Peer Evaluation
You may also want to include peer evaluation in this project. Keep a comment sheet or an envelope for peer comments next to the bulletin board for student use.

Customizing This Activity for Your Classroom
1. How could you make the guidelines for this activity (Figure 3.7) more specific? What additional information would help your students get the most out of this project? (Think about the integration of target language and culture, the visual presentation of the language, the use of additional images or pictures, and the like.)

2. These bulletin boards can assist the students in the class who learn best visually. How might you, as the teacher, capitalize on this valuable classroom resource during your teaching?
3. What specific goals do you have for your students as they carry out this project?
4. Do you foresee any challenges in this activity? How could you overcome them?
5. How can you ensure that the groups work as teams in this project?

Activity 3.4 STUDENTS' RIGHTS AND RESPONSIBILITIES

In the Villages

Many cabin counselors at Concordia Language Villages involve their villagers in the process of rule making on the very first evening of their stay in the village. Of course, some rules relating to health and safety are nonnegotiable. Villagers can't decide, for example, on rules that allow a 2 a.m. bedtime or leaving the cabin after lights-out. Discussions typically center on rules related to areas on which there *can* be flexibility, such as showing respect and courtesy towards one's living companions by keeping noise levels down during rest periods and not spraying insect repellant inside the cabin. The responsibility villagers feel in creating the kind of community in which they want to live usually translates into subsequent support for the rules. After all, the villagers had a say in coming up with the rules in the first place!

In the Classroom

In this activity, you will lead your students in a discussion of the role of rules in school classrooms. Under your leadership early in the school year, your students will identify a set of rules to guide life in your classroom. While its emphasis is on building community, this activity offers students important opportunities for target language practice and expansion of cultural knowledge.

Objectives
- ■ **Communication**
  - • Students will be able to state that a particular activity is allowed or prohibited.
  - • Students will be able to ask for and give permission.
  - • Students will be able to give a command to either start or stop an activity.

- **Connections**
  - Students will reflect on the motivation underlying school rules.
- **Comparisons, Cultures**
  - Students will be able to compare school rights and responsibilities within home and target cultures.
- **Communities**
  - Students will think about their immediate needs in the classroom, as well as issues of respect and responsibility within the classroom community.
  - Students will have a role in the design and implementation of classroom management, thereby supporting a positive classroom atmosphere.

Language Functions in Focus

- Asking for and giving permission
- Expressing opinions
- Giving commands
- Giving reasons
- Suggesting

Preparation and Materials

- Poster board or large sheets of white paper
- Colored markers

Before you get your students thinking about rights and rules, do a little brainstorming yourself. Think about rules in your life. What rules come immediately to mind? Which rules do you gladly follow? Which rules annoy you? Think back to the time when you were the age of the students in your class. Which rules did you want to fight against back then? Which rules were you happy to have in place? Can you think of a time when you had an argument with your parents or teachers about a particular rule? Who won the argument? Why?

How do rules relate to an overall discussion of rights and responsibilities? What rights are important to you? What responsibilities do you have related to these rights?

If you know about rules that typically exist within schools in your target culture, write down some of the rules you think your students would find most surprising. Think about similarities and differences between rules that guide school life in the target culture and those that guide life in the school where you teach.

Generating Interest

You may want to frame this activity in terms of famous rules, laws, or rights that the students are already familiar with, such as the U.S. Bill of Rights or traffic laws.

Lead a discussion to get your students thinking about the role of rules and laws in their lives. Gain insight into their knowledge and opinions by posing questions such as the following:

- Why do we have rules?
- What are some examples of rules?
- What kinds of rules exist in your home? Are these fair?
- What kinds of rules exist in school? Are these fair?
- What kinds of laws exist in our country? Are these fair?
- What happens if someone breaks these rules or laws?

Presentation and Practice

Now it's time to move from a general discussion to one focused on your classroom. First, make sure your students are prepared with the target language background they need to move ahead with the activity. Depending on the language level of your students, either introduce or review the following:

1. Ways to state in the target language that a particular activity is allowed or encouraged ("soft conversation allowed") or prohibited ("eating prohibited")
2. Ways to ask for and give permission in the target language ("May I . . . ," "Yes, you may . . .")
3. Ways to give a command in the target language either to start or stop an activity ("Stop talking right now!" "Begin discussing now!")

Take some time to practice these structures with your students.

If you know about rules that typically exist within schools in your target culture, bring these into the discussion now. Link the forms of these rules to the language lesson you've just given. Talk about some of the rules you think your students will find most surprising. Get their reactions to these rules. Give your students a sense of how classrooms and schools are run in the target culture, highlighting the similarities and differences that exist between those schools and the school in which you teach. If you've had personal experiences as a student or teacher of these in the target culture, tell a couple of stories that show how you reacted to these similarities or differences the first time you were confronted with them.

Now divide the students into small groups. Include in each one of the more responsible and respected students in your class. Designate these natural leaders as small-group discussion leaders. Ask each group to come up with three to five important rules related to behavior in your classroom. Write some sample rules on the board, such as the following, to provide students with target language models.

- Students should raise their hands and be called on by the teacher before they start speaking.
- Students should not chew gum during class.
- Students' cell phones should be turned off during class time.

Give the students some topics to think about during their discussion.

- Beginning and ending the class period
- Using the target language
- Eating, drinking, and chewing gum
- Talking in general, raising hands
- Homework
- Cell phones

Have each group write down the members' consensus choices and be prepared to present the reasons for its rule proposals. Beginning students may need to use primarily English to carry out this activity, whereas more advanced students should be able use the target language with occasional assistance from you.

After all contributions have been collected and shared with the class, have students vote on their favorites. Write the winners up in their order of preference (in the target language, of course!) on a piece of poster board or large piece of white paper. Hang the list on the wall and keep it there throughout the year. Have students come up with a fitting title for the rules. Some artistic students may wish to add colored illustrations to brighten the list and to clarify the meaning of the rules (for example, a pack of gum with a slash or × through it to designate no gum chewing in class).

Be prepared for some crazy answers from your students. While it is important to respect all contributions, you can counteract some of the more unusual ones with outrageous demands from a teacher's perspective, such as "Any student coming late to class must bring me a candy bar!"

Expansion

Have your students create an official handbook of the rules.

Revisit this activity throughout the year. Draw on the rules in subsequent lessons to review particular language forms, or remind students of their drafted rules at a later date as fitting occasions arise, such as tardiness or out-of-control talking during quiet work.

Have students create a set of rules for a fictitious community that fits with a course unit, such as a university, town, sports event, or government (see Activity 6.4).

Adaptation

Have younger and/or beginning students create a class list of Ten Things Needed for Success in School. Start off the students with simple phrases (an adjective and a noun): "an open mind" or "sharp pencils." Have them contribute the rest of the ideas. Think about supplying them with two sets of words (adjectives and nouns) from which to start.

World cultures have varied systems of rules and laws. Every culture has rules (written and understood); they not only take different forms, but also have different meanings. This would be a valuable opportunity to explore cultural differences beyond the school context.

Options for Evaluation

Expectations Rubric					
	Agree				Disagree
You showed that you can use the target language to state that a particular activity is allowed or prohibited, to give and ask for permission, and to give a command to start and stop an activity.	5	4	3	2	1
You have thought about the role of rules and laws in society and have come up with relevant examples.	5	4	3	2	1
You compared school rights and responsibilities in home and target cultures.	5	4	3	2	1
You have contributed actively to a discussion on school rules and how these relate to the rights and responsibilities of students and teachers.	5	4	3	2	1
You expressed your own classroom needs and recognized and respected the needs of others.	5	4	3	2	1

Student Journal Questions

1. How did you feel about writing up your own rights and responsibilities? Was it fun? Boring? Hard? Easy? Were some class rules easier than others?
2. What was your favorite rule? Your least favorite? Why?
3. If you had the opportunity to rewrite the rules, would you change anything? Why? Whom or what would your new rules affect?
4. Do you think we need laws and rules? Why or why not?
5. Give an example of a law or rule that you do or do not agree with. Explain your reasons.

Portfolio Entries

1. Include the list of rules and responsibilities created by the entire class.
2. Include the handbook described in the Expansion section for an advanced class.

Customizing This Activity for Your Classroom

1. Think back on your own learning experiences. Did your teachers ever give you a chance to help identify your own rules and responsibilities? If so, how did you view this? If not, would you have wanted your instructor to give you a greater voice in the classroom? Why or why not?
2. What language forms (vocabulary and grammar) tied to your specific target language could be introduced and/or practiced through this activity?
3. What kinds of challenges do you foresee in this activity? How could you overcome them?
4. Think about how various rules in the classroom might affect the 5 Cs. What sorts of rules could address goals of the communication standard? the cultures standard? the communities standard? Does the age or proficiency level of your students make a difference in your response?

It's Your Turn!

Customization. That's what the ideas in this chapter boil down to. How can you shape your tried-and-true ways of doing things—those things that work time and time again in the classroom—to the needs and interests of the students who are in your classroom right now? And why does it matter? Why is it critical that your learners have a consistent say in what they do in your course?

Obviously, you're the one with the experience and training, and very frequently you *do* know what is best for your students. On the other hand, your students know what their specific background knowledge is and what their motivations, goals, and interests are. The more information you have about these, the more effectively you can attune your teaching plans to your students. Recognition of the efforts you've made to incorporate their input will almost certainly lead students to become more invested in the course. They'll feel more comfortable within the classroom and sense that you're all in this learning endeavor together. The key is finding the balance.

It's not always easy to figure out how student interests and goals can be incorporated into your curriculum guidelines using the textbooks and other materials you have at your disposal. Remember, there *is* a middle ground. You may not be able to offer units on everything your students are interested in. In cases when particular student interests conflict with school or community standards, you can control their choices. You can still give learners options, but only within areas you're comfortable covering. Other student interests may be in areas in which you have no expertise at all. In these cases, you may be able to enlist the assistance of a student who *does* have expertise in the area or who at least has a sincere interest in developing such expertise. Getting students to share some of the responsibility of teaching may allow you to cover a great deal more material than you could alone. Students may have a special way of opening up the eyes of their fellow students to specialized topics through in-depth individual or small-group projects.

Student-generated topics also set the tone of a learning community where *all* participants are learning something—including you! Offering students opportunities to take on teaching roles allows them to grow personally in many ways and will enhance the classroom group as a whole.

Discussion Questions

1. The amount of responsibility students are given for their own learning varies widely around the world. Classrooms look very different in terms of the division of labor between teacher and students. In some classrooms, teachers have near total control, even talking almost 100 percent of the time. In other classrooms, students are seen to be actively learning from each other, with teachers off to the side gently observing and stepping in to redirect and guide as needed. The cultures associated with the language you teach may have a strong preference along these lines. If the societal pressures in these cultures lead to students taking much less initiative than in the United States, how can you deal with this? How can you let students know that they're learning the language of and about the target culture, but that the teaching they're a part of is necessarily more American than that of the target culture?

2. The notions expressed in this chapter are relevant to activities in other chapters in this book. Take a favorite activity from another chapter and look at it through the lens of learner investment. How can you incorporate the ideas from this chapter more integrally into those in the others?

3. Some teachers fear that putting students in leadership positions may result in chaos in the classroom. How can you find a balance? How can you ensure that student presentations will be of high enough quality to benefit the student audience? How can you make sure that time is managed wisely? How can you carry this off without losing your authority as a teacher?

For Further Reading

Brown, H. D. (2001). *Teaching by principles: An interactive approach to language pedagogy* (2nd ed.). Upper Saddle River, NJ: Prentice Hall Regents.

Chamot, A. U., Barnhardt, S., El-Dinary, P. B., & Robbins, J. (1999). *The learning strategies handbook*. White Plains, NY: Addison Wesley Longman, Inc.

Kagan, S. (1989). *Cooperative learning: Resources for teachers*. Riverside: University of California.

Nunan, D. (1998). *The learner-centered curriculum: A study in second language*. New York: Cambridge University Press.

Helpful Web Sites

Guide learners' research using a WebQuest: http://webquest.sdsu.edu.

A fun language-learning lesson plan for making rules with your students is on the Boggle's World Web site: http://bogglesworld.com/lessons/2002janfeb.htm

PART 2

Taking Off!

From our focus in chapters 2 and 3 on the creation of a welcoming and challenging classroom environment, we turn in the next four chapters to the implementation of activities tied to specific content areas in the service of the guiding principles of Concordia Language Villages. As they move through these activities, students are encouraged to reflect on similarities and differences between cultural products and practices in their target and home cultures. They are gently prodded into using the target language by feeling a real need to communicate, and they draw on all of their senses, not just those of sight and hearing, to experience the target language more holistically. Finally, they accomplish entire projects with their classmates through the systematic use of the target language.

Many potential connections exist between the activities in these Taking Off! chapters and those activities that were part of Setting the Tone. Some activities in this section will tie up quite naturally to the interests and ideas that surfaced in discussions with your students as part of Discovering Student Interests (Activity 3.1). Other activities will help students explore areas they identified as personal favorites for individual or small group work connected to the Superstar Obstacle Course (Activities 2.2), Students as Experts (Activity 3.2), or Creative Bulletin Boards (Activity 3.3). Still other activities (or portions of them) may assist the select group of students who decide to help younger or lower-level language students in the Student Mentors program (Activity 2.3).

You'll soon see that the 16 activities presented in Taking Off! vary widely in terms of duration and complexity from fairly minimal time commitments with relatively simple preparation in Telephoning (Activitiy 5.3) and Tracing Bodies (Activity 6.3), to the slightly more complicated Living Maps (Activitiy 4.2) and Sensory Path (Activity 6.1) to extensive, multifaceted projects such as Gardening (Activity 7.3) and Film Festival (Activity 7.4). This variation allows you to integrate just what you need for the amount of time you have. If you find yourself drawn to a particular activity but you don't have the time to carry it out in full, don't worry. In reading through the activities you'll see that you can focus your attention on specific tasks or stages. Additional time-saving tips are given in the Adaptation section of each activity. If you'd like to spend even more time with a given lesson, that's no problem either. Just look in the Expansion section of each activity for additional ways to help your students use the target language to investigate the topic in question.

And, whether relatively short or long, simple or complex, these activities offer your students opportunities for interconnected learning of the target language. As they participate in these activities, your students will make progress on multiple fronts simultaneously. The standards for foreign language learning related to the 5 Cs of the American Council on the Teaching of Foreign Languages (ACTFL)—communication, cultures, connections, comparisons, and communities—are all within reach. The activities allow for extensive and varied practice of the interpersonal, interpretive, and presentational modes, which are foundational to the success of any language learner. We encourage you to search for connections between the activities outlined here and the topics addressed in your course textbook or other educational materials you're already using. Implementing the activities in this book can enliven and add breadth and depth to the learning experiences of your students as you explore the relationships between language and issues connected to art, cooking, dancing, sports, geography, gardening, environmental issues, movies, restaurants, newspapers, and more.

As you provide your students opportunities to develop their use of the target language within rich, intriguing contexts, you are helping them see that initial insights into another language allow a peek into another way of doing things—another way of looking at life. Your students will learn that, as they make a commitment to be lifelong learners of another language, the initial peek will become a fuller and more complex understanding of another way of living. And what a precious gift that is!

chapter 4

Linguistic and Cultural Authenticity

It seems like such a basic idea—the notion that surrounding learners of a language with authentic language and culture is a good thing. Carrying on a conversation with a native speaker, reading a comic strip, watching a candy commercial, trying to play a balalaika, learning to play bocce, ordering from a menu—all in the target language—can really bring the language and culture alive. Adjective endings and verb conjugations leap right off the pages of the textbook and get put into active duty. The learner understands that the language is used by real people for real-world reasons; learning to use the right preposition at the right time doesn't just lead to an A on a test, but can actually make the difference between being understood or not.

In the language villages, however, this idea of surrounding learners with authentic language and culture means more than it might seem at first blush. It isn't enough just to learn about the standard language or about the culture of the early 21st century. Villagers are exposed to the range of variation in language and culture across both time and space. Counselors and teachers come from all over the world, so learners are often given opportunities to hear different regional dialects of their target language and to learn about regional differences in cultural products and practices. Learners use the language in a wide variety of situations during their stay in the villages, so they have a chance to try out different styles of the language as they relate to the formality of the situation. Some villages even have historical programs that enable learners to learn about their target language and culture at earlier stages of their history.

At this point you might be wondering how you can do all of this; after all, you're probably the only adult in your classroom and you probably don't have a budget that would allow you to go out and buy culturally authentic sports equipment or musical instruments. The four activities in this chapter are meant to help you brainstorm some creative solutions to these challenges, in some cases drawing on the Internet or native speakers of the target language in your local community.

Activity 4.1   SPACE AND TIME MUSEUM

In the Villages

Even without a time machine, participants in Concordia Language Villages programs regularly find themselves transported into faraway times and places. On special theme days, villages don a new look with intriguing decorations, special activities are built into the daily schedule, and even the kitchen staff uses its imagination to (re)interpret history! The themes range from particular artistic and musical movements to notable historical events of the target culture. All allow the villagers (and counselors!) a glimpse into the past by drawing on multiple senses, active participation, and some time for reflection.

In the Classroom

While you may not have the luxury of an entire village behind your efforts to recreate a historical event or celebrate an aspect of the target culture, you can create a museum to capture these points in time with the help of your students. The Space and Time Museum activity introduces students to famous works of art from one artistic movement and then enlists them as museum curators to carry out research on a second movement. Although the described activity focuses on art, you can easily shift the project's focus toward history or science.

Objectives

- **Communication**
  - Students will be able to describe and discuss works of art, artists, and important movements (or, alternatively, within history, science, or other disciplines).
- **Cultures**
  - Students will be able to identify and discuss major contributions of artistic movements to the target culture and modern society (or to learn about the cultural significance of particular historical or scientific events).
- **Connections**
  - Students will develop art history abilities by replicating artwork from a particular art movement (or a representative artifact of a historical or scientific event).

Language Functions in Focus

- Comparing and contrasting
- Describing objects
- Describing people
- Presenting information

Preparation and Materials

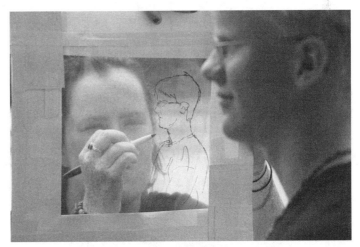

- Pictures of works of art that represent one of your favorite art movements in the target culture. These images can be copied out of library books or downloaded from the Internet.
- List of words and expressions to describe works of art (see Generating Interest for a model) written on an overhead transparency or on a large sheet of paper.

- Prepare short descriptive texts in the target language about the artists who created the works of art shown in your classroom gallery (see Generating Interest).
- Prepare a worksheet to be used to record student guesses when matching artists to works of art (see Generating Interest for a model).

After you've decided on the particular theme you'd like your class to explore, brainstorm relevant aspects of the artistic movement. Enlist help from your teaching colleagues in the art department during this stage. What do they consider the most important facets to be? And, just as important, what kind of knowledge do you want your students to derive from this activity?

Generating Interest

Since this activity has visual representations as its focal point, begin the project by introducing your students to prints of famous paintings, drawings, sculptures, or even architectural structures found within the particular artistic era of focus.

Once you've gotten your prints (or photocopies of the art representations), it's time to begin the classroom transformation by hanging them around the room for your students to see. To begin, have your students give titles to the paintings. It's a great opportunity to bring in more target language vocabulary! After they've shared their title ideas, let them know what the real titles are. Keep track of how many titles matched or came close to matching!

Next, have your students describe the works of art as a class. You should anticipate some of the words and expressions they'll need. Write these beforehand on an overhead transparency or on a big sheet of paper to be hung up so that you can refer to them when necessary. The sample vocabulary field shown in Figure 4.1 can be drawn on in your students' discussion of the artwork.

Beginning students can focus on adjectives and nouns related to the artwork, as well as the subjects of the paintings themselves. More advanced students can compare and contrast the paintings ("While the painting on the left depicts nature, the one in the middle is more abstract and uses bright colors and bold shapes.")

After they've had a chance to describe the works themselves, hand out short, descriptive texts about the artists responsible for the works of art shown in your gallery. In smaller groups or pairs, have the students read through these texts and determine which artists created which works of art. Have the students record their answers on a worksheet you have prepared based on the model shown in Figure 4.2. Discuss the answers as a class.

FIGURE 4.1   *Sample Vocabulary Field*

Describing art	Painting, drawing, sculpture, architecture, photography
Artists	A painter, sculptor, architect, or photographer
	Draws, creates, paints, designs, sculpts or shoots
	A piece/work of art, or masterpiece.
Subjects	Landscape, nature, cityscape, (self)portrait, still life, abstract, collage
	Impressionistic, surreal, abstract, classic
	Beautiful, breathtaking, captivating, interesting, disturbing, bland
	This piece captures, depicts, represents, or focuses on . . .
	The background, foreground, center, or focal point of the painting is . . .

Presentation and Practice

Time to switch roles, as your students become museum curators! First, divide the class into groups of three to four students. Each group is responsible for researching a famous artist (other than those already done in class) who represents an artistic movement different from the one focused on above. Choose two artistic movements that are related to each other in some way—the first movement acting as the topic for the first stage (Generating Interest) and the second movement as the focus for their group work. In this way, students can (1) compare and contrast the two movements and (2) see how the one influences the other.

Students should then find two to four artistic achievements of the particular artist or artistic group. Students will then recreate the artwork for an art exhibit, choosing any medium and any style. More advanced students can be asked to retain an element of the original piece in their own artistic representation. In addition to the artwork, have the students write up a background piece in the target language on both the artist and the respective works of art.

Finally, have each group of students display its work on a wall or bulletin board. If you can, showcase the work outside in the hallway or elsewhere in the school.

FIGURE 4.2 *Sample Worksheet for Works of Art*

Work of Art 1
Which artist do you think painted, drew, or sculpted this?

What information from the texts led you to believe this?

Work of Art 2
Which artist do you think painted, drew, or sculpted this?

What information from the texts led you to believe this?

Work of Art 3
Which artist do you think painted, drew, or sculpted this?

What information from the texts led you to believe this?

Expansion

Organize a field trip to a museum or concert that celebrates the target language. Have your students compare the presentation, content and style with their own museum.

Have groups of students give the rest of the class a guided museum tour of their particular artist.

Have students stage one of the famous paintings with themselves acting as subjects. Give them a handful of props to work with. Have them compare and contrast their reenactment with the original work of art. Take a photograph of the staging and hang it in the group's exhibit.

Have students create a brochure (or even an audiotape) for others in the target language to accompany their exhibit. The museum brochures can be used by other classes, particularly younger and beginning students. This could be done in conjunction with the Superstar Obstacle Course (Activity 2.2).

Add a musical dimension to the activity by having students choose music that corresponds historically or thematically to their art exhibits or artists.

Adaptation

For younger learners, simplify artists' profiles and worksheets by focusing on colors and favorite subjects, instead of artistic style or leitmotifs.

If you and your students prefer science to art, have students create an interactive science museum that represents inventors and/or inventions related to the target culture.

Similarly, you and your class can construct a history museum that depicts how life was lived during one of your favorite eras in the target culture. As an alternative, individual groups of students could focus on different turning points in the history of a country or city whose people speak your target language.

Options for Evaluation

Expectations Rubric					
	Agree				Disagree
You produced a well-written and relevant background piece on an artist from the target culture and his or her work of art.	5	4	3	2	1
You identified how an artistic movement shaped the target culture and modern society.	5	4	3	2	1
You worked cooperatively within your small group to create a representative piece of artwork for the art exhibit.	5	4	3	2	1

Student Journal Questions

1. What did your artist contribute to art of the target culture?
2. What other type of museum might your class create? How would it look?
3. Do you like the artwork created by the artist you chose? Why or why not?
4. What has studying art and artists taught you about the target culture?
5. Compare your target culture artist to an American artist you know about.

Portfolio Entries

1. Include the background piece written about an artist from the target culture.
2. Beginner learners might choose to put the warm-up worksheet in their portfolios.
3. Include a well-written response to a journal question to illustrate learners' reflective processes.

Customizing This Activity for Your Classroom

1. Reflect on the role that museums play in your target culture. What kinds of people go to museums? Do the museums charge admission fees?
2. What types of museums appeal to you? What ideas from your favorite museums can you share with your students to help model classroom exhibits?
3. Museums exhibit a variety of cultural products and perspectives related to art history, music, sports, aviation, culinary arts, ethnic studies and natural history. What types of museums fit best into your curriculum?
4. Do you have colleagues or native speakers in the community whose expertise you could draw on to create your museum?
5. Imagine your classroom transformed into the museum. What does it look like? Create a floor plan.
6. If you don't have a classroom of your own, how could you carry out this project?
7. How can students become guides for the museum?
8. Once your students have created their museum, how can you use it to introduce and practice the target language?
9. What can you foresee as the biggest obstacle in designing and building the museum? Brainstorm some ways to get past this.

Activity 4.2 LIVING MAPS

In the Villages

Maps of the countries or regions where the target language is spoken are often used to familiarize students with geography, but these maps do not need to remain abstract depictions used solely for reference purposes. Over the years, Concordia Language Villages counselors have found fun and innovative ways to interact with and learn from maps. Villagers are prompted to think about the differences in world view, emphasis, and perspective that are represented by different kinds of maps. And villagers are encouraged to use information from a variety of sources—personal experience, literature, travel guidebooks, reference works, and their imagination—to find the life hidden beneath the maps' symbols.

In the Classroom

In this activity, your students work in small groups to bring to life quadrants of a map you have selected to represent a country, region, or city where your target language is spoken. Each group identifies three or four tourist sites that fall within its quadrant of the map and decides how best to represent them by written texts and two- or three-dimensional graphics. Based on oral presentations of the sites, members of your class vote on their favorites and put together an itinerary for a dream class trip.

Objectives
- **Communication, Cultures**
  - Students will be able to identify, describe, and discuss (1) countries and regions of the target culture, (2) major tourist sites within the cities, countries, or regions, (3) differences across geographic regions, (4) currencies, (5) modes of transportation, and (6) the role of tourism.
- **Comparisons**
  - Students will be able to compare and contrast the home and target cultures with regard to geography, major tourist sites, currencies, modes of transportation, and the role of tourism.
- **Connections**
  - Students will be able to interpret information in maps and travel brochures.

Language Functions in Focus
- Comparing and contrasting
- Describing places
- Giving directions
- Giving reasons
- Presenting information

Preparation and Materials
- One large map of a country, region, or city in which your target language is spoken. Try to locate a map in your target language. (If you can't find a map large enough to hang up in your classroom, photocopy a smaller map onto an overhead transparency. Use this transparency to trace the outline of the map onto flip-chart-sized paper or butcher paper.)
- Divide your map into four quadrants: NW, NE, SW, SE. Make enough photocopies of each individual quadrant so that each student has his or her own copy of the quadrant being worked on in the small-group work described below (approximately one fourth of your students will be working with each of the four quadrants).
- Internet access or travel brochures containing texts about and pictures from countries, regions, or cities where the target language is spoken.
- Reference books on the areas represented by your map. Check these out of the library ahead of time if you'd like your students to get to work right away on their research; otherwise, students can be responsible for locating suitable references themselves.
- Post-It notes or index cards

Get in touch with tourist bureaus of towns, cities, regions, or countries where the target language is spoken in order to obtain travel brochures and maps for students to use. Further tourist information can be easily obtained from the Internet.

Identify one of your favorite tourist sites as represented on the map. Following the student instructions under Presentation and Practice, write up a text and create a visual representation. Attach these to the map as models for your students.

Generating Interest

Since this project addresses typical (and not so typical) tourist sites where the target language is spoken, it's a good idea to get your students thinking about tourism in general first. Begin by asking them what sorts of places are considered popular tourist sites in the United States, in their state or region, or in their local community. What makes these places so popular? What can an individual learn or do in these locations? What would the students show visitors to their own area, and why?

After this discussion, divide the students into small groups. If you have 16 to 24 students in your class, make four groups of 4 to 6 students each. (In this case, each group would work on a different quadrant of the map.) If you have more students say 24 to 32, you may find it works better to have eight groups of 3 to 4 students each. (In this case, two small groups would be working on each map quadrant.) Give each member in each group a photocopy of their section of the map to work with.

Standing at the large map at the front of the class, point to each of the four quadrants in turn. Ask which small group is working on each quadrant. Introduce the names and locations of a few highlights in each quadrant. Mention major cities, mountains, or bodies of water. If you have any personal experiences related to specific locations represented on the map, be sure to talk about them. Encourage students to get involved in this phase of the activity by noting travel experience or genealogical connections to locations represented on the map.

Presentation and Practice

Now it's time to get your students to work! Using reference books, travel brochures, and the Internet, have each group find three or four tourist sites to visit or activities to do within their quadrants. Some areas may be full of typical tourist activities; others may have less to offer to the typical tourist's eyes. You may have to encourage your students to think out of the box.

Once the sites have been selected, each group needs to decide how to represent each site on the map. Students should provide a visual representation of each tourist site and a short text describing it. Visuals can be as simple as a line drawing on an index card to more creative versions involving minisculptures made of clay or paper. Texts should be short and to the point because they will be written or printed onto Post-It notes or index cards, which will then be attached to the map at the front of the class. Be sure to show your model text and visual representation so that the students have a concrete idea of what to aim for.

In writing up their texts, students can use the questions in Figure 4.3 as a guide. Monitor the groups to be sure that the work is being distributed across all group members.

This activity should begin in class, but can be assigned as homework to complete. When each group has completed the texts and visual representations for each site, group members can attach their work in the appropriate geographic locations on the "mother" map at the front of the class.

Once all the information is collected, have each group come to the front of the class to introduce its sites. Ask students to take turns presenting the sites. Encourage them to speak freely, rather than to read directly from their texts. Students in the audience should take notes based on the categories used to write the texts (name of site, location, importance of site, activities, and cost). This information can be used as a reference point for the next stage of the activity.

Based on the oral presentations, have class members vote on the sites they would most like to visit. Following the vote, have class members discuss their reasons for their choices.

FIGURE 4.3   *Questions for Site Description*

What is the name of the site?

Where is it located?

Why is this site important?

What can visitors do there?

Does it cost anything to visit?

As a final important step, have each original small group put together an itinerary for a two-week dream class trip. Have each group include the top vote-getters in their itinerary, but customize the trip to take into account how long the group would spend in each location, how they would travel from site to site, what kinds of lodging they would have and how much free time, and so on.

Depending on how much time you would like your students to spend on this part of the activity, individual groups could create brochures advertising the trip or mark their proposed routes on the classroom map. Once each group has made its decisions, have your students compare and contrast their dream trips.

Expansion

Have students draw a map of a trip—one taken by an individual student or by the entire class on a field trip, or even one described in a book read in class. Have students label the different spots on their map with descriptive information about the trip and then write up their trips in narrative form.

Maps serve as excellent sites for practicing directions and language associated with travel. Puppets, stuffed animals, and even Bob, the Imaginary Fly (see Activity 2.4 for an introduction to this character) serve well as actors in narratives of trips that you and your students can co-construct. Place a large map of the target region on a table or the floor and use it to talk with your students about the travels of a stuffed animal or Bob the Fly. Engage the students by asking them questions or eliciting commentary about the travels. This is a great exercise for practicing prepositions of location and past, present, and future verb forms.

Adaptation

Simplify the activity for younger learners by using maps with fewer location references or maps that incorporate more visuals. Topographical maps work well, too!

More advanced students can write essays exploring more complex issues related to this activity. Possible essay prompts include these:

1. Why are certain tourist sites located where they are? What role does geography play? Mode of transportation? History? Social class? Other factors?
2. How are cities and towns typically situated? How do old cities differ from more newly planned ones? What could one expect to find in certain kinds of cities?
3. What do these tourist sites mean for the local people? Discuss the role of tourism in countries' economies, environmental impact, effects on city planning, and the like.

Options for Evaluation

Expectations Rubric				
	Agree			Disagree
You identified target culture countries and regions and their major tourist sites, currencies, and modes of transportation.	5	4	3	2	1
You discussed the relationship of major tourist sites to the cities, countries, and regions in which they reside, regional differences, and the role of tourism.	5	4	3	2	1
You compared and contrasted target geography to your home geography.	5	4	3	2	1
You interpreted information on target language maps and in travel brochures.	5	4	3	2	1

Student Journal Questions

1. Discuss two new things you learned about the geographic region you explored.
2. What city or region has this activity made you want to visit? What would you like to see there?
3. What was your favorite part of creating a living map?
4. How could this activity be made more interesting or more useful for students?

Portfolio Entries

1. Include copies of their written descriptions of tourist sites.
2. Include copies of the dream trip itinerary.
3. Include edited and revised answers to journal question 1 or 2.

Customizing This Activity for Your Classroom

1. Imagine your students creating living maps. What challenges do you foresee?
2. What map will you choose? Think about the implications of choosing a neighborhood map, a city map, a regional map, or a country map.
3. How can you incorporate a variety of cultures into this activity? (For example, do different cultural groups live in different regions of the city or country you selected? Is your target language spoken in more than one country?)
4. How can you highlight the language diversity within your target culture? (For example, what can you do to expose your students to dialects of your target language?)
5. What classroom management issues might arise during this activity? How might you prevent these problems?
6. How could you weave specific student interests into this activity?
7. Cross-disciplinary projects provide learners with multidimensional insights into material. What role could a social studies teacher play in this activity?
8. After reflecting on these questions, imagine the activity again. What is different?

Activity 4.3

CULINARY EXPLORATIONS

In the Villages

Food is a central part of Concordia Language Villages. Each village has its own kitchen staff that creates culturally authentic meals and snacks for the villagers. Having such different foods available provides villagers with important opportunities to learn about everyday life in the target cultures and to speak the target language in a natural setting. Some villagers go beyond simply *eating* these foods to learning in free-time cooking and baking activities/how to prepare them.

In the Classroom

Most students love to eat! Cooking, baking, and tasting treats are fun and enjoyable ways for your students to explore the target culture *and* to practice the target language. In this activity, your students begin by discussing their favorite foods, carry out detective work on an untitled target language recipe, prepare some culturally authentic food according to the recipe, and finally participate in a taste test by comparing foods from the target and home cultures.

Objectives

- **Communication**
  - Students will be able to use language constructions and vocabulary related to food preparation and eating.
- **Cultures**
  - Students will be able to prepare food from the target culture by reading and following a recipe written in the target language.
  - Students will be able to identify and discuss foods and culinary practices and traditions related to the target culture.
- **Comparisons**
  - Students will be able to compare and contrast cuisines and culinary practices representing the target culture and home culture.
- **Communities**
  - Students will work together as a class to produce a common product.

Language Functions in Focus

- Comparing and contrasting
- Describing objects
- Describing procedures
- Evaluating
- Expressing opinions
- Giving commands
- Giving directions
- Requesting

Preparation and Materials

Book the school cafeteria or the teachers' lounge kitchen if it's possible and practical. Otherwise, if you'll be carrying out this activity in your classroom, select a recipe that doesn't require refrigeration or use of a stove or oven during the food's preparation.

Find a recipe for one of your favorite foods from the target culture. (Check with your students to find out about any food allergies they may have so that you will prepare food that everyone in the class can eat.) If the recipe is already written in the target language, cover up the title of the recipe and photocopy it. If it's in English, translate it into the target language, leaving off the title, and then photocopy it. Make enough copies for each student in your class.

Identify and collect the ingredients and cooking utensils the class will need. Students will be working in small groups, so be sure to have enough bowls, spoons, and the like, for each group.

Depending on the background knowledge of your students, you may need to create a worksheet that introduces target culture measuring conventions and ingredients not typically used in the United States.

Generating Interest

Stage 1: Discussion

Start the activity off with a discussion of your students' favorite foods in the target language. This is a good opportunity to introduce and review food and cooking terms that will become important for the later stages of the activity. What do the students like to eat for breakfast? for lunch? for dinner? What are their favorite snacks? Are there foods that students particularly like to eat in the summer? In the winter? What are their favorite holiday foods? Have your students share culinary traditions that exist within their families.

Which of these favorite foods do they consider to be typically American? Which are foods that they perceive as coming from other cultures? Depending on the amount of time you have and how much interest there is among your students, you can open up a fuller discussion about the ethnic and regional backgrounds of food in America. Think about pasta, pizza, tacos, fried rice. Think about Philly cheese steaks, Cajun cooking, and Tex–Mex. What foods are popular in your geographic region that have been introduced by immigrants over the years? Which have been around for a long time? Which are relatively recent?

Following this preliminary discussion, ask your students if they've ever cooked or baked any of these foods themselves. If so, which ones? When? How often? Was it easy or hard? Did they run into any problems? What was their favorite part?

Presentation and Practice
Stage 2: Introducing the Recipe

Now it's time to introduce your own baking or cooking activity. It'll be more intriguing if you set this up as a bit of a mystery. First, divide your students into groups of four to six students each. Pass out copies of the recipe you'll be using, along with your worksheet highlighting unusual ingredients and measuring conventions. (If you are working with beginning language students, you may wish to introduce the material on the worksheet to the entire class before handing out the recipe for group work.) This is a good time to confirm with your students that no one in the class is allergic to any ingredient used in the preparation of the food.

Have students read through the recipe within their small groups. Since you haven't given them the title of the food they'll be preparing, they will need to put their heads together to figure out what it is, based on the ingredients it has in it and the food preparation steps. Ask the students to write down what they think the food is that they'll be preparing. What's their best guess?

Next, direct your students' attention to the front of the class. Asking for input from each group, have your entire class predict what food they'll be making. If there are different guesses, have each group state the reasons why they think its guess is the correct one. Now write the actual name of the recipe on the board (in the target language, of course!). Does this provide any more clues? Let your students in on the secret by identifying the food they'll be making and giving a little background. From what geographic region does the food originate? Where is the food typically eaten nowadays? When is it eaten? When and where have you eaten it? Why do you like it? Find out if any students are familiar with this food.

Then—staying in the target language, of course—have students list the ingredients needed, making sure that they've understood what each one means; the amounts needed of each, from most to least; the utensils needed; and the steps that will be accomplished in sequential order. Depending on the length of your class period and the amount of small- and large-group discussion, this may well be all that you can cover in one day. The next time you meet, have the students get back into their small groups and get ready to prepare the food. Since you're going to be modeling the food preparation, you'll need to decide on the best location for you to set up your demonstration area. If your classroom is large, it may work best for you to be at a table in the middle of the room so that all groups can see you.

Stage 3: Preparing the Food

Have students wash their hands before beginning this stage of the activity. Make sure each group has at least one copy of the recipe.

Depending on the amount of time you have, each small-group working area can be prepared in advance (with all necessary ingredients and utensils laid out) or each group can send a representative to a common area in the classroom to collect the ingredients and utensils needed for his or her group. If you choose the second option, have group representatives ask you in the target language for these ingredients and utensils. (Can I please have a carton of milk? Can I please have two eggs? Can I please have a mixing bowl? A measuring cup? Measuring spoons?)

If you've already completed the Living Map (Activity 4.2), be sure to use it as a resource in your discussion of the background of the food you're introducing!

If you're offering the Superstar Obstacle Course (Activity 2.2), one of your students may be your assistant chef for this project. He or she could help you to decide which recipe to use in class, translate the recipe (if necessary), help you gather up the ingredients and utensils, help distribute the materials in class, and even help with the demonstration!

When each group has what it needs, it's time to begin! From your location in the classroom, start off the demonstration as a cook might on a television show. Review in the target language what the food is called, where it comes from, when and how it's eaten, and what ingredients are involved in its preparation. Hold up each ingredient to strengthen the connection between word and food item. Have each group do the same. In terms of the actual instructions, make sure to structure the individual steps in the recipe with chronological markers, such as "first," "next," "then," and "finally." Stop after each step, giving each group sufficient time to carry out the task. Encourage each member of each group to get involved.

As students are actively measuring, pouring, mixing, cracking an egg, and so on, ask them in the target language what they are doing. Make sure they respond in full ("I'm measuring the flour," "I'm pouring the milk into the mixing bowl," "I'm cracking two eggs"). These answers will help both to reinforce the language being taught and to keep the students on task. If you notice that group members are starting to lose focus, direct your questions in the target language to them ("Christina, what is Kevin measuring?" "Adam, what is Rita mixing?"). These questions will allow students to practice not only first-person pronouns and verb conjugations, but third-person ones as well.

When you've come to the end of the preparation stage of the recipe, have each group bring their product to a designated area within the classroom and clean up their work areas. Remember that this cleanup period can also be a good opportunity for target language learning and practice. ("Who needs more paper towels?" "Remember to put all the milk cartons into the recycling bin!" "This table needs to be wiped up better.").

If you'd like to reinforce the material covered in the activity, you may wish to have your students complete a worksheet like that shown in Figure 4.4.

Stage 4: Actual Baking or Cooking Time

Unless you are preparing the food in a room that is equipped with ovens or stoves, you will need to finish the students' projects for them.

Stage 5: Eating, Comparing, and Discussing

When you see your students the next time, review with your students what they did the last time you were together. What was the product they were making? What ingredients did it contain? How much or how many of each ingredient? What steps were involved in the preparation? In what order?

With great panache, unveil the finished products! Hand out samples to everyone in the class. Once they've had a chance to taste their work, start up a discussion

FIGURE 4.4   *Sample Reinforcing Questions for Stage 3*

What was the name of the food we made today?

Where did it originate?

When is it typically eaten and where?

What were three ingredients we used today?

How much milk did we use?

Why did we separate the eggs?

Why did we melt the butter before we added it?

Where did we put the batter after we mixed it?

How long did it take to bake and at what temperature?

in the target language. Do they like how it tastes? If so, what do they like about it? If not, what's wrong with it? Are they surprised by how it tastes? If so, what were they expecting?

Now pass out a typical American product that shares some similarities with the product they made. (If they've made a cake, pass out bite-sized pieces of a typical U.S. cake; if they've made soup, pass out mini paper cups filled with an American-style soup.) Use this taste test as the springboard for a comparison between the two products. Which one would they rather eat? Why? Which one tastes sweeter? Which one is spicier? Encourage your students to use as many suitable adjectives as they can remember. Write these adjectives, as well as a few of your own, on the board for them to refer to.

If you are planning to integrate more than one cooking or baking activity into your curriculum, now would be an excellent time to get some feedback from your students. What kind of food would they like to make next? If the food this time around was a dessert, perhaps the next activity should focus on a snack or an appetizer. If you chose a food from the northern part of a target country this time, perhaps you could choose a food from the south next time around.

Expansion

For homework, have students translate their favorite heritage culture recipe and present it to the class. Showcase your students' work in a class cookbook.

Find a real cooking lesson on video (a lively and funny one may work the best) done in the target language. Showing a clip of the program in class is a good opportunity for students to become familiar with food and cooking terms in the target language. Have your students write down all the new terms they hear. Use this list to scaffold your discussion of the video.

If you have access to a video camera, your students can organize and make a cooking show video based on your demonstration. This is an excellent product to show at a parent–teacher night.

Invite parents, restaurateurs, bakery or gourmet shop owners, or other foreign nationals from the community to lead or contribute to future cooking or baking events. Work with ESOL (English for speakers of other languages) teachers and students to create an international day or evening.

Foreign language clubs can host target culture cooking lessons or meals. Consider combining the lesson or meal with the celebration of a culturally relevant holiday.

Adaptation

If you cannot spare class time for a cooking or baking lesson, organize an after-school club activity and offer extra credit for students who participate.

If your school does not have kitchen space available for your use, conduct a mock cooking lesson in your classroom and provide students with store-bought examples of the food.

For lower proficiency levels, scaffold instruction by providing fill-in-the-blank versions of the recipe and simplify follow-up questions.

Options for Evaluation

Expectations Rubric					
	Agree				Disagree
You read about and discussed food preparation and eating contexts in the target language.	5	4	3	2	1
You followed and prepared a target culture recipe.	5	4	3	2	1
You identified and discussed a variety of target culture foods and culinary traditions.	5	4	3	2	1
You compared and contrasted target culture and home culture cuisine.	5	4	3	2	1
You actively participated in your small group's food preparation.	5	4	3	2	1

Student Journal Questions

1. How would you describe American food to a person your age who lives in the target culture? Which part of your description do you think would be the most surprising to him or her?
2. How can learning about culturally authentic food and cooking help students gain insight into the target culture?

3. Describe the food you made in class.
4. Think about every stage of your cooking lesson. Describe the various ways this activity helped you learn the target language.

Portfolio Entries

1. Include an edited and revised copy of the worksheet they completed as part of Stage 3.
2. Include a polished response to one of the journal questions.
3. If your students created a cooking show video (see Expansion section), include a copy of it.

Customizing This Activity for Your Classroom

1. Visualize a cooking lesson in your school. What resources do you have available? What would you have to improvise?
2. Think about recipes and meals that could be integrated into your curriculum.
3. How could you best incorporate what your heritage learners know about culturally authentic foods and food preparation?
4. How could native speaker community members enhance this activity?
5. It is sometimes difficult to keep students speaking target language when they're carrying out a hands-on activity like food preparation. What might you do to discourage the use of English?
6. What classroom management issues might arise during this activity? How could you try to prevent them?
7. What extra-credit expansion activities relating to food and cooking could you offer your students?
8. Imagine this activity in a beginners' class. Now visualize it with intermediate or advanced learners. How did you scaffold the lesson differently?

Activity 4.4   VISITING EXPERTS

In the Villages

Concordia Language Villages encourages counselors to design and lead activities based on their own special talents and expertise. The counselors' diverse interests and perspectives on the target culture encourage growth and development in the village as a whole. Villagers learn language through culturally authentic content and real-life experiences while taking part in a wide variety of activities from cooking to fencing to building a tree house. Occasionally, the village circle of experts opens up to include visiting ethnic artists and musicians, foreign language educators, business people, and diplomats. And whether they stay in the village for a meal and an evening concert, to lead a model government simulation, or to deliver a lecture, they always discover how excited language learners are to have an opportunity to speak the target language with a visiting expert!

In the Classroom

This activity encourages you to reach out to parents of students in your school and other community members who speak your target language. By inviting them to come to talk as visiting experts with your students, you will add new dimensions and richness to your students' understanding of the target language and culture. Your guests can be encouraged not only to talk about their area of expertise, but also to teach your students a favorite song or game in the target language. These visiting experts can keep up their relationship with your students by assisting throughout the year with a variety of activities in this book, including Telephoning (Activity 5.3), Dancing (Activity 6.2), and even offering play-by-play commentary in the World Cup Soccer tournament (Activity 7.2).

Objectives

- ■ **Communication**
  - • Students will listen to and be able to understand (according to their language level) a native speaker's oral presentation.
  - • Students will be able to ask relevant and appropriate questions of a native-speaker guest.
- ■ **Connections**
  - • Students will develop knowledge about a particular job, hobby, or other area of expertise.
- ■ **Communities, Cultures**
  - • Students will be able to identify how the guest speaker's job, hobby, or other area of expertise contributes to the local and/or target culture community.
  - • Students will be able to access resources of the local and/or target culture community.

Language Functions in Focus

- ■ Asking for information
- ■ Expressing opinions
- ■ Expressing thanks
- ■ Greeting
- ■ Introducing oneself
- ■ Taking leave

Preparation and Materials

Locate parents of students in your school or other community members who speak the target language or who have spent a good deal of time in the target culture. Make contacts with consulates and tourist offices of foreign governments in your area, businesses that have contacts with regions of the world where your target language is spoken, or even local ethnic restaurants and grocery stores.

Invite these individuals to visit your class individually to speak in the target language about their jobs, hobbies, or other areas of expertise. Let each visiting expert know the language level of your students and describe the sorts of discussions or demonstrations your students would enjoy, such as learning a favorite song or game from the target culture. Encourage your visitor to use gestures and props as he or she speaks in order to help your students understand the presentation. Remind each speaker that a brief, interactive activity will be more effective than a lecture.

If possible, have your guest provide you with a basic outline of his or her presentation using simplified language. This outline will not only help the speaker adjust his or her language to suit the students, but will also provide you with target language you may need to teach ahead of the visit.

Generating Interest

Tell your students that you've invited a visiting expert to come to talk with them and that you're very excited that he or she has accepted your invitation. Talk a bit about who the speaker is, what he or she does, and the proposed topic of the presentation. Have your students brainstorm terms associated with the activity your visitor is planning to present. Provide words or phrases they aren't familiar with.

Encourage your students to look at magazine pictures or other materials on the topic. You can have them work in pairs or small groups to use the language from your brainstorming session to describe the pictures.

As a freer practice of the target language, you can also have students talk with partners about their own knowledge of or experience with the topic.

Depending on the language level of your students, introduce or review how one greets a stranger in the target language, introduces oneself, asks questions following a presentation, indicates gratitude at the end of a presentation, and says good-bye to a stranger.

Finally, have students prepare several questions in the target language to ask the speaker. These questions could address the specific topic of the presentation or the target language or culture in general.

Presentation and Practice

On the day of the visiting expert's visit, have your students greet the guest in the target language and introduce themselves to him or her. Encourage the students to have their questions ready to ask and to take notes during the speaker's presentation. Following the presentation and question–answer session, ask the speaker to reminisce and tell stories about his or her own childhood. This discussion may segue easily into an exchange of singing or playing of culturally authentic games. Have students show the visitor around the classroom, pointing out cultural and language topics already learned and activities carried out. Thank the visitor and say good-bye in the target language.

After the visitor leaves, have your students recap the presentation while it's still fresh in their minds. As a time-saver, you can create a worksheet with a few open-ended questions, such as the following, asking students to describe the day's activity.

- What did today's speaker talk to you about?
- What was your favorite part of the presentation?
- What are some of the things the speaker showed you in the presentation?

> *Although it is very important that your students get ample opportunities to speak with the visiting expert, don't underestimate the importance of giving them a chance to hear you and the guest speaking the target language with each other. After all, students only infrequently get to hear target language conversations with native speed and complexity. As long as you don't go on at such length that they tune out, many of your students will be listening intently to your modeling of the target language.*

> *What can you do if your speaker talks longer than you expected? If time is a concern for you, you should make your time constraints to your visitor very clear before he or she comes to the class. During the talk, you can always discreetly point to your watch to remind the visitor of the time. If you want your students to be able to ask more questions, politely interrupt the speaker and suggest that your class members would be interested in posing some of their questions.*

If the visitor leaves right at the end of the class period, consider giving your students these questions as homework to complete by the next time they come to your class.

Start the next class with a discussion about the speaker. Have students ask each other questions about the presentation and compare what people remember from the talk.

As a final step, have your students write thank-you notes to the speaker in the target language. Even beginning language learners can write a sentence or two. More advanced learners can follow a model note that you've written or just do the best they can on their own. Mistakes from young language learners within an expression of gratitude will almost certainly be endearing to the speaker.

Expansion

This visiting experts activity provides a wonderful opportunity for cross-disciplinary cooperation. Work with other faculty in your department or school to arrange for guests who can present in the target language on topics within the arts and humanities, social sciences, and natural sciences.

Encourage your students to invite (or come up with ideas for inviting) guests into the classroom. Ask students from the ESOL department for recommendations, too!

Provide extra credit to students who come up with an expert presentation of their own (See Activity 2.2, Superstar Obstacle Course and Activity 3.2, Students as Experts).

If the initial visit went well, consider inviting the guest back—possibly several more times. Having frequent visits will help students get over possible initial shyness or intimidation, and they will have more interesting questions to ask after they get to know each other a bit. Other activities in this book can benefit from the assistance of a native-speaking adult. Check out the possibilities within Eating Out (Activitiy 5.2), Telephoning (Activity 5.3), Dancing (Activity 6.2), Newspaper (Activity 7.1), World Cup Soccer (Activity 7.2), Gardening (Activity 7.3), and Film Festival (Activity 7.4).

Plan a field trip to visit the community guest at work or at home. Have students prepare for this visit by coming up with questions about the job or home environment.

Adaptation

If you're not the only teacher in your school who speaks your target language, invite another teacher to come to your classroom to demonstrate his or her special talents. This will be particularly effective because language teachers are very aware of the level and difficulty of the language they use.

If time or human resources run short, put on a different hat and do the presentation yourself! Introduce yourself as a guest and stay in character throughout the class period. See Activity 2.4 (Bob, the Imaginary Fly) for a discussion of the advantages of shifting in and out of your teacher role.

Options for Evaluation

Expectations Rubric					
	Agree				Disagree
You wrote up appropriate questions for the speaker in your target language.	5	4	3	2	1
You reported on what you learned from the guest speaker using key words introduced in the presentation.	5	4	3	2	1
You have demonstrated your knowledge about the speaker's job, hobby, or other area of expertise.	5	4	3	2	1

Student Journal Questions

1. Describe what your visitor presented today.
2. You prepared several questions for the presenter. Did you get to ask them? If so, how did he or she answer them? Were these the answers you expected? Why or why not?
3. What were some of the interesting things the presenter told you about his or her childhood?
4. If you had had more time, what other things would you have liked to have learned about the presenter?
5. When future speakers come, is there anything you or your teacher could do to make the activity less difficult, more interesting, or more useful?

Portfolio Entries

1. Include a written version of the visitor's presentation (answer to journal question 1) to help students remember what they learned and how much they enjoyed the experience.
2. Include a revised copy of the comprehension check homework assignment to keep the experience fresh in learners' minds.
3. Include the questions learners prepared before the visit and learners' interpretations of the presenter's answers (answer to journal question 2) to serve as a valuable representation of the expert's visit.

Customizing This Activity for Your Classroom

1. Can you imagine visiting experts coming to talk to your students? Do you have anyone in mind?
2. Think about what guests you might invite from your community. If you don't know anyone who speaks your target language, where might you seek help?
3. Involving other departments can strengthen a project. How might you make this a cross-disciplinary activity?
4. How can you prepare your speaker to appropriately tailor his or her comments for your learners' proficiency level?
5. How might you act as a visiting expert to your own class and present your hobby or interest to your own students?
6. Reflect on the value of guest presenters in encouraging lifetime learning among your students.
7. How often can you imagine inviting speakers into your class? For which topics in your curriculum?

It's Your Turn!

Immersing your students in both culturally and linguistically authentic environments is a true challenge. It can seem overwhelming to set up the conditions that allow your students to transport themselves mentally through space and time in order to capture a glimpse of what is it like in the target culture. Hearing English out in the hallways and over the intercom can be a severe jolt—and a ready reminder that one is still in the confines of the United States. It takes a great deal of imagination to "travel" to a museum in Mexico City or a kitchen in Tokyo.

What we've tried to impart in the activities outlined in this chapter is the absolute interconnection between cultural product and practice. When we begin to

understand products and practices, we begin to understand how others think. When we talk about cooking in the classroom, we're not talking about a quick diversion from everyday activities or even a reward for good behavior. We're talking about a springboard to discussions about how food fits into the daily life of a typical family in the target culture. How the eating of particular foods gives us insights into historical information or values surrounding holidays. How the labeling of foods gives us insight into the way food and nutrition are viewed relative to health.

Looking at a city map can lead to discussions of pros and cons related to differing modes of transportation—walking, subway, buses, cars. Where are the pedestrian zones? Who is in favor of them? Against them? Why? How can one find the historical center of the city on the map? Is there, for example, a street in the form of a circle that may indicate the presence of a wall around the city long ago? What are the oldest buildings within the city? Is there evidence of rebuilding? What is it? War or city renewal projects? Is there evidence of suburbs? Do people live near their places of employment or do they commute?

And on and on. Culture is so much more than a representative food or a type of clothing or an architectural style, although these, too, can be jumping off points for discovering related cultural practices, values, beliefs, and perspectives.

We encourage you to look outside this chapter for additional activities that highlight linguistic and cultural authenticity. Encourage your students to compare and contrast what they do in their everyday lives with what others in the target cultures may do. What kinds of restaurants do they have (Activity 5.2)? How do they use telephones (Activity 5.3)? What dances do they have, both traditional and modern (Activity 6.2)? How do their newspapers look (Activity 7.1)? What sports do they play and watch (Activity 7.2)? What kinds of gardens are popular (Activity 7.3)? What movies are classics; which are popular today (Activity 7.4)? These everyday comparisons are the first important steps to understanding and validating other ways of doing things and to understanding how the rest of the world may view us.

Discussion Questions

1. What can you do to learn more about the target culture if you haven't yet visited or lived in regions where the target language is spoken? If you don't have access to authentic materials from the target culture, what alternatives are there? What organizations might you contact for free or low-cost materials? How can you and your students transform items you do have into workable substitutes for cultural artifacts?

2. Some target languages are spoken in a variety of geographic regions representing a range of cultures. What criteria are important in choosing which linguistic and cultural varieties to include in your course?

3. Students often say they are more interested in current cultural products and practices than in older, more traditional cultural products and practices. Think about what kind of balance between traditional and modern you would like in your classroom. How might you excite your students about historically important products and practices? Are there any cultural or language organizations in your geographic area that could be approached for assistance?

4. Some teachers must follow very specific timelines and curricula. Sometimes this leads to a focus on language out of its sociohistorical context. How might you teach the aspects of the language that need to be taught, but within a cultural context that allows students to learn simultaneously about both cultural and historical content and language?

For Further Reading

Banks, J. A. and Banks, C. M. (Eds.). (2004). *Multicultural education: Issues and perspectives*. Boston: Allyn & Bacon (see especially chapters by Erikson, "Culture in Society and Educational Practices" and Ovando, "Language Diversity in Education.")

Blyth, C. (Ed.) (2003). *The sociolinguistics of foreign-language classrooms: Contributions of the native, the near-native, and the non-native speaker*. Boston: Heinle & Heinle.

Fantini, A. E. (1999). Comparisons: Towards the development of intercultural competence. In. K. Phillips (Ed.), *Foreign language standards: Linking research, theories, and practices* (pp. 165–218). Lincolnwood, IL: National Textbook Company.

Kramsch, C. (1993). *Context and culture in language teaching*. New York: Oxford University Press.

Lange, D. L. (1999). Planning for and using the new national culture standards. In J. K. Phillips (Ed.), *Foreign language standards: Linking research, theories, and practices* (pp. 57–135). Lincolnwood, IL: National Textbook Company.

Omaggio Hadley, A. (2001). *Teaching language in context* (3rd ed.). Boston: Heinle & Heinle. (See especially chapters 5 and 8.)

Helpful Web Sites

Start getting ideas here at the variety of museums that make up the Smithsonian Institution. http://www.si.edu/; then check out Web sites for museums in regions where your target language is spoken, such as the Prado, Louvre, or Uffizi.

National Gallery of Art online tours in five languages (many of which can be downloaded as PDF files): http://www.nga.gov/onlinetours/onlinetr.htm.

Check out the Global Schoolnet teacher-annotated resource page for reference tools such as maps, language translators, measurement, time zone, and currency converters to supplement your lessons: http://www.globalschoolnet.org/resources/index.html.

Find the map you're looking for at http://www.worldatlas.com.

A magazine site from any target culture, such as *America's Food and Wine*, http://www.foodandwine.com/, will provide great ideas for food-based lessons.

Would you like to bring target language television programming into your classroom? Contact SCOLA, a nonprofit educational consortium that receives and retransmits television programming from more than 70 countries at http://www.scola.org. SCOLA even offers a program called Insta-Class that prepares and distributes weekly lessons based on 5-minute transcripts of the programming in selected languages.

Yahoo! http://www.yahoo.com. Looking for authentic materials to expose students to the target language? The Web is an excellent source for articles, poems, music, travel guides, advertisements, and the like. Check out Yahoo's International sites written entirely in the target language. The Internet makes finding up-to-date materials on target culture current events, famous people, arts, and popular culture easy and, in most cases, free.

Argentina	http://ar.yahoo.com
Brazil	http://br.yahoo.com
China	http://cn.yahoo.com/
Denmark	http://dk.yahoo.com/
France	http://fr.yahoo.com/
Germany	http://de.yahoo.com/
Hong Kong	http://hk.yahoo.com
Italy	http://it.yahoo.com/
Japan	http://www.yahoo.com.jp
Mexico	http://mx.yahoo.com
Norway	http://no.yahoo.com/
Spain	http://es.yahoo.com/
Sweden	http://se.yahoo.com/
Taiwan	http://tw.yahoo.com

Association of College and Research Libraries provides a collection of literary texts in 17 Western European languages: http://www.lib.virginia.edu/wess/etexts.html

Covering animal vocabulary? Discover Sounds of the World's Animals. Make it a multimedia adventure by visiting Georgetown University's Sounds of the World's Animals Web site: http://www.georgetown.edu/faculty/ballc/animals/

chapter

5

Creating a Need to Communicate

When you were a student, did your teacher ever ask you a question to which he or she already knew the answer? *What's the capital of Alaska? What's the square root of 144? When was George Washington born?* Of course! In fact, many classrooms are made up of that kind of rhythm: teacher's question, student's answer, teacher's evaluation of the student's answer. Most students become accustomed to this rhythm and happily enter into its daily dance. And this type of routine certainly has its place in the learning cycle.

Activity 5.1 School Tour
Activity 5.2 Eating Out
Activity 5.3 Telephoning
Activity 5.4 E-Mates

But such questions can become stale after a while, leading some students to tune out. Sometimes such students seem to be asking themselves why they should bother answering a question publicly to which almost everyone in the classroom already knows the answer. It just doesn't seem worth it.

To combat this problem, many of us set up role plays that contain some sort of information gap. Typically in this type of role play, each student has a piece of information that the other student needs but doesn't have. Such a need propels the interaction, leading each person to continue to speak with the other until he or she gains the necessary information.

The activities in this chapter offer another way to address this challenge. They are based on interactions that occur naturally within the villages. As villagers move throughout the village over the course of a day, they ask and are asked many questions on topics that genuinely interest the questioner and to which he or she is in need of an answer.

Is there any more bread? (in the dining hall)
Who still needs to brush his teeth? (in the cabin)
What colors do you need for your painting? (in the arts center)
What kinds of chocolate do you have? (in the candy store)

This kind of needs-based give and take in the target language heightens student interest in designing an utterance that will serve its purpose and provides an incentive for the student to listen very carefully to the response. This move from unnecessary to purposeful communication can be enough to get even the most reticent students to focus and learn. Try it out!

Activity 5.1   SCHOOL TOUR

In the Villages

At Concordia Language Villages, counselors rely on the local environment as a daily resource for teaching and practicing the target language. To facilitate a smooth transition to this village life for incoming learners, cabin counselors accompany villagers on a tour of the site on the first evening of their stay. Villagers walking in small groups are introduced to components of everyday life, such as the dining hall, the health center, the bank, the store, and the beach. Staff members located at these stations occasionally take on character roles from the target culture to grab the attention of their audience as they outline important start-up information.

In the Classroom

This activity suggests how you can coordinate your own school tour for your language students. Include such places as the cafeteria, gymnasium, library, principal's office, health center, and more. Such a tour is a great way to introduce and practice target language vocabulary that will be meaningful to your students during every day of school life and will give your students some of the tools they need on a daily basis to avoid slipping back into using English in your classroom. After all, no matter how successful you are at turning your classroom into a culturally authentic oasis within your school, the context for much of what your students naturally talk about is the *rest* of the school.

Objectives

- **Communication**
  - Students will be able to identify and describe school spaces, furniture, and objects in the target language.
  - Students will be able to identify and describe individuals, courses, and activities associated with the school context in the target language.
- **Communities**
  - Students will develop an awareness of how the target language relates to their local environment.

Language Functions in Focus

- Describing places
- Giving directions (expansion activities)
- Narrating (expansion activities)

Preparation and Materials

- Camera (preferably Polaroid or digital)
- Index cards for descriptive texts (see Presentation and Practice)

Decide what areas of the school to include on the tour. Some areas to consider are the cafeteria, gymnasium, library, principal's office, health room, counseling room, art room, music room, drinking fountains, playground, recycling and trash bins, and parking lot. While you can spend as little or as much time at any one area as you'd like, you'll want to consider what kind of information is most relevant for your students within each area of the school, as well as the length of your students' attention spans. Three to five minutes at each site is probably just about right.

Be sure to discuss your plans and ideas with all relevant school administrators before the tour to prevent potential misunderstandings and to gain support.

Go around to these areas with your camera and take photographs of small details at each location (posters, signs, unusual doors or windows, tables, and so on).

Print these out and make photocopies of them to use with your students on the day before the tour.

Write up a brief description of one of the sites on an index card to serve as a model for your students (see Presentation and Practice).

Generating Interest

On the day before the tour (preferably in the first or second week of the school year), explain to your class that you are going on a tour. Brainstorm with them what possible tours one can go on, such as safaris or city (bus or walking) tours. Also ask them what purpose tours serve and what one typically does on a tour (take pictures, take notes, watch, enjoy).

Before embarking on the tour, hand out the photocopied photographs (as described under Preparation and Materials) of objects taken at different areas of the school to students. Next to each photograph, have the students write the name of the school location from where they believe that image comes. Encourage them to write this information in the target language. If they don't know a word or two, let them know that they'll be learning these on the tour. They will have the opportunity not only to check the accuracy of their guesses during the tour, but also to replace any words in English with the appropriate ones in the target language. This should help to sustain their interest in keeping a keen eye out and listening for the information they need.

Presentation and Practice

Walk with your students to the predetermined sites around the school. Have each student bring along the photocopied photographs and a pencil or pen on the tour. At each location, make sure that your presentation is as interactive as possible. Start off by asking the students what the place is called ("Where are we?" or "What is it called?"). Continue the conversation by asking who goes to this location, when and why. Ask who (if anyone) works at this location, what their names are, and the nature of their work.

At each stop on the tour, ask your students if any of them have identified an object within sight that was captured in one of your photographs. If so, ask several students to read what they wrote as their guess next to the identified photograph. See how many of the students guessed correctly—and knew the words in the target language. Give students who guessed incorrectly or who wrote the location in English an opportunity to write down the correct answer in the target language.

After you've visited all the sites on your tour, return to your classroom and have the students review vocabulary words from each site. Write these on the board below each school area name. Add any pertinent vocabulary that the students may have forgotten.

Divide the class into small groups or pairs, and make each responsible for describing one or more of the school areas visited. Pass out one index card per site. Have each group or pair write the name of the site in the target language on one side of the card and answers in the target language to the following sample questions on the other side.

- Where is it? ("between the principal's office and the cafeteria")
- Who works there? ("Mrs. Johnson" or "the nurse")
- Who goes there, and why? ("Students go there when they don't feel well or when they get hurt")

Provide your students with a model text for one of the sites.

Once all of the students have completed this activity, collect the index cards. You'll use these cards to create an interactive "Our School" bulletin board where students get the chance to show off their written texts *and* to create a guessing game for the classroom or even the entire school! Give each photograph you used on the tour a number; give each index card description a letter of the alphabet. Staple the photographs and index cards in random order on the bulletin board in your classroom or in the hallway. Students from the class, from other classes, or maybe even the entire student body can guess which photo matches which description. Have guessing sheets available in an envelope next to the bulletin board. List all numbers on the left-hand side of the sheet and all letters on the right-hand side. Students can draw lines connecting the numbers and letters to match their guesses. Have participating students put their name on the sheet and place their guesses in a box next to the bulletin board. Winners can be chosen at random from among those who made all the correct matches.

Not only will this competition be fun for your students, but the creation of such a contest can be great advertising for your language classes.

Expansion

Students can create a pamphlet or brochure introducing speakers of the target language to the major areas of the school.

Have students create decorative and useful signs in the target language for several areas of the school.

After your students have practiced the vocabulary of the school tour, recycle these newly learned words in subsequent lessons. If you're teaching prepositions and/or verbs of location and direction, for example, use the place names from the school tour to recreate the tour.

While this activity involves primarily descriptive language, you can alter the focus to narrative by having students create a story of their trip throughout the school. Reconstruct the story together as a class, or have individual students or pairs create more imaginative stories that involve elements from the places around school.

Have students create a board game based on your school, similar in format to Candy Land or Monopoly. Students should build relevant people, things, and reasons for being at the sites into their board games. At the principal's office, for example, they could write "Talked too much in class. Sent to prinicpal's office. Sit out one turn."

Adaptation

For beginning and intermediate learners, create detailed vocabulary and grammer worksheets for students to complete before visiting each room or area in the school. If you don't have the time to develop worksheets yourself, have your more advanced students create a worksheet for your beginning classes after you take them on the tour. You could also ask for permission to post signs at key points along the tour route before you actually take your class on the tour.

To work on prepositions with your intermediate and advanced classes, have your students describe their own movement (including in which direction) along the tour. Ask the students to give you continuous feedback on where you're headed. When you return to the classroom, have the students write up directions to each site. Then read them aloud and have the students guess which site is being described.

Consider your students' attention spans. For younger learners, you may want to divide the tour into shorter, more manageable parts or have them take the tour in groups of four to six students, each led by an older, advanced student of the language. This could be a part of the Student Mentors program (Activity 2.3).

Options for Evaluation

Expectations Rubric					
	Agree				Disagree
You identified and described school spaces, furniture, and objects in the target language.	5	4	3	2	1
You identified all important individuals within the school (principal, teacher, nurse, and others) and all relevant school subjects and school activities (lunch, recess, and so on) in the target language.	5	4	3	2	1
Your text about a particular school area includes the following information: Where the place is located within the school Who works there Who goes there, and why	5	4	3	2	1
You incorporated relevant vocabulary and grammatical constructions in your text and used them appropriately.	5	4	3	2	1

Student Journal Questions
1. Describe what it felt like to hear your school described in the target language.
2. Imagine that a native speaker of the target language visits your school. What areas of the school would you want to show him or her? What would you say?
3. What was your favorite part of the tour? Why?

Portfolio Entries
1. Include the texts describing various school areas along with relevant photographs. (You'll need to photocopy the index card for each member of the group responsible for its creation.)
2. Include the photocopied photographs with their target language labels.
3. Include any worksheets created for your beginning and intermediate learners, as outlined in the Adaptation section.
4. Include the individual or class narratives based on the school tour, as described in the Expansion section.
5. Have advanced students include their written directions to the school areas, as outlined in the Adaptation section.
6. Include a draft of their school board game, as outlined in the Expansion section.

Customizing This Activity for Your Classroom
1. What grammatical forms could be introduced and/or practiced through this activity?
2. Compare the language practiced in this activity to that highlighted in your textbook. What does the school tour activity provide your students that the textbook does not?

3. How can the language highlighted in this activity, particularly vocabulary, be recycled in later lessons? What sorts of benefits are there for recycling the language?
4. What other resources exist within your school to draw on in future lessons? Think about people, locations, and objects.
5. What kinds of classroom management issues might come up during the tour? What could you do to preempt these? How might you resolve them should they occur?

Activity 5.2   EATING OUT

In the Villages

Many villages have full-fledged restaurant evenings on the weekend. Villagers invite each other to go out to the restaurant and make telephone reservations for one of two or three seating times. The restaurants use actual menus with culturally authentic food choices: appetizers, entrees, desserts, and beverages. Cultural differences related to eating out are introduced in the small language groups the day before or on the day of the event. Villagers sometimes even work as servers during one restaurant shift and arrive as guests in another. Another less intensive but more frequent activity in the villages is found in the afternoon cafe. Some villagers work there as servers; others come to order cake and juice and linger to play games, listen to live music, or just chat with friends.

In the Classroom

Role plays of real-life situations, such as eating in a restaurant, help students experience and learn functional language. In this activity your students use the target language, along with their imagination and selected props, to choose a restaurant, reserve a table over the phone, read a target language menu, order a meal, and even pay the bill! Through eye-opening discussions, role plays, and reflection, students compare and contrast products and practices related to dining out in the target culture with their own experiences at home.

Objectives

- **Communication**
  - Students will be able to make a table reservation.
  - Students will be able to read a restaurant menu in the target language.
  - Students will be able to order food or take food orders in the target language.
- **Comparisons**
  - Students will be able to discover and discuss differences related to eating outside the home within the target and home cultures.
- **Cultures**
  - Students will gain insight into culturally authentic foods and restaurants.
  - Students will become familiar with the dining-out routines of the target culture.

Language Functions in Focus

- Comparing and contrasting
- Complimenting, complaining, apologizing (expansion activities)
- Expressing thanks
- Greeting
- Making reservations
- Opening and closing an interaction
- Requesting
- Suggesting
- Taking leave

Preparation and Materials

Collect a variety of restaurant props.

- Servers' notepads
- Aprons
- Tablecloths
- Dishes and silverware (paper and plastic are fine)
- Small vases with flowers
- Menus in the target language representing four different kinds of restaurants (in terms of type of food and price range)

> *If you don't have access to menus in the target language, you can find them on the Internet. Just go to a search engine that operates with information from your target culture (see Helpful Web Sites in Chapter 4 for information on these) and type in "menu" or "restaurant menus" in your target language. A few minutes spent checking out the resulting links should yield a number of usable menus.*

Create a handout containing a typical telephone conversation in the target language between a customer and an individual taking reservations at a restaurant. Include lines typically said by the restaurant representative, but leave the customer's lines blank (see Stage 2 of Presentation and Practice for details).

Create a second handout containing questions and answers in the target language that are typical of conversations between servers and their customers in a restaurant in your target culture (see Stage 3 of Presentation and Practice for details).

Generating Interest

Start the activity with a discussion in the target language about restaurants. What kinds of restaurants are there? As students come up with examples, sort them into categories, such as fast-food restaurants, diners, truck stops, chain restaurants, ethnic restaurants, and gourmet restaurants. What are some of the ways in which restaurants are the same? In what ways do they differ?

In what kinds of restaurants do your students prefer to eat with their families? To what kinds do they prefer to go with their friends? What do they consider when they are trying to decide where to eat out? Do they think about the type of food offered, the price of the food, the type of décor, the location?

Next, have students identify the steps involved in restaurant dining. Examples include calling ahead to reserve a table, asking for a table upon arrival at the restaurant, reading the menu, ordering food and drinks, taking part in conversation, and asking for and paying the check. As you write these steps on the board, encourage your students to brainstorm phrases in the target language that could be used for each. For example, you can have them think about different ways a customer could ask for a table. Discuss differences between formal and informal styles and vocabulary and how these may relate to different kinds of restaurants.

Presentation and Practice

The heart of this activity can be found in Stage 3, when students take on the roles of server or customer and role-play what goes on in a restaurant. If you're strapped for time, you can bypass the first two stages, which set the scene for the role play, and begin at Stage 3. Just choose one type of restaurant, have each group decide who will play the role of the server and who will play the customers, read through your handout on typical restaurant interactions, give the menus to the servers, and get started!

Stage 1: Choosing a Restaurant

First, divide your students into groups of approximately four students each. Each group should receive at least one copy of each of the four target language menus.

Have students read through the four menus within their small groups. Ask them to come to a decision regarding which of the four restaurants they would like to use in their role play and what occasion they'll be celebrating. Encourage each student to contribute to this decision by stating his or her preferences related to food choices, price of items, and the like. Ask each group what restaurant it chose and why.

Stage 2: Calling for Reservations

Now that the students have decided on the restaurant, it's almost time for them to choose a date and time for their reservation and to decide how many people will be in their party. Before directing their attention back to the small groups, however, you'll need to model the telephone conversation that typically takes place when a customer calls a restaurant to reserve a table. Be sure to include questions and answers regarding the date and time of the reservation, how many people are in the party, and the name of the person reserving the table.

Unless you happen to have an advanced student (this could be an activity for Activity 2.2, Superstar Obstacle Course) or a teacher's assistant to help you, you'll need to play both roles in this interaction yourself. You can signal the shift between roles by changing your posture and voice quality or accent. If you're feeling extra-confident, you can put on a chef's hat when representing the restaurant or a pair of glasses when talking as the customer. If you've been working with Bob, the Imaginary Fly (Activity 2.4), you can even have Bob take one of the roles!

After you model this conversation, have the students return to working in their small groups. Give each group a copy of the handout you've made of this conversation (see Preparation and Materials). Have the students in each group write their customers' responses onto the sheet and choose one group member to play the role of the customer.

When each group is ready, redirect everyone's attention to the front of the room where you are standing next to a telephone. Taking each group in turn, play the role of the reservations representative for each restaurant. Try to change your voice each time you need to represent a different restaurant.

Stage 3: Dining Out

Now that each small group has selected its restaurant and made its reservations, it's time to get ready for the heart of the activity. First, ask each small group to decide who in the group will play the server. The other students will then play the customers. Once every group has made this decision, distribute handouts containing useful questions and answers for the role play (see the sample role-play scripts shown in Figure 5.1 for ideas). Include typical exchanges between the server and

FIGURE 5.1 *Sample Role-Play Script*

Compare and contrast the target and home cultures according to how diners are seated. Do they sit on mats or pillows on the floor or do they sit in chairs? Are strangers sometimes seated together at the same table?

1. Upon arrival at the table

   Server: **Good evening. Welcome to _____ . Here are your menus. What can I bring you to drink?**

   Customer: I'd like _____ , please.

   Think about any cultural differences related to beverages at mealtime. For example, is water typically served and, if so, is it bottled or tap water? What do children and teenagers typically drink at mealtime? Are beverages served with ice cubes or without? At what temperature are beverages served?

2. When the customers are ready to order

   Server: **May I take your order please? Would you like any appetizers? soup? salad? entrees?**

   Customer: Yes, I'd like _____ , please.

   Compare and contrast the target and home cultures according to the number of courses typically served at one sitting and the types of food that belong to these courses. For example, is salad usually part of a restaurant meal and, if so, is it served before the entree, at the same time, or afterward? Is bread usually brought to the table? When? Is dessert usually eaten? If so, what are typical desserts?

3. When the server brings the food to the table

   Server: **(distributes the food) Here you are. Is everything to your satisfaction? Can I bring you anything else?**

   Customer: It looks wonderful.

   Server: **Enjoy your meal!**

   Is there a particular phrase in your target language that is used at the table when food is passed or placed in front of a person? Is there a particular phrase in your target language that is used to wish "bon appetit"? Think about the eating utensils and how they are used throughout the meal. Introduce and practice any differences here.

4. When the diners have finished eating

   Customer: Excuse me. May we please have the check?

   Server: **Yes, of course. Your total comes to _____ .**

   Customer: Here you go.

   Server: **Thank you. Have a wonderful evening.**

   Customer: Thank you. Good-bye!

   Highlight practices in your target culture that have to do with paying for the meal. How do the diners find out what they owe? Does the server leave the check on the table? Do customers signal when they are ready to pay? Whom do they pay—the server, a cashier, or someone else? Is a tip included? How much is a typical tip?

his or her customers at the following points: (1) upon arrival at the table, (2) when the customers are ready to order, (3) when the server brings the food to the table, and (4) when the diners have finished eating.

Read through the handout, stopping to highlight any relevant cultural practices. Have your students repeat the lines related to the role they'll be playing. Emphasize that all students need to be paying attention to *both* sets of lines, as they will need to *understand* the lines they're not responsible for producing.

After you've gone through the practice dialog, have each small group set up a table with the props you've brought in. Make sure the students playing servers have enough copies of their restaurant's menus to distribute to their customers. Have these students stand with menus in hand a few feet away from the table they'll be responsible for.

When the tables are set and the servers are ready to go, let the role plays begin! If you'd like things to be a little more orderly in your classroom, you can stand in a central location and play a kind of all-purpose host or hostess. Have the customers representing one small group at a time come up to you. After greeting them, you can lead them to their table and signal their server to start the role play. Return then to your host or hostess location and wait for the next group of customers to arrive. If you don't want to spend so much time getting the groups organized, just ask each group of customers to sit down at its table once it's set. The servers can then take their cues and begin.

Now it's your turn to stand back and watch things unfold! If things go as planned, students will combine the functional language they've practiced with their own imagination and sense of humor to transform your classroom into one or more lively restaurants! Stay in your role as host or hostess and wander around from table to table. Listen in on the conversations, encouraging students to assist their classmates if they get stuck on certain phrases or vocabulary during their role playing.

If there's sufficient time and interest, shake things up a bit! Have customers regroup themselves and head off to sample another restaurant within the classroom. They'll have a different server and maybe even a different menu. If you think they've had enough practice in their roles as staff and customers already, have one of the customers in each group change places with its server. Now have everyone order something crazy—start off the meal with dessert or substitute chocolate sauce for cheese sauce!

Stage 4: Reflecting on the Process

Once all the customers have had their opportunity to order, eat, and pay for their meals, direct their attention back to you. Help them to reflect on the experience. First, ask the servers how things went. Did they have any trouble remembering the language they were to use? Did they have trouble understanding anything their customers said? Next, turn to the customers. Did they find it difficult to order from the target language menus? Did they have trouble understanding anything the servers said to them? In what ways was this experience similar to their own experiences going out to eat with their families and friends? In what ways (besides not having real food!) was this experience different from what they're used to?

Expansion

Invite parents, community members, or students from other classes to eat in your restaurants (as long as they speak the target language, of course!).

Have students switch roles and replay the restaurant scene in a different tone. Students will have fun making up part of a mystery or a soap opera.

Share personal anecdotes with your students about eating in restaurants in the target culture. Invite guests from the community (see Activity 4.4, Visiting Experts) or students from other classes who are familiar with the target language and culture. What differences did they notice in the way meals are shared?

Adaptation

For lower-proficiency-level classes, divide the activity into two lessons. On the first day, students can brainstorm ideas, meet in role groups, and then write simple restaurant dialog. Between classes, make copies of these scripts for each member of the groups. In the second lesson, have the groups perform their role plays one by one.

For your more advanced students, you can turn the role playing up a notch by having students try to deal with more challenging restaurant situations. Once the students have had a chance to practice their roles in their spontaneous skits, pass out cards indicating specific situations that they are to act out. Have one group try to deal with the wrong entree, another with a forgotten wallet, and a third with loud customers at a nearby table.

Although props can help set the mood, imagination is the key to role playing. If your classroom has limited resources, challenge your students to create a restaurant scene from whatever you have. For example, students can create a table by drawing plates and silverware onto a big piece of butcher paper.

Options for Evaluation

Performance-Based Assessment

Take advantage of this role-playing activity to conduct an informal, performance-based assessment. This is a good opportunity for teachers to evaluate and monitor students' speaking ability.

Consider videotaping the role plays so that students can later evaluate their own language performances.

After the first set of role plays, have students meet in their role groups (customers versus servers) to discuss how they think they did and what they still need to work on. Are any words, phrases, or pronunciation giving the students trouble?

Expectations Rubric					
	Agree				Disagree
You successfully made a table reservation in the target language.	5	4	3	2	1
You ordered or served food in a restaurant using the target language and displaying appropriate cultural practices.	5	4	3	2	1
You identified and discussed culturally authentic foods, restaurant etiquette, and dining-out routines of the target language culture(s).	5	4	3	2	1

Student Journal Questions

1. Compare eating out in the target language culture with eating out in your local area. Think about similarities and differences in terms of food, the service, tipping, and the like.
2. Which expressions and vocabulary practiced in the skits do you think would be most practical to know for dining in a restaurant of the target culture?
3. Imagine that you are a server in a restaurant where only the target language is spoken. What three food items from the menu would you recommend to your customers and why?
4. If you could open up a restaurant, what kind would it be and how would it look?

Portfolio Entries

1. Include the brief restaurant dialog as described in the Expansion section.
2. Include a written response to one of the journal questions.
3. Include a list of target language expressions and phrases used in restaurant situations collected by the students.
4. If you videotaped the role plays (see Performance-Based Assessment) include a copy of the tape.

Customizing This Activity for Your Classroom

1. What kinds of eating venues exist in your target culture? How do these compare to your students' own culture?
2. Think about some of the major differences in eating out in the target culture(s) and the students' native culture(s). Do differences exist in service expectations? In seating arrangements? In length of time customers can remain in a restaurant? In tipping? In meal options, such as vegetarian? What three aspects of dining out would most likely shock your students? How could you incorporate some of this knowledge into the class lesson?
3. What kinds of ethnic restaurants (from the perspective of the target culture) exist in the target culture? Brainstorm the advantages and disadvantages in terms of using a restaurant in this lesson that serves food other than what one typically considers the cuisine of the target culture.
4. How could you highlight table etiquette in this activity? What types of table manners would be important for your learners to know? Would you want to compare table manners to the students' own culture?

5. What kinds of resources could you draw on in your school to carry out this activity?
6. Think about the role scaffolding plays in this role-playing activity. What would the role play look like *without* prior preparation in language and content? Conversely, what would the learning process look like *without* the role play?

Activity 5.3

TELEPHONING

In the Villages

Talking on the phone in the target language can be a real challenge. It can be daunting to try to understand conversational partners without the help of facial expressions and other clues from the immediate physical context. Additional challenges include cultural differences in the way dial tones and busy signals sound and in the types of language used to open and close telephone conversations. At Concordia Language Villages, learners have a chance to practice talking on the telephone in the target language when they make telephone reservations for restaurant evenings (see Activity 5.2) and when they confirm their end-of-session travel plans over the phone with a travel agent.

In the Classroom

In this activity, your students will have opportunities to practice and become comfortable with practical uses of the target language by identifying and role-playing real-life telephone situations, such as asking for information, making arrangements to meet someone, and even just chatting on the telephone. The performance-style practice of target language telephoning outlined in this activity will help your students with one of the potentially most anxiety-producing contexts of speaking a second language and have fun doing it!

Objectives

- **Communication**
  - Students will be able to make and receive telephone calls in the target language.
- **Cultures, Comparisons**
  - Students will discover and discuss cultural differences in telephoning practices.
- **Communities**
  - Students will become comfortable with target culture telephone etiquette in preparation for interacting with members of the target culture.

Language Functions in Focus

- Asking for information
- Comparing and contrasting
- Greeting
- Introducing oneself
- Opening and closing an interaction
- Making dates or appointments

Preparation and Materials

- Plastic hand-held telephones for all of your students. (Don't worry! If you don't have the time or money to get these props, just have the students pretend.)

Locate a brief video or DVD excerpt (from a movie or a television show) of individuals talking on the telephone in the target language.

Prepare a worksheet and overhead transparency that provide a transcription of portions of the dialog in the video or DVD excerpt (optional: see Presentation and Practice for more detail).

Prepare a handout with the target language equivalents of useful words and phrases, such as shown in Figure 5.2.

Generating Interest

Start off this lesson with a short brainstorming activity in which students in small groups put together a list of reasons why people use telephones. Discuss the groups' answers and provide target language phrases to describe the most common answers, such as *arrange to meet a friend, find out store hours, get a phone number from directory assistance*, or *make a doctor's appointment*. This list is potentially endless; this fact alone should drive home the point to your students how much we depend on telephones in our daily lives and why it is important to learn how to talk on the phone in the target language!

Ask your students if anyone has ever had to make a telephone call in the target language (or another language they are just learning). If no one has had this ex-

FIGURE 5.2 *Useful Words and Phrases When Telephoning*

Nouns	Verbs	Useful Expressions
telephone	to call	Hello.
cellular telephone	to dial	Goodbye.
pay telephone	to ring	_____ speaking.
telephone call	to pick up	May I speak with _____ ?
local call	to hang up	May I ask who's calling?
long distance call		This is she (he). (Speaking.)
collect call		Yes, she (he) is.
emergency call		Just a minute, please.
dial tone		Would you like to leave a message?
busy signal		Can I leave a message, please?
white pages		You must have the wrong number.
yellow pages		This number has been changed.
		This number is no longer in service.

perience, ask if anyone can recall having had a telephone conversation with someone who didn't speak English very well. Ask the students to describe some of the difficulties they had and to think about their possible sources. These answers can serve as springboards to identifying important differences between talking on the telephone and talking in person.

Presentation and Practice

Now that you've discussed both the need for telephone conversations and the possible difficulties associated with them, your students will be ready to focus on learning and practicing the target language within this important context.

Begin by asking your students to identify as many structural parts of a basic telephone call as they can. Examples include picking up the receiver, waiting for the dial tone, dialing the number, waiting for the other party to pick up the phone and answer, identifying yourself as the caller, asking to speak with a particular person, opening the conversation, carrying out the conversation, mutually closing the conversation, and hanging up the receiver. By naming the components of a typical conversation together with your students, you'll all have a chance to see a telephone script emerge from the discussion. You can use this script to compare and contrast telephone practices across cultures if you'd like and to situate the target language that corresponds to the various steps of talking on the phone.

Pass out your worksheet (Figure 5.2) on useful words and phrases connected with telephone calls. Use it to reinforce information that has already been identified by the students and to bring up areas not yet covered.

Now show the video or DVD excerpt (or perform your role play as described in the sidebar) one time through without the sound. Have students guess what's happening in the excerpt. Who are the people? Where are they? And why are they talking on the phone? Write these answers on the board. (This activity also lends itself well to small-group work. Students can compare their answers with each other before talking as a class.) Have your students try to identify what clues they are drawing on to make their guesses.

Watch the video or DVD excerpt a second time through, this time with the sound. Have the students write down how the speakers introduce themselves, ask to speak with a particular person, open the conversation, say goodbye, and so on. Depending on the length of the excerpt and the speed of the conversation, your students may need a good deal of help with this. You may find it useful to provide students with a partial transcript of the interaction (see Preparation and Materials on page 112). Type up the majority of the dialog and ask students to fill in the missing lines. Play the excerpt several times so that students have a chance to complete the activity.

Using an overhead transparency of the written transcript of the dialog, have students compare their answers with each other. Be sure to identify and highlight uses of any words and phrases in the dialog that were discussed earlier based on your handout of useful words and phrases. Once agreement has been reached regarding what was actually said in the interaction, compare and contrast the dialog with the students' initial thoughts based on the silent viewing of the conversation. What do your students think now about the context of the telephone conversation? Do the individuals know each other? What is their relationship to each other? Why are they talking on the phone? This is a good place to talk about the differences in the formality of language used between people who know each other well (such as family members and friends) and those who are relative strangers.

Now that you've given your students some building blocks, it's their turn to try their hand at it. Seat pairs of students back to back and have them act out the phone conversation on the video or DVD. Reassure them that their conversation doesn't have to match the conversation in the excerpt exactly. Invite students to improvise a little as long as they stay in the target language.

What can you do if you can't locate a target language video or DVD containing a telephone conversation? Ask a student from a more advanced class to role-play such a telephone conversation with you. (You could videotape this role play in advance if you have time.) But what if you can't find a student to help you? Then just take on both roles yourself, using two different telephones and two different hats or pairs of eyeglasses to distinguish between the two roles. The students will laugh at the difficulty you're having changing phones and hats or glasses so quickly.

Have students find a new partner and sit back to back. Using the list of what we do on the telephone, have them improvise a new telephone conversation. Make sure they take time before they act out the call to decide what the purpose of the call is and which person is playing which role. Here are several ideas to get them started:

- Call directory assistance to find out the phone number of a specific store; then call that store to find out the hours it is open.
- Call your favorite restaurant to reserve a table for the coming weekend (see Eating Out [Activity 5.2] for more ideas).
- Call your friend to find out if he or she can go to a movie with you; figure out what movie you'd like to see, what time you'd like to go, and how you're going to get there.

After a few minutes of pair work, invite two or three pairs to reenact their favorite conversation for the whole class. Following each pair's performance, ask audience members questions about the context of the conversation they just heard. Who are the individuals talking on the phone? How well do they know each other? What language clues are the audience members relying on to determine these answers? What is the purpose of the telephone conversation? What was decided during the conversation?

Expansion

Locate community members who speak the target language and are willing to have short phone conversations with your students as part of a homework assignment. Give your students specific information to ask for. This is excellent practice and fun, too! If you've had a visiting expert (Activity 4.4) talk to your class, try to set up some phone calls with that person.

If you have access to telephone books from the target culture, either pass them around for students to examine or make photocopies of different kinds of entries (residential, business, government, advertising, and the like). Lead a discussion of differences noticed by the students. Are the phone numbers shorter or longer than American phone numbers? Are all numbers the same length? Does there seem to be an equivalent to our area code? Are the pages color-coded (is there anything like our yellow pages)?

Have students create short phone drama skits they can perform for the rest of the class. Encourage them to make the scenes melodramatic—like a soap opera. Fellow students can read the dialog first so they will understand the scene as it is performed.

Try some speed dialing! Have small groups pull telephone conversation scenarios out of a hat and give them 3 to 4 minutes to act the scene out within their individual groups. Set a timer and offer four or five rounds. After the final round, give the groups 8 to 10 minutes to perfect their single most favorite scenario for performance in front of the class.

Adaptation

For lower-proficiency-level classes, consider allowing students to use notes or printed dialogs in their practice. You can even write a few key phrases for each step in a phone conversation onto flip-chart paper and hang it up in class so that students can refer to it when necessary. Use two separate class sessions for learning about and practicing formal and informal telephone conversations.

Adjust the topics of conversation to suit the age of the learner. For example, younger learners may invite a friend for a sleepover, while a teenager might practice making plans to go shopping or out to a movie.

Incorporate this activity into specific thematic units. If you're doing a unit on health, for example, have your students role-play making a doctor's appointment on the telephone. If you're doing a unit on restaurants (see Activity 5.2), students can practice calling restaurants to make a table reservation.

Options for Evaluation

Expectations Rubric					
	Agree				Disagree
You made and received telephone calls using the target language.	5	4	3	2	1
You showed evidence of understanding telephoning practices within the target culture.	5	4	3	2	1
You compared telephoning practices of the target culture with those of your own culture.	5	4	3	2	1

Student Journal Questions

1. What was it like to talk on the phone in the target language? What was hard? What was easy? What do you think you need to work on more?
2. Compare telephoning practices in the target culture with those in your own community. Describe two similarities and two differences.
3. Reflect on the difference between telephoning and talking to people face to face. Which is easier for you? Why? What are some advantages and disadvantages of communicating in these two ways?
4. Think about the difference between talking on the phone with a good friend and talking with someone you don't know. In what sorts of situations would you talk on the phone with a person you don't know? What is the language like? Why is it different from when you talk to a good friend?
5. What three pieces of advice would you pass on to someone who wants to make a phone call in the target language?

Portfolio Entries

1. Include lists of phrases students used to carry out a typical phone conversation in the target language.
2. Include two telephone dialogs, one informal and the other formal.

3. Include scripts from students' phone drama skits, as described in the Expansion section.
4. Include a written response to one of the journal questions.

Customizing This Activity for Your Classroom

1. Think about your own experiences telephoning in a foreign language. What was the most difficult aspect of it for you? If miscommunication occurred, at what point(s) in the conversation did it surface? How did it come about?
2. Why is telephoning considered more challenging than face-to-face coversation? Do you agree with this assessment?
3. What parts of the activity do you anticipate your students having the most and least difficulty with?
4. How could you incorporate native speakers into this activity?
5. What would this activity look like with students who are heritage speakers? What kind of information could they add to the activity? What kind of information would they need for telephoning that they wouldn't otherwise know?
6. What telephoning situations are your students likely to encounter and need in the target culture?
7. What specific grammar and vocabulary items from your target language could be practiced using this activity?
8. Where in your syllabus would this telephoning activity best fit?
9. What sorts of challenges do you foresee using this activity with beginning language learners? How could you overcome them?

Activity 5.4

E-MATES

In the Villages

So often needs-based learning is thought of in terms of functional language in service encounter situations, such as stores, banks, and movie theaters. But there is another important aspect of needs-based learning: developing relationships between individuals. One of the greatest strengths of Concordia Language Villages lies in its focus on the human connections and cultural bridges created among counselors and villagers alike.

In the Classroom

How might you recreate within *your* classroom the informal, friendly interaction that occurs among people from a wide variety of backgrounds at Concordia Language Villages? One way is to implement an E-mates exchange program with a class studying the same target language as you, but in a very different part of the world. In this activity, we take the traditional pen pal idea a few steps further by using the target language to highlight students' developing awareness of other cultures (not necessarily only the target culture) and by introducing writing conventions associated with e-mailing in the target language.

Objectives

■ **Communication**
- Students will be able to write and read e-mails in the target language.
- Students will become familiar with e-mail and writing conventions of the target language.

■ **Cultures**
- Students will become acquainted with young people from a culture other than the home and target cultures by using the target language.
- Students will become acquainted with cultural products and practices of a culture other than the home and target cultures by using the target language.

■ **Comparisons**
- Students will be able to identify and report on similarities and differences across cultures.

■ **Communities**
- Students will develop friendships with other learners of the target language through use of the target language.

Language Functions in Focus

■ Comparing and contrasting
■ Describing people
■ Expressing opinions
■ Introducing oneself
■ Opening and closing an interaction

Preparation and Materials

■ Computer access for students (in- or outside class)
■ An e-mail text written in the target language. A text that contains abbreviations and emoticons (a sequence of ordinary characters on a computer keyboard that are combined to create an icon—a smiley face, for example—that expresses emotion) typical of the target language will be especially useful in your class discussions—see Generating Interest.

Locate an instructor of the target language who would like to partner with your class on this program. Local or national language teaching organizations may be helpful in establishing this link. Such organizations often know about teachers in other countries who want to set up communication with a class abroad. To make this a needs-based program for both partners, it is a good idea to find a class that has neither English nor your target language as a native language. That way, both classes will benefit from student-to-student communication in the target language. Students will also have valuable opportunities to use the target language to learn about other cultures and peoples.

Once your partner class has been identified, find a map that contains the city in which your partners live, along with some photographs from the region. Learn a few common phrases in the native language of your partners (for example, *Hello, What's your name?, My name is. . . , Good-bye*) to share with your students. You can use the Internet or travel books to locate this information (see Presentation and Practice).

> *If you can't locate a target language class in a region outside both the United States and your target language regions, set up an e-mates program with another class in the United States that is studying the same language you are—and at approximately the same level. You can learn about a different geographic region of the United States that way, but you may have to keep reminding your students to use only the target language in their correspondence.*

Write a brief text in the target language to introduce yourself to the partner class. This text will be used as a model for your students in the Presentation and Practice section of this activity.

Create an e-mate preference list form (Figure 5.3) to be used by your students in the selection of their e-mates (see Presentation and Practice).

Generating Interest

A great way to introduce this project is by talking with your students about the nature of e-mailing and the conventions associated with it.

Ask your students how people communicate in the world and why they communicate in these ways. Some responses may include letter writing, e-mailing, faxing, talking, sign language, and telephoning. Probe more specifically for e-mail by asking your students these questions:

- Who has used e-mail before?
- To whom do you typically send e-mail?
- What kinds of things are talked about in e-mail?
- What are some of the advantages of e-mail (for example, speed, cost)?
- What are some of the disadvantages of e-mail (for example, sometimes miscommunication occurs because you cannot see or hear the conversational partner)?

These questions can lead nicely into a discussion of emoticons and abbreviations in e-mailing. Ask your students if they have any favorite emoticons they use when e-mailing or other signs when they write notes or letters. Ask what kinds of abbreviations they're familiar with (for example, BTW, lol).

If you've been able to locate an e-mail text written in the target language, print it out and share it with your students. Point out how the message is opened and closed. If the text you found contains abbreviations and emoticons typical of the language, have students guess what these mean.

Introduce computer and e-mailing terminology in the target language (*keyboard, typing, to send/edit/save an e-mail,* and so forth).

Presentation and Practice

Depending on how tech-savvy you are, you may want to set up a Web page introducing the class, complete with photographs.

Introduce your students to the e-mate project. Tell them a little about the culture of the corresponding class. Identify the city where your partners live on a map. Share photographs of the region if you can locate some in books or on the Internet. Teach a few common phrases in the native language of your partner class.

Suggest to the language instructor on the other end that students from both classes write up a short text introducing themselves. Provide your students with a sample one—make one for yourself!—so that they have a sense of how to construct their paragraphs. Give students feedback so that they can make language corrections.

FIGURE 5.3 *E-Mate Preference List*

Name: _____

I would like to correspond with (in order of preference):

1)

2)

3)

4)

Once the texts have been written and traded with the other class, have each of your students read one text from the other class aloud. After everyone has heard the students' self-descriptions, have each of your students fill out a form such as the one shown in Figure 5.3.

Suggest to the other teacher that he or she do the same. Get responses from the teacher and determine the best student matches.

> *Matching students may be a little tricky, especially if you are working with class numbers that do not match up evenly. In these cases, suggest that some people double up with a correspondent.*

To get the ball rolling, it's a good idea to establish guidelines for appropriate e-mail behavior. For more subtle supervision, give the students a list of information they need to find out each week from their e-mate. This can be in the form of an actual checklist from which students can choose to ask questions. If you want to zero in on particular language forms or functions, you may decide to suggest that students perform certain tasks that are more likely to contain these forms or functions (for example, descriptions are more likely to contain adjective endings, and stories about a trip are more likely to contain past tense and prepositions). Have your students "cc" you on every message they send. In this way, you can monitor your students' messages to make sure that the content is appropriate.

To encourage students to get to know each other relatively quickly, ask your students to try to find out one or two pieces of new information about their e-mate every week.

Here's an example of topics to start off with:

Favorite interests and hobbies:
Favorite sport:
Favorite food:
Parents' names:
Siblings' names and ages:
Best friends(s):
What the e-mate wants to be when he or she grows up:
Pets:
Favorite music, singer, or group:
Favorite city:

Every once in a while, get feedback from your students to find out how the project is developing, to motivate those who are not participating enough, and to highlight the similarities and differences your students are discovering between the e-mates and themselves. Here are some questions to guide you:

- Does anyone have an e-mate with the same favorite sport, food, or hobby, and so on?
- Does anyone have an e-mate with the same number of siblings?

- What have you learned about the culture of the e-mate (school, home, or the like)?
- Has anyone learned new words in the target language through the e-mate?
- Has anyone learned new words in the native language of the e-mate?

Expansion

Have students write up biographical sketches of their e-mates and make photocopies of the collection for each of your students.

Why not do some snail-mail? Have your class design postcards to send to their new friends abroad.

Create a bulletin board devoted to the project: Post a map of the geographic region where your e-mates are located. Hang pictures of the region and post photographs of the e-mates, and any postcards received from them.

Have extra-motivated students write a report on their experiences for the school newspaper (see Activity 7.1), possibly as part of the Superstar Obstacle Course (Activity 2.2). Send a copy to the correspondence group.

Adaptation

If your students do not have access to e-mail outside the class, devote 10 to 15 minutes a week of class time for students to write to their new e-mates. In this way you will be available to help your students should they have specific questions.

If your students do not have the opportunity to work regularly on computers, traditional pen pals are a lot of fun, too. Everyone loves receiving postcards and letters through the mail!

For beginning students, write the first few e-mails as an entire class, with individual students filling in specific focused information, such as age, hobbies, numbers of siblings, and favorite subject in school.

To challenge your more advanced level classes, provide specific topics for your students to address in their correspondence that fit those dealt with in instruction. Perhaps students in both classes could read the same poem or short story or even see the same film, if such coordination is initiated early enough in the school year. An intriguing e-mail discussion responding to the text or film could develop!

Options for Evaluation

Expectations Rubric					
	Agree				Disagree
You wrote and read e-mails in the target language, and you learned the e-mail and writing conventions of the target language.	5	4	3	2	1
You learned about your e-mate's language and culture through your shared target language on e-mail.	5	4	3	2	1
You learned about your e-mate's interests and family through your shared target language on e-mail.	5	4	3	2	1

Student Journal Questions

1. What are you learning about your e-mate? What have you learned so far about your e-mate's home and culture?
2. What is your favorite part of this project? Your least favorite? Why?
3. Is it getting easier to write? Are you ever frustrated? Why?
4. Can you see your use of the target language improving through this project? If so, in which ways?
5. What kind of advice can you give next year's students about participating in a writing project like this?

Portfolio Entries

1. Include students' self-introductions to their e-mates.
2. Have beginning and intermediate students fill out a worksheet based on information about their e-mates.
3. Include biographical sketches of the e-mates, as described in the Expansion section.
4. Include written responses to the journal questions.

Customizing This Activity for Your Classroom

1. Think about your own experiences corresponding with others in a foreign language. What was your medium of choice? Why? Was the correspondence voluntary? Did you encounter any hurdles to corresponding? What did you learn from the experience?
2. How can you keep your students' interest going throughout this project?
3. Keep a learning journal throughout this project. At the start of it, write down your specific goals and expected outcomes for the project. What do you expect your learners' level of participation to look like throughout the process? What kind of information do you think your students will learn? What kinds of language forms do you expect them to practice? Do you expect their language to develop in terms of complexity and accuracy? Address these points throughout the project. Upon completion of the project, compare your initial thoughts to those at the end of the semester. Were your original goals met? What did your learners get out of the experience?
4. What advantages and disadvantages do you see in having students write e-mails on their own? Can you think of any solutions to the challenges you foresee?
5. How would this activity look for younger learners? How could you scaffold this activity to meet their needs?
6. What sorts of knowledge about e-mailing can you expect your students to have before entering the classroom? How could you tap into this background knowledge?
7. What cultures would be interesting for you and your learners to work with in this e-mail exchange program?
8. Since your students will be communicating with students who also are not native speakers of the target language, inaccuracies in the language are bound to come up. How might you address errors in this project without losing students' confidence and reducing their comfort level? Do you even want to address errors in this activity?

IT'S YOUR TURN!

It can be very scary to step out of the airplane into a foreign airport or to get on a train in one country and get off in another. As we like to say at Waldsee, the German language village, there is no ticket counter for beginning German students in the Hamburg train station! Using a language other than one's mother tongue to negotiate the twists and turns of everyday life can be a real challenge. Knowing exactly what to say and do at every moment of the day can sometimes seem more difficult than curling up in an armchair with a novel or composing a poem in the target language.

Even fairly proficient language users may feel a pit in their stomach when faced with making a telephone call in another country. *How do I greet the person who answers the phone? What do I do if the person I'm hoping to talk with isn't in? How do I leave a message? How do I close the conversation—neither sounding too formal, nor too informal?* Normally confident speakers of the language may feel a bit panicked when arriving at a restaurant in another country. Perhaps knowing the language isn't enough. *Do I just head for an open table or wait for a hostess? How do I get the check? Whom do I pay?*

The activities in this chapter are all about offering learners an important bridge between what they're learning in the classroom and real life out there in the target culture. They're meant to give learners a safe haven in which to practice, to prepare for the move into the real world. It's the crucial middle ground between insulating someone from reality and pushing him or her off the proverbial cliff.

Discussion Questions

1. Think about a typical day in the life of a tourist in your target culture. What information, both linguistic and cultural, does the tourist need to know to get along? What is absolutely critical? What is important to a comfortable visit? What would help the tourist to get the finer points right? Using the activities in this chapter as models, devise communicative activities to help out students with these new situations.
2. Some of your students may have spent time in your target culture. How can you use their knowledge of these needs-based situations to help other students in the class?
3. Many movies and books set in today's target culture are full of scenes that display these important ways of speaking: people making phone calls, ordering meals in restaurants, going to the doctor, shopping in a department store, and buying a ticket to a movie. Think of ways to use these resources to help teach your students about such needs-based language use.

For Further Reading

Canale, M., & Swain, M. (1980). Theoretical bases of communicative approaches to second language teaching and testing. *Applied Linguistics, 1,* 1–47.

Ellis, R. (2003). *Task-based language learning and teaching.* New York: Oxford University Press.

Savignon, S. J. (1997). *Communicative competence: Theory and classroom practice* (2nd ed). New York: McGraw-Hill.

Helpful Web Sites

The wonderful list of guiding questions for speaking activities on The Internet TESL Journal Web site can be used for all languages! http://iteslj.org/questions/

E-pals is one of the many commercial organizations that can put learners in touch. Visit http://www.epals.com

The Learning Scenarios Web page from the Languages Other than English Web site is a wonderful instructional resource that provides thematic, integrative units of study for foreign language teachers in Arabic, French, German, Japanese, Latin, Russian, and Spanish: http://www.sedl.org/loteced/scenarios/welcome.html.

A wonderful list of emoticons and *assicons* is available at http://www.netlingo.com/smiley/cfm

chapter
6

Experiencing the Language

Engagement. That's what this chapter's all about. How do we get learners to dive headfirst into their learning? To be alive in the moment—to be ready with open minds to *really* learn? We're not talking about sponges sitting in their chairs ready to soak up whatever we may offer them. We're talking about *active, curious, searching* minds, ready to interact with us in the learning process.

Activity 6.1   Sensory Path
Activity 6.2   Dancing
Activity 6.3   Tracing Bodies
Activity 6.4   Simulations

When I think back—more than 30 years!—to my high school days, two images pop up almost immediately: the first is of my sophomore English class producing a video of our 1970s version of *The Great Gatsby*; the second is of my junior chemistry class filling a balloon with two parts hydrogen and one part

oxygen and imploding it to produce a tiny bead of water. As hard as I try, I can't come up with the name of another book we read in that same English class or recall the details of a single paper-based assignment in chemistry. The whole-body experiences that produced the film and the water helped to make the knowledge stick.

And that's what we hear from many of the learners at Concordia Language Villages: learning the language in this experiential way helps it stick in their minds. They contrast this way of learning with cramming for pencil-and-paper tests; the aspects of the language that helped them to get an A or B on the test seem to disappear within a week or so. They simply don't stick.

Through the activities in this chapter, you'll explore ways to teach the language that give learners the opportunity to experience the language hands-on and with their whole body. They'll use all their senses, not just the seeing and hearing most typically associated with language instruction. They'll be able to draw on all their intelligences, not just the analytical or reasoning strengths so often highlighted in language learning. Musical intelligence, kinesthetic intelligence, interpersonal intelligence, spatial intelligence, naturalist intelligence—these can be integrated into a holistic language-learning experience.

So, get out there and *move* with your students! It's good for learning, and it's fun, too!

Activity 6.1

SENSORY PATH

In the Villages

The woodsy environment of Concordia Language Villages is a resource that is regularly drawn on by counselors for language teaching purposes. Because the outdoors offers a number of different sounds, sights, smells, and things to touch, villagers are encouraged to relate the target language to their senses in a range of activities. A nature trail provides especially good instructional props for teaching the target language in a hands-on manner and offers the added benefit of giving villagers an opportunity to develop experience-based environmental awareness.

In the Classroom

This activity brings elements of nature indoors to your classroom. Students begin by using the target language to describe the natural materials, such as leaves, sticks, rocks, and water, they see in front of them. In response to your prompting, they then begin to think about how the objects feel, smell, and sound. Soon they'll be working in pairs—one blindfolded student working with a sighted student—to discover what lies along a mini-sensory path you've laid out for them. Based on these common experiences, each of two larger student teams constructs a more elaborate sensory path for the other team. All these integrated activities lead to the same important place—the development of students' target language abilities through the creative use of all their senses.

Objectives
- **Communication**
  - Students will be able to identify objects from nature.
  - Students will be able to describe how these objects are perceived through the senses.
- **Connections**
  - Students will be able to use senses other than sight to perceive the environment.
  - Students will reflect on what it is like to learn a foreign language without sight.
- **Communities**
  - Students will develop trust with other students by working together cooperatively.

Language Functions in Focus
- Asking for information
- Describing objects
- Giving commands
- Giving directions
- Narrating

Preparation and Materials
- Several large fabric bed sheets
- Small scarves to be used as blindfolds
- Materials found in nature, such as sand, leaves, rocks, bark, moss, sticks, flowers, water, and mud

- Bowls or pans to hold materials
- Old towels or bed sheets to cover up the stations (to keep them a secret!)
- A clean-up station with soap, water, and towels to clean up afterward (if you don't have a sink in your classroom)

Prepare handouts for student teams to use to display the map of the stations on their sensory paths (see the Presentation and Practice section for a model).

Generating Interest

Bring some natural materials to class (sand, leaves, rocks, bark, moss, sticks, flowers, water, and mud) and ask the class to describe them to you in the target language. Write their answers on the board. Most likely, the students will focus on the visual characteristics of these objects. Ask them to think about how these objects feel, smell, and sound. Give students these words, and write them on the board for all to see. Make sure to include vocabulary that the students are likely to encounter in the following stages of the activity as detailed later.

Introduce or review simple command forms and directions (straight, to the left, to the right, up, down, and so on). Students will need to give each other directions (for example, "Go straight three steps," "Turn to your right," "Move your hand down a little bit") over the course of this entire activity.

To spark interest in your students and prepare them for the type of language you would like them to use, prepare a mini-sensory path for the class that involves them touching (and possibly smelling!) objects placed on a larger table. Pair students up and blindfold one person in each pair. There should be as many objects as there are pairs. Have the seeing student ask questions such as "What do you feel?" or "What does it feel like?" and the blindfolded one describe the object in the target language.

Have student pairs move after approximately 1 minute to the next object along the path. About halfway into the path, have the students switch roles. Now the student who was blindfolded is the guide, and vice versa. After they've completed the path, have the blindfolded students take off their blindfolds. Ask all your students to look at all of the objects on the table and identify those that they touched. As a follow-up and vocabulary review, hold up a few objects and ask who touched them and how they described them.

Presentation and Practice

There are different ways for you to go in this activity. You can either have your students make up a planet or other imaginary place or have them create a trip around the world that involves going through different terrain. At the center of this activity is the students' ability to use the target language in ways other than those associated with the visual.

Divide the class into two teams. Tell the class that each group is responsible for creating a sensory path or nature trail for the other team. Students will be blindfolded and barefoot and will literally step into different worlds and environments. For this project, each group must (1) decide on the materials to be used (sand, rocks, water, mud, and so on), (2) create a narrative or descriptive text for the students as they step into the different pans,

FIGURE 6.1 *Map of the Sensory Path*

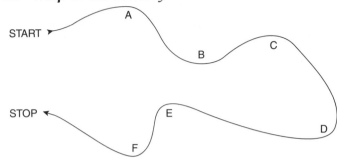

What object was at this station?

What was the station called?

What did you experience there?

such as "You are now entering the Amazon. Be careful of the quicksand as you step," and (3) draw a map of the path with the stations marked but not labeled on a handout based on the example shown in Figure 6.1.

As each station is completed, have students cover it with a towel or sheet so that the other team members won't see it. When both teams are done with all parts of their project, you're ready to begin.

Choose one team's path to start with. Just as in the mini-sensory path described in Generating Interest, students take turns guiding blindfolded students in pairs along the sensory path. The team members who created the path serve as guides for the other team's members. Each guide carries a copy of the map along with the narrative or descriptive texts to be read at each station. The other team members put on their blindfolds. Each student finds a partner and off they go!

At each station along the trail, guides narrate or describe stations using the texts they wrote as a team. In response to questions about what they're feeling at each station, the blindfolded students describe what they are experiencing. Upon completing each station, guides will need to direct the blindfolded students to the next station. Be sure students are continuing to use the command forms and directions (right, left, straight, up, down, and so forth) you introduced and reviewed earlier.

As each pair finishes the sensory path, have them meet in an area of the classroom away from a view of the path. Have the blindfolded students take off their blindfolds and try to describe what they experienced. To help them remember, hand out copies of the map of the different stations. Have them jot down what they remember about each station along the trail. What object was at each station? What was each station called? What did they experience there?

Lead a discussion of the experiences. As you find out how many students guessed all objects correctly or whether some objects were easier to guess than others, be sure to incorporate the guides' experiences as well as the blindfolded students' experiences. They were the ones, after all, who got to see what the blindfolded students tried to do in an attempt to figure out what the object was. They also got to hear a lot of funny guesses!

Tie this discussion of experiences back to the activities in the Generating Interest phase of the activity. Compare and contrast what students said on the mini-sensory path with what they said on the larger trail. Was it easier to recognize the objects the second time around? Was it easier to describe the objects the second time around? Notice how much more easily the descriptive adjectives and nouns roll off your students' tongues!

If there's time, have the team switch roles and begin the exploration of the second team's path. Otherwise, wait until the next time you meet to unveil the second trail.

Expansion

If your resources allow for it, set up a more permanent version of the sensory path outdoors in the schoolyard.

Have students create and guide sensory paths for younger classes (see Student Mentors, Activity 2.3).

Have students write stories about their travels along the sensory path. Make sure they describe in detail what kinds of textures, smells, and sounds they experienced. Encourage them to be imaginative in recreating their journey—they can add other characters and a plot to make the unseen environment really come alive!

Adaptation

If you don't have the space to create an all-out sensory path, create a sensory tasting (or, alternatively, smelling) trail. Have blindfolded students taste (or smell) different foods (or spices and flowers) that are laid out on a table. The foods can be as simple as fruits and vegetables (or typical spices and flowers) found in the target culture. Keep the same format of questions and answers as from the activity above. Check ahead of time for any student allergies!

Have beginning students sit blindfolded at a table. Pass basic objects (such as a coin, ball, fork, candy bar, or Frisbee) one at a time from person to person. Stop after each object has been passed and ask students to describe what they had in their hands. This should be relatively easy to do and will focus the students on the names of objects and basic adjectives in the target language. The next round can include objects that are more difficult to identify (such as remote controls, corkscrews, or chess pieces). Increase the level of richness of decription for more advanced students.

Instead of using blindfolds, you can place objects into cloth or opaque plastic bags. Have students try to identify and describe the objects by feeling them through the bag.

If you're interested in showcasing the environment, create a sensory path on the school playgrounds and fields. You may even wish to incorporate the idea into a field trip to a local nature park! Ask students to walk barefoot and have them guess what they are feeling: pine needles, bark, grass, mud, and so on. Of course, you'll need to check ahead very carefully to ensure that nothing dangerous (glass, nails, or the like) is on the pathway.

Options for Evaluation

Expectations Rubric: Individual Learning Assessment

This assessment can be used to evaluate learners after the initial blindfolded activity from Generating Interest.

	Agree				Disagree
You identified the objects from nature covered in the activity.	5	4	3	2	1
You asked questions about how things feel, smell, and sound in the target language.	5	4	3	2	1
With the help of others, you described how various objects feel, smell, and sound in the target language.	5	4	3	2	1
You worked cooperatively with your partner during the blindfolded activities.	5	4	3	2	1

Expectations Rubric: Group Learning Assessment

This assessment can be used to evaluate learners at the end of the entire activity.

	Agree				Disagree
With your peers, you narrated a story in the target language.	5	4	3	2	1
As a guide, you asked questions about how things feel, smell, and sound in the target language.	5	4	3	2	1
While blindfolded, you described how various objects feel, smell, and sound in the target language.	5	4	3	2	1
You showed a willingness to discuss with others your experience of being blindfolded and reflected on the experience of learning a language without being able to rely on sight.	5	4	3	2	1
While blindfolded, you cooperated by letting your guide partner guide you through the activity.	5	4	3	2	1
As a guide, you helped your blindfolded partners with the target language. For example, if they were searching for a certain word, you helped them.	5	4	3	2	1

Student Journal Questions

1. Describe two stations on the sensory path that you designed. Now describe two stations on the sensory path you experienced blindfolded.
2. Did wearing a blindfold change how much you relied on your other senses? How?
3. What other sensory paths could you take to help you learn the target language? Describe your ideas.

Portfolio Entries

1. Include the map of the sensory path labeled with the student's recollections of the blindfolded experience.
2. Have each guide include a map of the path he or she helped to design, along with the narrative or descriptive texts that accompany each station.
3. Include a written description of how a blindfold affected students' senses (answer to journal question 2).

Customizing This Activity for Your Classroom

1. Think about your local environment. Now imagine taking your students on a sensory walk. What issues might you face?
2. How can heritage learners take a leading role in this activity?
3. What personal knowledge and experiences could you draw on to make the sensory path more effective?

4. How do you think a trust activity like this one will help give learners courage to speak the target language?
5. Think about classroom management issues that might come up over the course of this activity. What could you do to prevent problems from occurring?
6. How can you and your class link issues related to your local environment to environmental issues in the target culture?
7. After reflecting on questions 2 through 6, how has your image of this activity changed?

Activity 6.2   DANCING

In the Villages

Learners are exposed to a wide range of dancing opportunities at Concordia Language Villages. Some villagers prefer to learn ethnic folk dances, while others want to learn ballroom dances. Still others want only to find out how young people in the target countries dance when they go out with their friends on weekends. After learning these dances, villagers then have many opportunities to try them out—during enactments of cultural holidays and festivals, during performances for visitors from neighboring language villages, or when top hits from the target culture get them onto the floor at a weekend village dance!

In the Classroom

The music starts and the beat kicks in. Students stop what they're doing and look around for clues. They're ready to get up and move to the music if you just signal. In this activity, your students talk about what they already know and like about dancing and then have a chance to learn the moves to a popular dance from your target culture. If you're careful to attune your choice of music and dance to their interests, this activity can do wonders to increase your students' enthusiasm for the target culture. The repetitive nature of most dances can be accompanied by repetition of relevant aspects of the target language—but this kind of repetition isn't tedious. Because it's tied to physical movement and energetic music, students can practice and become proficient at aspects of the target language and not even be aware that they're doing so. And, if that weren't enough of a motivation, dancing ties in well to other units in your syllabus, including history, geography, festivals, music, and popular culture.

Objectives

- ■ **Communication**
  - • Students will be able to comprehend oral dance instructions.
  - • Students will be able to describe movements involved in dancing.
- ■ **Cultures**
  - • Students will be able to describe and perform dances from the target culture.
- ■ **Comparisons**
  - • Students will be able to compare dances from the target culture with those of their home culture.
- ■ **Connections**
  - • Students will develop an artistic appreciation for dancing.
- ■ **Communities**
  - • Students will develop a sense of community through goal-oriented group work.

Language Functions in Focus

- ■ Comparing and contrasting
- ■ Describing procedures
- ■ Giving directions (expansion activity)

Preparation and Materials

Multimedia resources such as the Multicultural Folk Dance Treasure Chest by Christy Lane provide not only videos, music, and written directions for dances representing a wide variety of cultures, but also relevant geographical, language, and cultural background information. Check other sources on the Internet, such as Human Kinetics, for this and similar resources.

Select a dance that you would like to have your students learn. Concordia Language Villages counselors have found that circle and line dances work best for younger groups of students or for any students who might feel uncomfortable in pair situations.

Use library or Internet resources to learn enough about the dance so that you can do the basic steps and provide some information about its history.

Locate music that is appropriate for the dance. Many large music stores have international, folk, or world music sections.

If possible, locate a video showing young people doing the dance and/or a dance instruction video. Students will identify with a TV or movie clip showing young people dancing; a dance instruction video offers step-by-step vocabulary practice. Using both is ideal, but either alone is valuable.

Generating Interest

As a class, have students list and discuss popular dances in their own culture and break them down into discrete steps using relevant vocabulary. Depending on the language level of your class, you may need to introduce students to vocabulary, such as right and left, hand and foot, and the names of dance movements, such as turn, hop, skip, slide, and step. Practice integrating these vocabulary items into command forms (*"Take two steps to the right," "Hop twice," "Turn around"*). If you have time, you can use the game Twister© or Simon Says© to make this learning fun and effective.

After discussing dances in their own culture, have students brainstorm what they already know about music and dance in countries where the target language is spoken. List important points on the board and refer to them, as appropriate, in upcoming stages of the instruction.

To introduce the actual dance you'll be learning, you can either give your students a brief description and history of the dance, show a video of it, or both.

Experiencing the Language

Presentation and Practice

Begin the dance lesson by playing one time through the music that accompanies the dance. As the music plays, you can call out the dance steps at appropriate places in the music.

Next, demonstrate the dance yourself. If you need a partner or several students for a line or circle dance, consider having one or more of your students learn the dance ahead of time as part of Activity 2.2, Superstar Obstacle Course.

For the next stage, turn the music off. Take the students measure by measure through the various steps, moving slowly and repeating frequently.

As the students become more familiar with the dance, turn on the music and give it a trial run. Call out the different steps above the music ("Two steps to the right!" "Change partners!"). Encourage students to participate orally as they dance by asking questions such as "Which foot do we lift first?" "Which count do we jump on?"

When you think the students have internalized the dance, step back, turn on the music, and see what happens without oral tips from you. Have fun!

Expansion

If the dance you teach involves fancy footwork, have your students draw a numbered dance-step poster with a brief description of each step written next to the shoe prints. They'll have fun trying to transfer the steps to paper and tracing their shoes!

Your older students will have a blast creating their own dance instruction video! They can teach the dance learned in class or even create their own.

Have a native-speaker community member come to teach the dance or sport to your students (see Activity 4.4, Visiting Experts).

Nothing beats showing off what one has learned! Have students perform their dance(s) for other classes, at a school assembly, or for their parents.

Adaptation

Have beginners concentrate on directions (right, left, forward, backward) and simple body parts (foot, leg, arm, head). Intermediate and advanced students can focus more on describing their actions.

Have your middle school students create a new dance using their newly learned dancing vocabulary in the target language. Students can work in groups and eventually teach the dance to the rest of the class. Give out prizes to the funniest, wildest, fastest, most graceful, and most complicated dances.

Have older students compare the dance they learned (or created) to popular dances. Encourage them to reflect in their journals on how culture influences dance and music.

Got two left feet? Try adapting this lesson to a different physical activity more suited to your own interests. Think martial arts, yoga, even self-defense—anything that involves coordinated movement and reflects aspects of the target culture.

Options for Evaluation

Expectations Rubric					
	Agree				Disagree
You followed oral dance instructions in the target language provided by the teacher.	5	4	3	2	1
You described basic dance steps by referring to direction (left and right) and relevant body parts (feet, legs, hands) in the target language.	5	4	3	2	1
You participated in the various stages of the activity, from the brainstorming session to the actual dancing practice and demonstration.	5	4	3	2	1
You discussed the similarities and differences of dances from the target culture to dances in your home culture.	5	4	3	2	1
You have developed a further understanding of dance as an art form.	5	4	3	2	1

Student Journal Questions

1. How has acting out moves helped you learn language?
2. What other physical activities could you do to help you learn language? Describe one activity you can imagine doing in class.
3. How has this activity helped you learn about the target culture? How might you learn more about music and dancing of the culture?
4. How would you describe American dancing to a teenager from the target culture?

Portfolio Entries

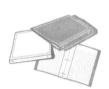

1. If small groups create videos, include a copy in each learner's portfolio.
2. Have learners turn journal entry 4, a description of contemporary American dancing, into a letter to a teenager from the target culture.

Customizing This Activity for Your Classroom

1. Can you imagine your learners doing this activity? What might you do to tailor it to their needs and interests?
2. Could you ask a native speaker from the community to help you teach a dance lesson?
3. Think about dancing you have seen or experienced in the target culture. Where could you find more information on that type of dance?
4. If dancing isn't your thing, what is? Would you prefer to demonstrate tai chi, mime, or yoga? What other activities would work?
5. How could learners do some cultural research to enhance this activity?
6. How can you make sure that your students are continuing to hear and speak the target language throughout the lesson?
7. What classroom management challenges might you face with this activity? Think about what limits and rewards you could establish to keep your students on task.
8. Take a minute to picture how much fun you and the students will have during this activity!

Activity 6.3

TRACING BODIES

In the Villages

The Concordia Language Villages' principle of experiential learning comes to life literally when villagers use their bodies to learn and practice the target language. Villagers trace each other's bodies directly onto the village square or onto large sheets of paper as they review basic body parts, colors, and numbers. And long after it has come to an end, colorful target language traces of the activity remain to elicit smiles from passersby—at least until the next rainstorm!

In the Classroom

In this activity your students enjoy working cooperatively to learn and practice the target language by first outlining their bodies and then filling in details with markers and paper in the classroom or chalk on the playground blacktop. While beginning students focus on basic nouns, adjectives, and numbers, more advanced learners use this activity to learn specific vocabulary ("eyebrows" and "fingernails"), practice comparatives ("Her arms are longer than his arms"), and imperatives ("Draw blue hair!") or as the first step to flesh out characters for a target language cartoon or short story.

Objectives

- **Communication**
  - Students will be able to identify parts of the human body in the target language.
  - Students will be able to describe people's physical appearance in the target language.
- **Communities**
  - Students will develop teamwork skills.

Language Functions in Focus

- Describing people
- Narrating (expansion activity)
- Presenting information

Preparation and Materials

- Large pieces of colored chalk (if the activity is done outside on blacktop or concrete)
- Butcher block paper or other very large sheets of paper (if the activity is done on paper)

■ Colored markers or crayons (if the activity is done on paper)
■ Target language dictionaries
■ Anatomy Web printouts or anatomy books (optional)

Decide whether you'll be taking your class outside to draw on a blacktop or concrete surface or whether you'll be drawing on paper on the floor in your classroom.

Generating Interest

As a class, provide target language terms for body parts by pointing to your own facial features and body. Have students answer chorally or one at a time. Don't let them crack a book!

Ask students to identify situations in which we need to know how to name parts of the body. Have some in mind in case you need to elicit them, such as learning a dance ("Hop on your right foot"), going to a doctor's office ("My knee hurts"), or learning a sport ("Don't bend your elbow").

Presentation and Practice

To begin, divide students into pairs. Place large sheets of paper on the classroom floor or take your class outside onto a blacktop or concrete surface, such as a basketball court, playground, or terrace.

Have each pair decide who will be the model and who will be the artist for the first round of drawings. Have all the models lie down on the paper or ground. The artists then trace around the models using markers, crayons, or chalk. Encourage the artists to change colors often to make the verbal descriptions more interesting. When the outlines are complete, have the students switch roles. Now the original artist is the model, and vice versa.

When all the outlines are complete, have students fill in their own features, including hair, eyes, nose, and mouth. Again, encourage your students to be creative in their use of colors and shapes. This way they'll be able to have a little more fun with their descriptions and comparisons. If you have time, encourage the students to add clothes, jewelry, shoes, and the like, onto their outlines.

After all the drawings are done, the students should label the posters or blacktop using target language dictionaries and anatomy resources.

When everyone is finished with the labeling, bring the whole class together. At this point, you should provide a physical description of your own body, such as "I have long fingers but short arms. I have very long legs and feet."

Students can then take turns describing their drawings. If you don't have too many students in your class, you can walk as a group around to each drawing and listen to each person's description individually. If your class is too large, you can divide the students into groups and have them visit two or three drawings each and listen to descriptions of these drawings.

Beginning students can limit their descriptions to simple sentences including colors, numbers, and names of basic body parts: "I have blue hair, two orange hands, and ten purple toes."

More advanced students can be asked to compare their drawing to the one next to it. Whose drawing is more colorful? Whose hair is longer? Whose legs are straighter?

For homework, have beginning students practice the language they've learned in this activity by writing a description of their own body. You can ask them to describe their favorite clothing as well. More advanced students can be asked to incorporate two or three of their favorite figures into a creative poem, short story, or cartoon.

If you have intermediate or advanced students, they can give directions to each other regarding the colors, shapes, types of clothing, and so on, to be drawn onto the figures. For example, "Draw the left thumb purple." "Make the left shoe red and the right shoe yellow." This is a good way to practice command forms. Encourage these more advanced students to look up words they might not yet know, such as "fingernail" or "eyebrow."

Expansion

Challenge advanced students by having them find expressions in the target language that include different body parts. (Examples in English include "Cross your fingers!" and "Don't roll your eyes at me!") Have the class write these expressions directly onto the tracings. This can lead to an interesting discussion on the relationship between the body and the target language. For example, if hands come up prominently in expressions, have your students try to figure out what these expressions have in common with each other, in which situations they are used, and what the underlying meaning of hands might be.

Students love game shows and competitions! Create a *Jeopardy* game based on the four to six major body areas that the students are likely to include in their self-descriptions (for example, hair, legs and feet, arms, and face). Transform the blackboard into a game board and read parts of the student descriptions as they fit the various topics. Just as in the TV show, students respond with a question, such as "Who is Marie?"

The traced bodies can serve as great props for a murder mystery story created and performed by the students in which they're asked to incorporate some of the language they've just learned.

Adaptation

Have beginning students focus on the body parts by pointing to the drawn model and asking straightforward questions like "What's this, class?" You can also use a partly labeled worksheet to scaffold the information.

If you're short on time and space, have students trace each other's hands onto paper. Label the fingers, thumb, palm, and wrist. Younger students may enjoy drawing in details on each finger to make finger puppets. These can then be used as actors in an impromptu skit.

In small groups, have students draw basic features of an internal body system such as the nervous, respiratory, circulatory, or digestive system. Provide anatomy books in the first or second language for easy reference (or pull the information off a medical Web site). Give students the necessary words, either on the board or on a handout, to help them complete the activity.

Tracing and drawing are great activities for labeling parts. Instead of bodies, you can have your students trace or make rubbings of different leaves collected on a field trip, for example. Another variation can involve classroom objects. Introduce or review objects (scissors, tape, pencils, notebooks, and so on) by having students create posters by labeling and coloring various objects.

Options for Evaluation

Expectations Rubric					
	Agree				Disagree
You can identify different parts of the human body in the target language.	5	4	3	2	1
You described your body and appearance in an oral presentation of the drawing you produced with a partner using the vocabulary introduced in class.	5	4	3	2	1
You worked cooperatively with your body-mapping partner.	5	4	3	2	1

Student Journal Questions

1. Describe yourself using the terms you learned tracing a body.
2. Write a funny short story or poem using as many body terms as you can.
3. Discuss how this activity has helped you learn the target language.
4. Think of some artistic ways to learn about astronomy, furniture, animals, or cars. Pick one and describe how you could do this in your language class.

Portfolio Entries

1. Include a written response to journal question 2.
2. Include a labeled worksheet-sized version of the body.
3. Take a Polaroid or digital photograph of every student (or ask learners to draw silly caricatures of themselves). Have them paste it under their self-description (answer to journal question 1).

Customizing This Activity for Your Classroom

1. Imagine your learners tracing bodies. Can you think of any adjustments you would need to make to this activity to suit their age, hobbies, areas of interest, and language level?
2. How can you make sure that every student participates fully in this activity?
3. Activities involving the human body might lead to behavior problems among your students. How might you structure the activity to prevent problems of this sort?
4. How could a biology or gym teacher help you expand this activity?
5. Now that you have considered some of the logistics, imagine your class completing this activity again.

Activity 6.4   SIMULATIONS

In the Villages

Simulations are an integral part of the Concordia Language Villages curriculum and underscore its mission: to prepare young people for responsible citizenship in our global community. Since languages embody how people think and act, as well as how they speak or read, learning another language means gaining a deeper appreciation for the cultural, political, and historical background of target language countries. Simulations and role plays offer creative and effective ways to bring these issues to life. Historical and political role plays encourage villagers to consider difficult real-world tradeoffs. Cross-cultural and global awareness simulations offer villagers time-compressed experiential opportunities to consider the world from another perspective. Villagers might create their own fantasy cultures, learn how to act appropriately as a guest in a foreign culture, gain a better appreciation for the unspoken and unwritten norms of their target culture, represent their country's position on a major international issue at a model United Nations summit, or relive major historical moments.

In the Classroom

The main idea behind most simulations is to allow students to experience a new perspective and expand their world view. Participants take on roles of different personalities, customs, and cultures. Although simulations involve role play, they operate within the constraints of a predesigned set of rules. A certain degree of ambiguity in these rules, as well as provision for open-ended outcomes, can give students room to bring their own creativity, prior experience, and personal values to the activity. Good simulations can be powerful educational tools and have the capacity to generate strong thoughts and feelings among participants. You should be prepared for this possibility and always ensure that there is time for a concluding discussion or debriefing. The following is a cross-cultural simulation appropriate for all languages: XYZ Land.

Objectives
- **Communication**
  - Students will be able to express needs and viewpoints in the target language.
  - Students will be able to negotiate their needs and viewpoints with others in the target language.
- **Comparisons, Cultures**
  - Students will be able to identify and report on similarities and differences across cultures.
  - Students will reflect on the varying resources and needs of different cultures.
- **Communities**
  - Students will develop a respect for different beliefs, traditions, and perspectives among world cultures.

Language Functions in Focus
- Asking for information
- Comparing and contrasting
- Describing people
- Describing places
- Describing processes
- Presenting information

Preparation and Materials
Collect objects that represent water, land resources, and grain for trading, such as these:

- Small paper cups of water or small pieces of blue construction paper
- Small plastic bags filled with dirt or small pieces of brown paper
- Pieces of bread, popcorn, or small pieces of white paper

In preparation, make enough copies of the Role-Play Sheet (Figure 6.2) for all your students. Provide an example of Culture A based on this sheet to share with your students before they devise Cultures X, Y, and Z at the beginning of the role play.

Depending on how many students you have and the size of your classroom, you may need to reserve three separate rooms close to each other or three areas of a larger room in your school, such as an all-purpose room, a gymnasium, or a cafeteria.

Think about the amount of time you have to work with. This activity usually takes about one and a half hours, including the debriefing. If you need to spread the activity over two class periods, consider using the first class period for set up and creation of the three cultures and the second class period for the actual simulation and debriefing. It is important *not* to split up the actual simulation and the debriefing.

Generating Interest

Often the key to successful simulations is to thrust students into a role-play situation before they have had much time to prepare. Once they have experienced another perspective or world view, they often are very engaged and eager to find out more about cross-cultural differences. The concluding discussion or debriefing is therefore an important time to engage students and to encourage them in further activities focused on cultural similarities and differences.

Simulations can be emotionally powerful. Those that deal with such important issues as hunger, conflict, or discrimination can have an extraordinary impact on participants. Although a simulation can never duplicate the complexity of a real event or teach specific facts, it may allow students to exercise problem-solving skills and experience the feelings that may occur in a real event.

Presentation and Practice

Divide the group into three cultures, X, Y, and Z. Each culture should have at least 5 to 6 members and could have up to 30 to 40 members. Hand each group the role-play sheet given in Figure 6.2, and before you send them away to the place where their culture will be, tell them they will have 20 minutes to devise answers to the questions on the sheet. It's a good idea to provide an example of a Culture A for your students so that they will understand the kinds of choices they will have to make in the creation of their respective cultures.

Conducting the Simulation

After each group has had enough time to devise its culture and practice it within the group, it may send emissaries to visit other cultures or to seek the resources it needs. Visits should be limited to 4 to 5 minutes, and emissaries should stay true

> Tell your students that they can use any language or symbolic gestures to communicate, as long as they don't speak or write English. Given the time constraints, groups usually choose to communicate with a small set of made-up gestures and spoken words that only they know the meaning of. Common words and phrases include translations of "Hello," "My name is . . . ," "What's your name?" "Where are you from?" "Do you want to trade?" "Please," "Thank you," "Yes," "No," "Good-bye," and any others that students predict might be useful based on the task.

FIGURE 6.2 *Role-Play Sheet for Cultures X, Y, and Z*

Role-Play Sheet

How do you communicate? (no English please)

What are the prevalent social relationships in your culture? (Are leaders born into their positions or selected by the people? Do certain age groups have higher status than others? Do certain jobs or professions have higher status than others?)

What type of political system do you have?

What type of economic system do you have? What are items of value in your culture? How are goods and items of value exchanged among members of your culture?

Are there any particular symbols (banners, flags, songs, music, chants, gestures) of your culture?

Some facts about the three cultures in this activity:

Culture X is rich in grain and water, but poor in resources to build your land.

Culture Y is rich in resources to build your land and abundant in water, but poor in grain.

Culture Z is rich in resources to build your land and abundant in grain, but poor in water.

to their culture at all times, communicating *only* in the way the group decided on—never in English. After each round of visits, emissaries should have 1 to 2 minutes to relay their experiences to members of their culture before a new round of visits is started. (Beginning language learners should be allowed to use English for this short relaying of experience; more advanced learners should be expected to use the target language here.)

After everyone has had a chance to visit another culture, call the cultures together. Make sure each culture sits together for the debriefing.

The debriefing is the key to the simulation, allowing you to channel the students' enthusiasm for the simulation experience into a discussion about other cultures—and their own. Unless your students' target language abilities are very advanced, you should consider conducting the discussion at least partially in English. This will allow the students to focus on the cultural comparison goals of the activity. This would be a good opportunity to work with a social studies teacher so that the English would be coming from him or her—and not necessarily from you!

- Ask a representative from Culture X or Culture Y to describe Culture Z.
- Ask a representative from Culture Y or Culture Z to describe Culture X.
- Ask a representative from Culture Z or Culture X to describe Culture Y.
- Then ask a representative of each culture to describe his or her own culture.

Compare some of the initial impressions with the final explanations. Why might there have been some misunderstanding? How were members of one culture able to function in the other culture? Did any of the cultures obtain the resources they needed?

Now take the discussion a bit further by asking whether anyone in the group has traveled abroad. Were there aspects of the cultures they visited that reminded them of the imaginary cultures in XYZ Land? Have they considered how such deeper cultural differences as notions of beauty, modesty, time and space, or social relationships might influence their target language? What aspects of their target language culture intrigue them? What aspects do they want to learn more about?

Expansion

Older, more mature students can colead this activity for slightly younger classes. Make sure the students have a clear understanding of the goals and steps of the activity before undertaking it themselves (see Activities 2.2, Superstar Obstacle Course and Activity 2.3, Student Mentors, for additional ideas as to how to make this work).

Use this simulation to help students explore cultural differences. Have them list some stereotypes of your target culture. Then ask a guest from another country to list some stereotypes of American culture. Compare the lists. Do they feel there is any truth behind these stereotypes? How could one build down such stereotypes? Discuss in small groups.

A related exercise is to ask your students to name 10 things representative of U.S. popular culture. Have them identify the values behind the objects by asking them why they are popular. Fast-food restaurants, for example, might be associated with convenience and our concept of time. Invite comparisons with your target culture.

Adaptation

If you don't have much time to spare, you can turn XYZ Land into a much shorter simulation. Write some basic elements of an imaginary culture and tell two or three students to practice their new culture and language for 5 minutes. The imaginary culture should contain a few elements that would not be apparent to Americans. Tell two other students that they are Americans stranded 80 kilometers from their hotel, without money, in this imaginary culture and that their goal is to convince the local inhabitants to loan or give them enough money for bus fare back to their hotel. Bring the two groups together and see what happens. Guide the ensuing discussion, interweaving audience commentary with the perspectives of each small cultural group, about cultural differences with the entire class.

If you'd like to focus the simulation specifically on your target language and culture, you can replace the imaginary culture in the adaptation above with your target culture. In this way, two or three of your students would be asked to act in ways they think are representative of the target culture and to speak the target language exclusively. The two students who play the stranded Americans would have the fun of pretending that they can't understand the target language they're learning! During the debriefing, you can ask what the actors did to depict the target culture and why. What did the audience think about the portrayal of the target culture and language? What might they have done differently had they been chosen as actors? What challenges did the students playing the stranded Americans face? Expand these points into a larger discussion of stereotypes and perceptions of others as related to both cultures. How is the target culture perceived by many Americans? How are Americans perceived by many within the target culture? Speak from your personal experience when appropriate and encourage any students with relevant experiences to add this valuable information to the discussion.

If you'd like to bring some more play into the simulation, you can turn XYZ Land into a game based on the German tale *The Neverending Story* by Michael Ende.* Both the book and the resulting films are popular with young people. The goal of the game is to save the world of fantasy by inventing a new one. Introduce the main character, Bastian, a human child, who becomes sick in the fantasy world and soon dies. It is now up to the students in your class to devise a new world. Divide students into five small groups, each being responsible for preparing an aspect of the new world. The first group decides who lives in this world and how they clothe and feed themselves. The second group considers where they live and how they protect themselves. The third group considers what the environment will be like, including weather and landscape. The fourth group considers social relationships, such as rules or laws. The final group considers how and when this world began. Have each group introduce its individual aspect and have a narrator (either you or another student) weave the elements together into a story of the new fantasy world. The final discussion can address similarities and differences between the fantasy world and the real human and natural worlds.

Options for Evaluation

Traditional evaluation methods may not be appropriate for simulations. Many teachers have found an effective evaluation to be journal entries or other writing exercises in which students summarize their insights from the activity and the debriefing. If you would like to use a rubric, we offer the following option.

Expectations Rubric					
	Agree				Disagree
You worked cooperatively with your group expressing and negotiating your needs and viewpoints with others in the target language and in the new communication system you devised for your culture.	5	4	3	2	1
You identified the similarities and differences of the varying resources and needs of different cultures.	5	4	3	2	1
You summarized the simulation and the debriefing in your journal entry.	5	4	3	2	1
You connected the simulation to larger cultural issues in the world by either making explicit comments and/or raising questions in your journal entry.	5	4	3	2	1
You displayed a deeper understanding of different beliefs, traditions, and perspectives among world cultures.	5	4	3	2	1

*Ende, Michael (1979). *Die unendliche Geschichte*. Stuttgart: K. Thienemanns Verlag; English translation: Ende, Michael (1997). *The Neverending Story*. New York: Puffin Books.

Student Journal Questions

1. Summarize the simulation and its debriefing.
2. Describe the culture your group created for Culture X, Y, or Z.
3. Has this activity changed your view of the world? If so, how?
4. How can people help solve big world problems by doing small things in their own community?

Portfolio Entries

1. Include a summary of the simulation and the debriefing based on journal question 1.
2. Include a reflection on how the XYZ simulation has changed learners' views of the world (answer to journal question 3).
3. Include photocopied worksheets completed by the group as part of Presentation and Practice to accompany the summaries and/or reflections.

Customizing This Activity for Your Classroom

1. Imagine you and your learners at each stage of the simulation. What specific language and content problems might your students face? How can you scaffold the activity to resolve these issues?
2. How do you imagine students of different ages will respond to the challenge of creating a new culture? How do you think elementary school students might answer the questions? How might the approach of high school students differ?
3. Discussions of complicated topics are great opportunities to let heritage learners shine. What leadership roles could heritage learners take in this simulation?
4. What examples from your local community could you provide to help your learners understand varying perspectives on a given issue?
5. What visuals could you find to help stimulate learners' imaginations in the brainstorming phases? How might print, video, and cyber materials help make this simulation more lifelike?
6. Make a list of the challenges you anticipate regarding this simulation. Ask a senior teacher to help you face these challenges.

FURTHER RESOURCES

XYZ Land is just one of many simulations used within Concordia Language Villages. Cross-cultural, historical, and political simulations related to a variety of languages and cultural groups have been brought together within two Concordia Language Villages resource manuals entitled *Simulations* and *Global Awareness*. For information on these manuals, contact the administrative office of Concordia Language Villages, Concordia College, 901 8th Street S., Moorhead, MN 56562, USA (telephone: 800–222–4750 or 218–299–4544).

IT'S YOUR TURN!

Have you ever noticed the difference in the way you talk about something that happened to you directly compared with the way you retell what happened in a movie you saw or a book you read? When you're telling a story about something that happened directly to you—that you experienced directly when you were part

of the action—you have all your senses to draw on. How things sounded, how they looked, how they felt, how they smelled and tasted. It's much easier to get wrapped up in the telling and provide all sorts of details and animation. This is the difference we're aiming for in the activities in this chapter.

In so many existing classroom activities, learners don't own the activity. They first have to get into the mind of the character before they can try to carry out the requested task ("Imagine that you are Carlos, or Michele, or Toshiko"). In our activities, students participate fully—with their whole bodies—in a learning experience, going blindfolded along a sensory path, learning a new dance, tracing a body, or taking part in a cultural simulation. None of these activities can be done while sitting at a desk. None of these activities can be done while daydreaming. All of these activities demand full mind–body engagement and enable the learner to have a deep, visceral connection to the language learned. When a blindfolded learner touches the sticky sap within the bark of a tree and smells the pine fragrance, he or she will never forget the words associated with this experience. When a dancer hears over and over again—along with the rhythms and the tones of the music— left foot, right foot, jump, turn to the right, one-two-three, the repetition that is a natural part of the activity helps to connect the language to muscle memory. The next time the music is heard and the dance is begun, the words just start to flow.

Discussion Questions

1. This whole-body, full-senses approach can be helpful to any learner. But it can be the pivotal difference to some. Perhaps you have students who seem not to be able to live up to their potential in your class because of difficulties they have with reading or writing—or possibly with being able to focus fully on the unsupported spoken word. The experiential approach, with its supporting information streaming into the mind from all the senses, may be the trick that helps to unlock these students' potential—and helps them succeed in learning a foreign language. Identify someone who might be especially helped by this approach and devise an activity to supplement existing classroom activities.

2. Identify a set of vocabulary words, a language function, or a grammatical feature that you want your students to learn especially well. Figure out a way to link your area of focus to an experiential activity—sports or dancing work especially well—that includes natural repetition. If you'd rather not be so rambunctious, many board games and card games can be adapted to include any type of vocabulary, function, or feature; the repetition will help it settle in.

3. Look at the types of textbook activities you usually make available to students. How can you make them more experiential so that they draw on more of the students' senses? Or get students to use more of their intelligences?

For Further Reading

Asher, J. (1982). *Learning another language through actions: The complete teacher's guidebook* (2nd ed.). Los Gatos, CA: Sky Oaks Productions.

Gardner, H. (1993). *Frames of mind: The theory of multiple intelligences* (10th ed.). New York: Basic Books.

Gardner, H. (1999). *Intelligence reframed: Multiple intelligences for the 21st century.* New York: Basic Books.

Kolb, D. A. (1984). *Experiential learning: Experience as the source of learning and development.* Upper Saddle River, NJ: Prentice Hall.

Krashen, S. & Terrell, T. (1983). *The natural approach: Language acquisition in the classroom.* Hayward, CA: Alemany Press.

Vygotsky, L. S. (1978). *Mind in society: The development of higher psychological processes.* Cambridge, MA: Harvard University Press.

Helpful Web Sites

Check out the Environmental Protection Agency's Environmental Kids Club at http://www.epa.gov/kids/ where you'll find wonderful teacher resources and student activities.

Stuck on how to find a dance you'd like to teach? Start by visiting http://www.humankinetics.com. Check out Christy Lane's *Multicultural Folk Dance Treasure Chest,* volumes 1 and 2, which include videos, CDs, and guides with background information and dance instructions. Also search for Web-based dance magazines from your target culture.

To find anatomical drawings and terms for the Activity 6.3, start with *Gray's Anatomy* online at http://www.bartleby.com/107/ and then search for similar sites in your target language.

Supplement your simulations using information from the United Nations: http://www.un.org

To read an interview with Howard Gardner on his theory of multiple intelligences, go to http://www.nea.org/neatoday/9903/gardner.html

chapter 7

Learning within Extended Projects

Have you ever built a tree house from scratch? No, not by driving to the lumber-yard and picking up some two-by-fours, but by hiking out into the woods and lo-cating just the right trees, cutting them down, stripping the bark, and moving on from there? Have you ever learned to play the balalaika well enough to join with others to make beautiful music? Have you ever woven a rug based on your own design and painstaking precision? Have you ever worked as the editor of a com-munity newspaper?

Many villagers take part in such projects each summer and they do so by using the target language. Most of them come away from the project not even knowing how to express what they've done in English; the only way they know how to talk about carpentry or weaving is in the target language.

Such project-based learning makes good sense for a number of reasons. First, working on a project provides a coherent focus for the learner. Rather than learning a wide range of disparate and unrelated aspects of the target language, the learner is able to work consistently and repeatedly with a manageable range of vocabulary and language functions. Second, a project offers the learner a way in which to link the use of the language to the acquisition of another domain of knowledge or skills, such as newspaper editing or playing the balalaika. Third, participating in such projects offers a wonderful and seamless way to build the kind of learning community we talked about in chapter 1. Each member of the community uses language in concert with others to produce a product—one as fleeting as a moonlight concert, another as long-lasting as a stained glass window built into a residence hall.

The activities in this chapter offer you the chance to see your students in action, all working together on a multifaceted project that will leave a positive mark on your school. And I'm willing to bet that two very important serendipitous effects of the common work will be increased enthusiasm to use the target language with fellow students along with a deepened sense of community in your classroom. Perhaps younger students will see this energy and want to join in the fun!

Activity 7.1   NEWSPAPER

In the Villages

In many Concordia Language Villages programs, learners design, write, and publish weekly or biweekly newspapers that are read in small language groups, cabins, and cafés. Advanced villagers contribute substantive news articles,

intermediate-level villagers conduct and write up interviews, and beginning-level villagers write top 10 lists or draw cartoons. Photographs of evening programs and cabin groups help make such newspapers favorite reading material on the drive home from the village and valuable keepsakes long after the summer is over.

In the Classroom

This activity helps you guide your students through the entire process of designing, creating, and distributing a newspaper in your target language. Following initial comparisons of American and target culture newspapers, your students divide up and take on responsibilities related to producing a paper. Some students investigate and write reports. Others serve as editorial assistants. After cartoons, puzzles, horoscopes, and ads have been added, your students are ready to distribute the paper and then sit back and read their joint accomplishment. They complete the project by reflecting on the process and the important role they played in it. What a great way to build, maintain, and energize your learning community!

Objectives

- ■ **Communication**
  - Students will be able to read newspaper articles and additional features in target language newspapers.
  - Students will be able to write newspaper articles (and additional features in a newspaper) in the target language.
- ■ **Cultures**
  - Students will be able to identify newspaper sections, features, and careers associated with the media in the target language and culture.
- ■ **Comparisons**
  - Students will be able to compare and contrast newspapers from their home culture with those from the target culture.
- ■ **Connections**
  - Students will explore how information is packaged in newspapers.
  - Students will develop knowledge about specific content areas investigated in students' articles and stories.

■ **Communities**
  • Students will become acquainted with a variety of local community resources.
  • Students will work together collaboratively.

Language Functions in Focus
  ■ Asking for information (Expansion activity)
  ■ Comparing and contrasting
  ■ Expressing opinions
  ■ Narrating
  ■ Reporting

Preparation and Materials
  ■ Four to eight newspapers in the target language and English (number depends on class size)
  ■ Access to computers for word processing
  ■ Photocopier
  ■ Specific software for creating newspapers or newsletters (optional)
  ■ Scanner (optional)

Prepare a handout with guiding questions in the target language about newspapers. This questionnaire is to be used as part of the Generating Interest section (see Figure 7.1 for a model).

Prepare a worksheet to facilitate comparison of target language and English newspapers as part of the Generating Interest section (see Generating Interest for a model).

Prepare a model newspaper article in the form of a report or story about your class. You'll be using this model in Part B (Playing Reporter) of Stage 2 (Designing the Class Newspaper) to help your students visualize how their products will look.

Generating Interest
Stage 1: Talking about Newspapers

Have your students brainstorm terms associated with newspapers so that everyone has a common base vocabulary to work from. Provide some community and school newspapers as props in case your students get stuck. Be sure to elicit major newspaper sections, jobs and responsibilities associated with the print media, processes of writing and publishing newspaper articles, and ways of reporting information.

In smaller groups, have your students answer some guiding questions about their interests in newspapers. This will get them thinking about their own potential roles in the creation of a class newspaper. You can use the questionnaire shown in Figure 7.1 in the target language to get them started.

Now it's time for the students to take a peek at some actual newspapers and look for similarities and differences between papers from the students' native culture and those from the target culture. Divide the class into groups of three or four and give each group one paper in the target language and one in English. Give each group a worksheet based on the following model to guide their analysis. Notes

> *To make the comparisons in this exercise more interesting, have your students use newspapers that were published around the same time.*

FIGURE 7.1 *A Questionnaire Guide about Newspapers*

A newspaper's main function is:

A newspaper should have the following sections:

The most important sections of a newspaper are:

My favorite sections of a newspaper are:

If I worked for a newspaper, I would most likely be (circle one):

- A news reporter
- A sports reporter
- An editor
- An advice columnist
- A layout specialist
- An entertainment guide writer
- An opinion columnist
- Other:

The best way to distribute a school newsletter is:

should be written in the target language to give students an opportunity to practice the vocabulary introduced earlier.

Have the class come together and discuss their answers. The discussion should address the major similarities and differences between papers in the two cultures. Not only should this get the class thinking about how papers may be constructed differently across cultures, but it also gives them ideas for the development of their own newspaper.

	Newspaper in English	Newspaper in the Target Language
1. What is the name of the newspaper?		
2. What are the different sections of the newspaper?		
3. What types of articles are found on the front page?		
4. Are there photographs? What are they of? Are they in black and white or color?		
5. What is the most interesting headline?		
6. What countries outside the United States are mentioned in the newspaper?		
7. What kinds of advertisements can be found in the newspaper?		
8. What's the longest newspaper article?		
9. What kinds of people are likely to read the newspaper?		

Presentation and Practice

Stage 2: Designing the Class Newspaper

A. The Planning Process   At this point, you'll want to explain the newspaper project in greater detail to your students. Get input from the class on sections to include in the paper and the paper's likely audience. Depending on the age and language level of your class, you may want to include sections devoted to world or national issues, not just local ones centered on the classroom or school.

List the different jobs and responsibilities required for the project (see Figure 7.1 for ideas) and have students volunteer for the various positions. You, as the teacher, will most likely want to take over the position of final editor, although you can always have editorial assistants to help assemble the actual paper further down the road. The way this activity is set up, each student has the opportunity in Part B to write up a story or report for the paper. Part C, then, involves creating nonnarrative sections of the newspaper.

B. Playing Reporter   On an individual basis or in pairs, have students investigate and write up a report on a topic of their choice. Make sure to first provide a model text for your students. You might want to write up a report or story about the class, such as life in school from the teacher's perspective. After you have pointed out the structure of the article, let the students begin their work. Point your students to the expectation rubric for this phase of the project (see Options for Evaluation) for further details.

After you have given the students feedback on their texts as editor-in-charge, have them revise their drafts before publication. It's best if the students have access to a computer to revise these texts. It will make the eventual layout much easier for you when assembling the entire newspaper. Encourage them to use photos or illustrations to accompany their texts.

C. Additional Aspects of the Newspaper   After the students have written up their first articles, it's time for them to try their hand at creating nonnarrative texts typically found in newspapers, such as cartoons, crossword puzzles, horoscopes, weather reports, and advertisements. You can use model texts from a target language newspaper to guide them in format and language for these different sections. Otherwise, you can have students interpret these genres in their own way, as they're likely to already be familiar with them in their own culture(s).

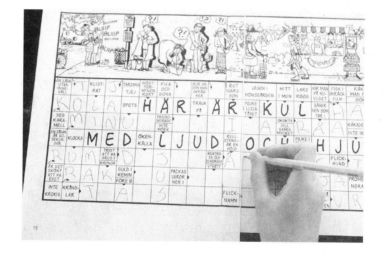

Stage 3: "Extra, extra! Read all about it!" Distributing the Newspaper and Reflecting on the Process

Putting the newspaper together will take a significant amount of time. At this stage, you might want to call on some volunteers from the class to help with the layout. (This could be part of the Superstar Obstacle Course, Activity 2.2.) Use a scanner for pictures and photographs, if you have one available. If you don't have access to one, leave room on the page layout to paste in graphics.

Once the newspaper is photocopied and ready for distribution, you can have students visit other language classes or speakers of the target language in your community to advertise the paper.

Now sit back and relax. Give your students time to read and enjoy the final product. Let them laugh about the top 10 lists and fill out the crossword puzzle. Have them read the articles and discuss their contents. Use the newspaper as you would any other written material in your course. You can even assign comprehension checks or responses to articles as homework.

Once the paper has been read and enjoyed, engage the class in a final discussion of the project. Which parts of the process did they like best? What parts didn't they like as much? What aspects were difficult? Easy? Interesting? Finally, what suggestions do they have for future classes interested in making a newspaper?

Expansion

Work with other faculty in your language department to coordinate and establish a continuous newspaper and award extra credit for contributions.

Participants in Concordia Language Villages programs are often exposed to languages and cultures outside those found in their own village. You can bring other languages into your classroom by collaborating with other foreign language teachers to create a foreign language school newspaper. Each language classroom can contribute its own news in the target language to the paper. In class, have fun trying to translate the Spanish classroom's headlines into French! This is a great way to highlight the multicultural aspect of your school.

Elicit the help of faculty in other departments and target language speakers from the community to provide ideas and input. Your students can conduct (and audiotape) interviews with speakers of the target language to include in the newspaper. More advanced learners could develop these into human interest pieces.

Engage older students in a discussion of social perspectives and political stances that leading newspapers in the target language tend to take. This discussion can take place in English or in the target language, depending on the language levels of your students. Compare these perspectives and stances to those found in newspapers from the students' own culture. This comparison can lead to a discussion of the roles and responsibilities of journalists and the differences between reporting and opinion formation.

Adaptation

If you're worried about saving trees, you may want to consider creating what many news sources around the world do to advertise their printed products—put newspapers on public display in showcase windows! Glue your students' newspaper pages onto poster board and display them in the classroom or school hallway. Get other foreign language teachers to participate so that stories in different languages can be read.

Your newspaper can be as elaborate or as simple as you'd like, ranging from cutting and pasting articles typed by different students to downloading photographs from the Internet or integrating digital photographs into a newspaper produced using specific journalistic computer software.

You can have beginning and intermediate students develop their newspaper pieces in pairs or small groups. More advanced learners can write articles on their own as homework.

With younger students, you'll probably want to focus on happenings close to the class and school.

Older, advanced students can read their local newspapers and revise these stories for a target language audience. This would require students not only to translate the text, but also to think about what additional background information they would have to include in the article to make it understandable to readers. These same students can read newspapers in their target language on the Web and condense and simplify the news stories for inclusion in the class or school newspaper.

Options for Evaluation
Expectations Rubrics
Stage 1: Talking about Newspapers

	Agree				Disagree
You identified different newspaper sections and careers associated with the media in the target language (as part of the first worksheet).	5	4	3	2	1
You compared and contrasted a newspaper from the target culture with one from the native culture (as part of the second worksheet).	5	4	3	2	1

Stage 2: Designing the Class Newspaper

A. The Planning Process: Group Assessment

	Agree				Disagree
You worked together with your peers to plan out the sections and responsibilities for the newspaper.	5	4	3	2	1

B. Playing Reporter (Newspaper articles, first and second drafts; this rubric can be adapted to assess other newspaper features, such as horoscopes, weather reports, and puzzles): Individual or Pair Assessment

	Agree				Disagree
Your newspaper article contains the following: A clear beginning, middle, and end An awareness of audience A clear understanding of the event or person written about	5	4	3	2	1
You incorporated relevant vocabulary and grammatical constructions in your newspaper article and used them appropriately.	5	4	3	2	1
You drew on local resources, that is, the class, school, or wider community, in your article.	5	4	3	2	1

Student Journal Questions

1. Compare and contrast newspapers that are read in the United States to those that are read in regions of the world where your target language is spoken. Is their outward appearance different? What kinds of topics do they deal with? What sections do they typically contain?
2. There were many stages to creating a class newspaper. What was your favorite part of the project? Least favorite? Why? What aspects were difficult? Easy?
3. What characteristics do you think a good news reporter has to have?
4. Do you think newspapers should be politically neutral? Explain your answer.
5. Think about all the things you learned through working on the newspaper. Did your language abilities develop through the project? If so, how? What did you learn about newspapers that you didn't know beforehand?
6. What kind of advice would you give future classes interested in creating a newspaper?

Portfolio Entries

Portfolios are ideal for long-term projects like this one because they help to show your students how small steps can contribute to an impressive end product. What is more, the different items that contribute to the portfolio build on each other and reveal development in language abilities and content knowledge. A journal entry that reflects on the entire process (such as the answer to journal question 5) would make an appropriate ending to the other items.

1. Include students' initial brainstorming questionnaire from the first stage of the project.
2. Include students' comparison grid of English and target language newspapers from the first stage of the project. Have your advanced students develop this into a compare-and-contrast essay.
3. Include students' first and second drafts of their narrative reports, as described in the second stage of the project.
4. Include students' additional newspaper sections.
5. Include the final class newspaper in its entirety.
6. Include journal entries in answer to one or more questions above.

Customizing This Activity for Your Classroom

1. What kinds of school resources could you draw on in this project? Think about individuals, places, and objects.
2. What aspects of this project do you think would help students the most in terms of their language development? What aspects would you expect students to enjoy the most?
3. Think about newspapers and magazines that are popular in regions where your target language is spoken. How would you characterize them in terms of their content, writing styles, formats, intended audiences, and political slants? Which newspapers would be appropriate and relevant to this project to show your students in class? What information would you want to highlight in class?
4. Think about the individual learning styles and aptitudes of your students. What roles would you give individual students within the project's framework to develop their language abilities *and* bolster their comfort level in using the language?
5. Where in your class syllabus would this long-term project best be situated? Think about the content matter, the language features, and the time commitment involved.
6. How can you keep your students' interest throughout the entire project?
7. Think about assessment. What are the advantages of assessing students' work throughout the project over assessing it at the end, and vice versa?

Activity 7.2   WORLD CUP SOCCER

In the Villages

Participants in Concordia Language Villages eagerly anticipate soccer games, both within a single village and in friendly competition with other villages. The sports events capture the fury for "football" that exists in many countries outside the United States. Villagers prepare by practicing aspects of the target language that are needed to play the game, designing and painting team jerseys and signs, coming up with target language cheers and songs, and even making and selling refreshments!

In the Classroom

In this activity, your students will play in a soccer tournament that includes teams from the other foreign language programs in your school. But before the teams actually hit the field, they'll engage in several language-learning and community-building exercises. First they'll learn about the cultural significance of soccer in regions where your target language is spoken. They'll vote to choose the country they'd like to represent in the tournament—along with team name, colors, and mascot—and then learn terms and phrases necessary to play the game. Game rules will be reviewed in the target language, and language rules will be added to discourage the use of English on the field. Once team jerseys and signs have been made and target language cheers and songs have been learned, it's time to blow the whistle and take part in some friendly competition. Perhaps you or another speaker of your target language can deliver play-by-play commentary over the school's public address system as your team scores—Goal! Tor!

Objectives
- **Communication**
  - Students will become acquainted with the rules of soccer in the target language.
  - Students will be able to communicate with team members and officials in the target language while playing soccer.
- **Cultures**
  - Students will become acquainted with the cultural significance of and the practices associated with soccer in the target language.
- **Comparisons**
  - Students will be able to compare cultural practices associated with soccer in the target culture with those associated with the home culture.
- **Communities**
  - Students will develop community spirit through teamwork.

Language Functions in Focus
- Asking for information (Expansion activity)
- Attracting someone's attention
- Comparing and contrasting
- Requesting

Preparation and Materials

- Collect as much soccer paraphernalia as you can find (for example, soccer balls, magazine and newspaper articles, pictures and interviews, Internet reports, sports videos)
- Gather materials for T-shirt design (for example, enough white T-shirts for each class member, fabric paint, and brushes for decorating the T-shirts)
- Gather materials for posters (for example, paint, butcher block paper or poster board)
- Have national flags of countries represented in the tournament to be flown during the tournament and awards ceremony (optional)
- Have audiotapes of national anthems represented in the tournament available to play at the awards ceremony (optional)
- Trophies and/or medals for winning teams (optional)

Talk with teachers from other foreign language classes about the tournament. Try to get at least three other classes to participate. This way you can have two games whose winners go on to play each other in the finals. If you can get more teams, great! Share this activity description with participating teachers so that your students will be prepared in approximately the same way.

If you'd like to use a public address system during the tournament (see Presentation and Practice, Stage 4), arrange for this ahead of time. Invite speakers of the target languages involved in the tournament (language teachers or members of the community) to give the play-by-play commentary.

Generating Interest

Stage 1: Talking about Soccer

Introduce the project by telling students about the soccer competition between classrooms. Have the students first list all countries in which the target language is spoken, and then have a classroom-wide vote to choose which country they'd like to represent in the tournament. After the country has been identified, vote on the team's name, colors, and mascot.

Since soccer has gained in popularity in the United States in recent years, your students are likely to know a lot about the sport already. Draw on their knowledge in a brainstorming session on the cultural significance of soccer in the United States and abroad. How popular is soccer in the States? How popular is it in the target culture(s)? Have the students been to soccer games? What are the games like? Have they played soccer? This discussion can lead to individual conversations on soccer between your students and their e-mates (Activity 5.4).

Presentation and Practice

Stage 2: Introducing the Language and Rules of the Game

Devote sufficient class time to teaching the target language terms and phrases that are necessary for participation in the game. Draw a layout of a soccer field on the board and write in the different positions. Make sure to include all of the action verbs typically involved: kick, run, pass, score, and so on. Teach your students phrases that teammates and coaches can use with each other during the game, such as "Good try!", "Over here!", "Time out!" You can also throw in some hand signals that referees use.

After the useful terms and phrases have been introduced, it's time to go over some of the basic rules of the game. Write the rules in the target language on the board or on a large piece of paper. Again, your students will likely be able to draw on their own experiences playing the game. It's just up to you to give them the target language tools to be able to talk about the game. Some points you'll want to be sure to cover are the goal of the game, number of players on each team, duration of the game, how to score, and what counts as a penalty.

Have your students decide on language rules for the tournament. What will happen if a player speaks English on the field during a game? What will happen if

Don't forget that you can incorporate the expertise of the soccer aficionados in your class by encouraging their participation in the Students as Experts program (see Activity 3.2) or the Superstar Obstacle Course (see Activity 2.2).

a member of the crowd cheers in English during a game? (See Activity 3.4, Students' Rights and Responsibilities, for tips on running such a discussion.) In some villages, speaking English means a penalty kick for the opposing team!

Stage 3: Preparation for the Tournament

Two or three outdoor practice sessions should be held to review both the rules of the game and the target language to be used on the field. Let the students know that they need to follow both game *and* language rules. Though not all students may want to take part in the tournament (some may wish just to cheer on their team), it's important that everyone have a chance to play during practice. Don't forget to stretch, and in the target language! This is another great way to build language into the activity.

Decide what each student would like to do during the tournament: player, scorekeeper, coach, coach's assistant, or crowd member. Depending on the size of your class, several students may play the role of coach for each team.

A few days before the first game of the tournament have the students create team T-shirts or jerseys for the players and signs in the target language for the supporters. At this time, introduce songs or chants from the target culture that are fun to learn and use during the game.

Stage 4: The Big Day!

On the day of the tournament, make sure that you have a referee (you, another teacher, or an older student). Students who signed up to officiate can be scorekeepers.

Play the games, ending up with the championship. Keep the target language coming, on both the field and the sidelines. Encourage cheers and songs!

If you have access to a public address system, invite language teachers or target language speakers from the community to give play-by-play commentary in one of the target languages of the game and to do pre- and postgame interviews with the coaches and selected players. If two target languages are represented on the field, switch commentators at half time, so that both languages get to be heard by the spectators.

Following the championship game, have an awards ceremony. Wave the flag of the winning team, play the team's national anthem, and present the team trophy or individual medals in the target language.

Have fun!

Stage 5: Post-tournament Wrap-up: Reflections

After it's over, ask students to reflect on the game and the tournament as a whole. How much target language did they speak? How many penalty kicks did they get for speaking English? What was hard about using the target language during the game? What parts did they especially enjoy? Which team had the best jerseys? The best signs? The best cheer?

Expansion

Make the World Cup tournament an annual event, and start preparations as early as the first day of class each year!

Your more advanced classes can conduct postgame interviews with the players. Have a few students audiotape or videotape the dialog to incorporate into an article for the student newspaper (see Activity 7.1) or create a television news segment (as part of the film project described in Activity 7.4). Not only will this give your students an opportunity to practice their sports vocabulary, but they'll get a big kick out of doing the postgame wrap-up, too!

Sports enthusiasts can earn extra credit doing what they love to do. Introduce your students to some of the major soccer teams and stars in the target culture. Students can keep track of scores and report these in the school newspaper (see Activity 7.1).

Adaptation

If the activity cannot be coordinated with other classrooms, one class can be split into teams and the activity done on a smaller scale.

Soccer may not be for everyone, and it may not be the dominant sport in the culture of the language you teach. Depending on the size of your class and other resources, you can easily adapt this activity to fit another sport, such as volleyball or table tennis. If your students have varying sports interests, consider coordinating with other foreign language teachers to create two different sports teams, such as table tennis and soccer. Each of you can referee one event.

Encourage other foreign language instructors in your school to create a schoolwide Olympics! Incorporate flags, national anthems, and cheers from the cultures of each target language.

Options for Evaluation

Expectations Rubric					
	Agree				Disagree
You communicated with team members and officials in the target language while playing.	5	4	3	2	1
You were able to explain the rules of the game in the target language.	5	4	3	2	1
You displayed understanding of the role of soccer in the target culture.	5	4	3	2	1
You compared the role of soccer in the target culture with soccer in your native culture.	5	4	3	2	1
You worked together with your peers in creating T-shirts and team signs.	5	4	3	2	1
You actively took part in the postgame wrap-up of the match, in which you reflected on class members' participation in the game.	5	4	3	2	1

Student Journal Questions

1. Compare and contrast the role of soccer in the United States with its role in the target culture. What are the fans like? The players? The games?
2. Explain what it was like to play soccer in the target language. Was it easy? Difficult? Fun? Were you able to avoid speaking English entirely?
3. What was your favorite part of this activity?
4. Explain how the team name, colors, and mascot were chosen.
5. What other sports or activities from the target culture would you like to learn next?

Portfolio Entries

1. Include a list of useful target language phrases for playing soccer created by your students.
2. Include a drawing of a soccer field with player names and positions identified in the target language.
3. Include the class rules for playing soccer.
4. Include a copy of the video- or audiotape postgame wrap-up, as described in the Expansion section.
5. Include a report of soccer scores in the target culture(s), as described in the Expansion section.

Customizing This Activity for Your Classroom

1. Think about your students' interests. How many play sports? How many play soccer? Does playing soccer make sense for your class? Would another game work better?
2. What would you anticipate as the most difficult aspects of this activity? How would you deal with these challenges?
3. How might you gain support from school officials for this activity? With whom might you have to speak? How would you make your case for teaching language through soccer?
4. How could the activity be structured to incorporate language classes of different proficiency levels?
5. Are there native speakers from your community or other teachers who would be interested in helping? What could they contribute to the activity?
6. How could you encourage more speaking of the target language on the playing field? On the sidelines?
7. How could you weave language and content from this project into subsequent lessons?

Activity 7.3 · GARDENING

In the Villages

The organic and ever-evolving culture of Concordia Language Villages is due in great part to the sense of stewardship that is nurtured among villagers throughout their stay. One way lessons of stewardship are brought to the forefront is for counselors to involve villagers in extended projects that leave a lasting imprint on the village. Extended projects in the villages have included gardens, nature paths, stained-glass windows, and wall mosaics.

In the Classroom

In this activity, you guide your students as they plan, plant, and nurture a school garden. The project begins with a discussion to find out what your students already know and like about gardening. What plants are found in regions where your target language is spoken? Which ones can be grown in your own environment? Once they have been exposed to the target language terms they need to talk about plants and gardening, small groups of your students become responsible for planning and planting sections of the class garden plot. Students chart the growth of their plants and write a final report. How rewarding it is when your students begin to see how their hard work affects their local community!

Objectives

- **Communication**
  - Students will be able to identify different plant types in the target language.
  - Students will be able to describe plant life and growth in the target language.
- **Connections**
  - Students will be able to design, build, and tend to a garden.
  - Students will become acquainted with botany through the target language.
  - Students will be able to gather and analyze scientific data in the target language.
- **Communities**
  - Students will become active members of a community through teamwork and stewardship.

Language Functions in Focus

- Describing objects
- Describing processes
- Giving reasons
- Reporting

Preparation and Materials

- Plot for garden
- Variety of seeds
- Planting soil
- Watering cans
- Small wooden stakes
- Poster board
- Lamination materials

> *If you do not have adequate space or resources to create a garden such as the one described here, you may wish to consider an indoor garden box. See information under the Adaptation heading.*

FIGURE 7.2 *Plant Checklist*

Plant name:

Description:

Season:

Climate (including temperature range, humidity and watering, soil):

Light:

Pests:

Special care:

Uses for:

- Gardening books, magazines, and seeds envelopes in the target language
- Camera

Prepare a planning worksheet to be used by your students as part of Stage 1 under Presentation and Practice (see Figure 7.2).

Prepare a growth chart to be used by your students as part of Stage 3 under Presentation and Practice (see Figure 7.3).

Before you involve your class in this project, think carefully about the type of garden (flower, herbal, vegetable, butterfly, or other) that you would like to grow. A number of factors should be considered. Here are some questions to help you in your decision:

- What plants grow best in our climate during the time of year we expect to work in the garden?
- What seeds are available?
- How much time will we have?
- How much space will we have?
- What is the soil like?
- Is water available on site?
- Is there wildlife that may potentially damage the garden?
- What kinds of gardens exist in the cultures where the target language is spoken? What are the soil and climate like there? Which, if any, of their plants would be adaptable to the climate of my school area?

FIGURE 7.3 *Plant Growth Chart*

GROUP _____									
Student Names:									
Name of Plant:									
Date:									
Color:									
Height:									
Other interesting observations:									

Generating Interest

Introduce the project to the students through a brainstorming of all plant types they know in the target language. List them on the board according to their major groupings, for example, fruits, vegetables, flowers, or trees. Ask students which plants are found in the target culture(s), as well as which could be grown in your own environment. This should lead to a short discussion of climate and agricultural practices in both the target culture and your own. Write all relevant vocabulary on the board for your students.

Presentation and Practice

Stage 1: Planning the garden

To spark interest in your students and to get an idea of the different ways of creating a garden, take your class on a field trip to a nearby garden or park. Check with your local garden community for names of close and interesting garden sites. Search for speakers of the target language who could accompany you on a visit and field questions, and involve parents who like to garden.

Have students take notes on the sorts of plants they like, as well as on the layout of the garden. Make sure they note sun exposure, watering needs, and the like.

Divide the class into smaller groups. Each group is responsible for one section of the garden plot and decides (with your guidance) what kinds of plants to grow. Let students know what types of seeds you have to choose from. Provide students with garden books (in the target language) or printed information from the Internet. Though difficult to track down, seed envelopes in the target language found in gardening stores are ideal for this stage in the project, because they provide your learners with pictures of the flowers or plants and relevant language.

You can provide your students with a checklist in the form of a worksheet, such as the one shown in Figure 7.2, as they decide on plants they want to include. Have each group propose three different plants from among those that you have available.

Once they have conferred with you about their choices, have your students create a visual design of their garden plot with appropriate labeling.

Have each group write very short descriptive texts in the target language about their plants to be attached to stakes for marking the garden. Make sure to laminate against rain.

Stage 2: Planting Seeds

Set aside one class period or a time after school to prepare the garden. Have your students plant the seeds. Be sure to use the target language both to advise the students and to ask them what they're doing as the process unfolds. Have them mark the plots with their stakes and descriptive texts.

Once the seeds are in the ground, have students speculate which plants will begin to surface first or last. Write these up in hypothesis form on poster board and hang the poster up in the classroom.

Stage 3: Charting Growth

Have the students chart the growth of the plants. Provide students with a form for each plant. These can be posted on a wall, or possibly attached to a clipboard, with notes recorded weekly. Include relevant vocabulary for students to use. Figure 7.3 shows a sample chart.

Take photographs of the plants at regular intervals to include in the final report (see Stage 4).

Enlist the help of your fellow teaching colleagues in biology or other teachers interested in science for related experiment ideas.

If you want to focus more specifically on the scientific aspects of plant growth, you can build a biology experiment into the project. Have your students try to grow one or two of the same plants from the outdoor garden without one of the plant's life-sustaining variables (the lack of sunlight being one of the more interesting to observe; the plant should grow quite high and lack a greenness in color). Have students then chart both plant sites and compare and discuss. The findings from this analysis can be written up in a short descriptive text or displayed on a poster for all to see.

Stage 4: Everything in Full Bloom—Reflecting on the Process

Have each group write and present a final report on their plants. These texts should draw on all the language and vocabulary that the students have developed over the course of the project. If the plants did not grow as expected, students can provide their own hypotheses as to why not. Have students include drawings and photographs of the plants at various stages in their development.

Expansion

Have students conduct research to find out the cultural significance of different kinds of flowers and plants within the target culture. Are some plants thought to bring good luck? Are certain flowers given only to loved ones? Are others typical of funerals?

If your students grow herbal plants that are used in the cooking of the target culture, have your class use them later in recipes (see Culinary Explorations [Activity 4.3]). For example:

■ Make salsa with cilantro for Spanish classes
■ Make a pesto sauce out of fresh basil for an Italian class
■ Make a fresh salad or a stew with tarragon for a French class
■ Make a dill–cream sauce for a fish dish for a Norwegian class
■ Make mint tea for a German class

If you are growing a flower garden, teach the class or interested students how to dry and preserve flowers.

For extra credit, have interested students design posters or handouts for the class on related topics, such as these:

- A chart listing the various meanings attached to particular plants in the target culture
- A labeled diagram of a plant or flower
- A picture depicting photosynthesis
- A diagram of a food chain involving plants (this one in particular has the potential to invite creative variations from your students!)

These are excellent projects for the Superstar Obstacle Course (see Activity 2.2).

Adaptation

Many varieties of plants can be grown indoors. Herbal plants are especially hardy in this way, as they need little soil. Just make sure to provide them with enough sunlight, and avoid over- and underwatering.

Have younger and/or beginning language learners write a collective narrative of their plants' lives in lieu of the final report. Students can draw pictures at various stages of growth to make into a book. Similarly, students can write a sample how-to book for future classes, incorporating illustrations.

If gardening is not your thing, but you would like students to develop a sense of stewardship by giving back to the school, there are a number of other projects that you can develop. Work with your school's art teacher to create a mural for the school hallway or have students help with a school or neighborhood cleanup.

Options for Evaluation
Expectations Rubrics

Because there are several stages to this project, you'll want to give feedback on a number of activities to the small groups.

Stages 1 and 2: Planning the Garden and Planting the Seeds					
	Agree				**Disagree**
You identified the major parts of a flower or plant in the target language (as part of a worksheet to be filled out during a field trip to a garden or park).	5	4	3	2	1
Your group incorporated relevant vocabulary and grammatical constructions in answering the questions (as part of a worksheet for the group garden plot).	5	4	3	2	1
Your group's plant choices make sense given the local environment of the proposed garden (as part of a worksheet for the group garden plot).	5	4	3	2	1

For the descriptive texts:

	Agree				Disagree
Your group's text includes information about the following: The plants' expected appearance (height and color) The plants' natural habitat (where it typically grows) The plants' specific needs (sunlight and water)	5	4	3	2	1
You incorporated relevant vocabulary and grammatical constructions and used them appropriately in your texts.	5	4	3	2	1

Stages 3 and 4: Charting the Growth and Everything in Full Bloom (Final Report)					
	Agree				Disagree
Your group observed and charted the growth of your plants, including writing up the observations.	5	4	3	2	1
Your report answered the following questions: Why your group chose the plants it did What the group did to prepare its garden plot The observations the group made Possible reasons why the plants did or did not grow as expected	5	4	3	2	1
Your report drew on vocabulary learned throughout the entire project.	5	4	3	2	1
Your entire group worked together on the plant observations and the report.	5	4	3	2	1

Student Journal Questions

1. Describe the class field trip to the garden. What did you do there? What kinds of plants did you learn about? What was your favorite part of the trip?
2. Think about all the things you learned through growing the garden. Did your language abilities develop through the project? If so, how? What did you learn about plants that you didn't know beforehand?
3. Discuss your hypotheses about how the plants would grow. Are you surprised by what happened? What did you learn from the experiment?
4. What advice would you give next year's class for creating a garden? Think about plant choices, teamwork, and the observation process.
5. What role do plants play in our lives? How do you think your class garden will be used within your school community?

Portfolio Entries

1. Include the students' garden checklist and visual plan, as described in the first stage of the activity.
2. Include students' short descriptive texts of their chosen plants, as described in the second stage of the activity.
3. Include the class hypotheses about the expected growth of the plants, as described in the second stage of the activity.
4. Include the group charts of the growth of the plants.
5. Include the final reports prepared by each group.
6. Include any of the extra credit projects discussed in the Expansion section, such as labeled plant diagrams or pictorial representations of food chains.

Customizing This Activity for Your Classroom

1. What grammatical features of your target language do you expect your students to practice and learn through this project?
2. Brainstorm other possible botany experiments you could conduct through this project. Ask your fellow science colleagues for ideas, and find out in which grades these topics are covered. Is cross-disciplinary coordination possible?
3. Can you see any hurdles in this project? How could you overcome them?
4. Beyond gardening, brainstorm possible ways you and your class can act as stewards to your school or local community. What opportunities for personal growth and language development would come about as a result of working on these projects?
5. Think about your school's resources for creating a garden. Is there space? Is there someone to help prepare the soil and maintain the plot? Would you involve the students in these stages? Why or why not?
6. How would this activity look for a beginning language classroom? An intermediate and advanced language classroom? What would be the specific communication, connections, and communities goals in these classrooms?
7. How could environmental issues be incorporated into this project?

Activity 7.4   # FILM FESTIVAL

In the Villages

Several Concordia Language Villages' programs hold film festivals in which small groups of villagers write screenplays and produce short films that are viewed by the entire village and judged by a jury of "prominent" villagers. A glitzy awards ceremony, complete with the arrival of the stars in "limousines" and the presence of paparazzi, celebrates the young film makers and their efforts.

In the Classroom

In this activity, your students are motivated and challenged to get involved and push their target language levels to new heights. First, students view a popular film in your target language and discuss what contributes to making it so successful. Students then work in small groups on the production of original 5- to 10-minute films. Each step of the project offers wonderful opportunities for language development—from deciding on characters, setting, and plot, through writing the script and practicing lines, to the final performance captured on videotape. Once all films have been made, your students screen the final products, write movie reviews, and vote for awards in a variety of categories. The project reaches its high point in the long-awaited awards ceremony, complete with a student master of ceremonies and stars from the target culture to present the awards. Which group will win funniest film? Or best integration of a pink flamingo? The categories are up to your students and you'll all have a blast!

Objectives

- **Communication**
  - Students will be able to comprehend authentic oral target language.
  - Students will be able to write a screenplay in the target language.
  - Students will be able to speak the target language by performing a role in a film.
  - Students will be able to write a film review in the target language.
- **Cultures**
  - Students will become familiar with a film of the target culture.
- **Connections**
  - Students will be able to identify the elements of a film story line.
  - Students will gain knowledge about the making of films (that is, the different stages and jobs involved).
- **Communities**
  - Students will develop community feeling within the classroom and the school through teamwork that results in a publicly presented product.

Language Functions in Focus

- Describing people
- Evaluating
- Expressing opinions
- Giving directions
- Introducing someone else
- Narrating

Preparation and Materials

- Video camera
- Blank videotapes
- VCR and television for viewing films
- Video or DVD of a target language film (see Generating Interest, Stage 1)
- Target language movie review (to be used as a model for students in Presentations and Practice, Stage 3)
- Trophies, medals, or others awards (optional) for the final awards ceremony

If you do not have films in the target language at your disposal, enlist the help of your school or town librarian, or check with national language teaching organizations.

Prepare a handout to assist students in taking notes on the film they will watch as part of the Generating Interest section (Characters, Setting: Time and Place, Major Events).

Generating Interest

The first stage of this project, Viewing and analyzing a target language film, prepares students for the heart of the activity (Stage 2, the making of a movie) by giving them the experience of watching a film in a language other than English and getting them to think about the work that goes into the making of a film. If you're having difficulty locating a suitable film for this first stage, or you don't have the time to spend viewing and analyzing a film, simply bypass this stage and begin with Stage 2. Try to leave time, though, for the awards ceremony described in Stage 3. It will be an absolute highlight of the project!

Stage 1: Viewing and Analyzing a Target Language Film

Have your students watch a portion of a target language film in stages. Consider the following factors when choosing a film to be used in class:

- Choose a relatively recent film that will appeal to both young men and women.
- Check to see that the language, content, and camera shots of the film are appropriate for your community, that is, students, parents, and school.
- Make sure that the story line is not too complicated and that the language is mostly comprehensible. For beginning students, keep in mind that films with more action are easier to understand that those with lots of dialog. Dubbed versions of an American film that the students are likely to be familiar with, such as *Star Wars*, also work well for lower-level language students.

Start the project off by muting the audio of the film for the first few scenes. Have students guess what is happening. This allows relevant vocabulary to be introduced and gives students an edge in comprehension once you play back the audio–video version. Supply your students with background information surrounding the film (history, geography, famous individuals represented in the film, and the like) if this information is critical to basic comprehension of the story.

Have students determine the basics of the film after the first few scenes have been shown: (1) characters, (2) setting (time and place), and (3) major events in the unfolding of the plot. It's helpful to give your students a handout with these categories so that they can take notes for themselves while watching. During the discussion, have the class give titles to some of the scenes.

Have them guess what happens next. Ask about each of the main characters. If you have time, and your students are enjoying and understanding the film, show the rest of the film, stopping every 10 minutes or so to check comprehension and get some feedback. At the end of the film, stop at the credits, point out the various roles involved in creating a film, and elicit from students the responsibilities of each position.

For intermediate and advanced students, this is an excellent place to introduce and/or practice relative clauses. For example,

A movie editor is a person who cuts and splices film.
A movie director is the person who yells "Action!"

Remind the students that they will eventually be performing some of these same tasks in their own projects.

Presentation and Practice

Stage 2: The Making of a Movie

In groups of five or six, students decide on the basics for their movies. This is a good place to discuss different movie genres. Provide the groups with guidelines regarding movie length, setting, number of actors, content, and language to be used.

You may wish to use a list of requirements and questions like this:

To spark additional creativity, you could require that each film contain a particular prop, such as a soccer ball, a pink flamingo, or an item found typically in the target culture, such as a jar of Nutella or a pair of chopsticks. Alternatively, to reinforce language previously worked on in instruction, you could provide students with a list of required words, phrases, or grammatical structures to be incorporated into their individual scripts.

Film Requirements

- Movies should be 5 to 10 minutes in length.
- All group members should take part in the script writing and acting out of the film.
- Every character in the film should have a speaking role.

Questions to Answer

- What kind of movie genre is it (comedy, adventure, drama, mystery, musical, adventure, thriller)?
- Who are the main characters?
- Where does the movie take place?
- Will you use more than one physical setting?
- When does the movie take place?
- What is the general plot?

Once the ideas have been proposed and submitted to you for feedback, have the groups write their film scripts. Make sure they include both dialog and film directions. Give your students feedback on their scripts so that they can revise them before going into production.

Give your students time to practice in class and encourage them to continue practicing on their own time. Create a timetable for videotaping each film. Decide whether you will do the taping, whether the films can be recorded by your school's media specialist, or whether the students will need to organize this by themselves. Consider having the groups tape one scene at a time, rather than waiting to tape the entire performance at once. More frequent taping of shorter segments will allow students to polish a smaller number of lines at a time, will facilitate the sharing of the video camera, and is also more like the filming process of a real movie!

Stage 3: At the Movies

Once all the videotapes have been submitted, make time during class to view the films. Since each film should be very short, you could either view all the films during one class period or schedule one film at the beginning or end of the class period everyday for a week or so. A member of the group responsible for the film to be shown should make a brief oral presentation to introduce it to the students in the audience.

Have students choose one student film to review. Provide a model movie review from a target language entertainment magazine or newspaper—or even from the Internet. If you can find a written review of the film that you showed in Stage

1 of the project, all the better! Point out the structure, content, and particular language features used in the movie review genre so that your students can produce a more authentic version of their own. Collect the reviews and keep them for possible use in the upcoming awards ceremony. If you have a class or school newspaper, a review or two could be included in an upcoming edition (see Activity 7.1).

Have students brainstorm award categories to use in a film competition. Possible ideas include best film, best actor, best actress, best costumes, best set design, and alternative categories such as scariest movie, best screen couple, and funniest scene. Make up a ballot containing the categories decided on by the group and have all students vote for their selections ahead of time. Select a small group of students to count up the votes and to determine the winners in each category. This information should remain a secret until it is revealed in the awards ceremony to come.

Plan the details of the awards ceremony. Have students decide who will be the master of ceremonies and which stars from the target culture will present the awards (and which students will play those stars). Choose a student to be in charge of selecting and showing film clips during the ceremony. Have a creative student or two design invitations and/or posters announcing the big event. Send invitations home with your students and encourage them to invite their friends and family members.

The opening night can begin with a reception and a showing of the films, if you have enough time to do so. When the ceremony is about to start, the stars begin to appear, appropriately dramatic music begins to play, and the master of ceremonies begins to speak. Once the audience members (including those nominated in the various categories) have gathered, it's time to open up those envelopes and discover the winners!

Expansion

Share this idea with your colleagues who teach other languages, including English as a Second Language, and turn Stage 3 into an International Film Festival. The students will have a great time listening to clips of winning films that represent all the languages in your school!

This project can be linked to other projects done previously in class. Have students create films based (strictly or loosely) on texts that you as a class have already read together. Fairy and folk tales serve as great examples and can be manipulated to fit alternative time frames, physical spaces, genres, and the like. This is a wonderful way to let students' individuality and creativity shine. Furthermore, vocabulary can be reviewed and expanded as you have students compare and contrast texts with their film adaptations.

If you decide not to include the movie review in the project, you can offer it as an optional extra-credit activity, one that could eventually be placed into the newspaper (see Activity 7.1) or as a task for the Superstar Obstacle Course (see Activity 2.2).

Adaptation

If videotaping is not a possibility for you, you can guide a live theater performance or a variety show for students to showcase their acting talents. Just make sure to create enough space for a stage and invite a live audience! Students can also produce a playbill, complete with descriptions of the acts and credits.

Don't have much time for an all-out film festival? Consider creating a foreign commercials festival in which students create shorter videoclips advertising products found in the target culture. This would work well across different language programs and may be easier for beginning and intermediate language learners.

With its emphasis on film technology, this project will probably work better with older students. You can adapt the activity to younger children by having them create their own puppet shows in the target language.

If your class is studying current events, you can shift the content focus to create a news program or a documentary in the target language. Just make sure to have appropriate text models in the target language for the students to work with.

Options for Evaluation
Expectations Rubrics

As there are three stages to this project, you'll want to give feedback on and evaluate a number of activities.

Stage 1: Viewing and Analyzing   Worksheet on characters, time and setting, and story line (grading optional)

Small-Group or Pair Assessment					
	Agree				**Disagree**
You identified the time, setting, and major characters of the film, as well as the basic story line of the film.	5	4	3	2	1
You identified professionals who are typically involved in film making.	5	4	3	2	1

Stage 2: The Making of a Movie   Student Group Proposal of Film (Worksheet)

Small-Group Assessment					
	Agree				**Disagree**
Your group provided information on the following: Movie genre of your film Description of the main characters Time and setting(s) of the film General plot of the film	5	4	3	2	1
The entire group participated actively in the project proposal.	5	4	3	2	1

Film Script (Drafts 1 and 2)					
	Agree				**Disagree**
Your film script includes the following: A clear story line or plot Clear film directions Speaking roles for all group members	5	4	3	2	1
You incorporated relevant vocabulary and grammatical constructions and used them appropriately.	5	4	3	2	1
The entire group actively participated in writing the script.	5	4	3	2	1

Stage 3: At the Movies (Film Review)

	Agree				Disagree
Your review text includes the following: Summary of the film reviewed High and low points of the film Who would enjoy the film	5	4	3	2	1
You incorporated relevant vocabulary and grammatical constructions learned through the project and used them appropriately.	5	4	3	2	1

Student Journal Questions

1. Explain some of the choices your group made for the film. Why did you choose the genre you did? The characters? The plot? The time and place?
2. What part of your movie are you most proud of? Why?
3. There were many stages to making your film. What was your favorite part of the project? Least favorite? Why? What aspects were difficult? Easy?
4. Describe the awards ceremony. What was it like? Were you surprised by the outcomes?
5. Think about all the things you learned by making your film. Did your language abilities develop through the project? If so, how? What did you learn about films that you didn't know beforehand?
6. What three pieces of advice would you give future classes interested in making a movie?

Portfolio Entries

Portfolios are ideal for long-term projects like this one, because they help to show your students how small steps can contribute to an impressive end product. What is more, the different items that contribute to the portfolio build on each other and reveal development in language abilities and content knowledge. A journal entry that reflects on the entire process (such as the answer to journal question 5) would make an appropriate ending to the other items.

1. Include class or individual notes about the foreign film shown in class, as described in the first stage of the activity.
2. Include a list and description of jobs associated with film making, as described in the first stage of the activity.
3. Include group proposals for the films, with your feedback, as described in the second stage of the activity.
4. Include first and second drafts of the film scripts, with your feedback, as described in the second stage of the activity.
5. Include a copy of the finished film.
6. Include the students' reviews of each others' films, as described in the third stage of the activity.
7. Include the invitations to the award ceremony and a list of the class winners.

Customizing This Activity for Your Classroom

1. Think back on your previous language-learning experiences involving film and video. What kinds of movies did you watch in the target language? What was the experience like? Did you have comprehension problems? Did you like the films? What did your instructor(s) do with the films?

2. Similarly, think back on your experiences acting in a foreign language. Were these primarily skits? Did you ever participate in a play or movie? Did you ever perform a song in the target language? What was the experience like? What do you attribute to the success—or lack of success, as the case may be—of the performance?

3. How are the three communicative modes of the National Standards (interpersonal, interpretive, presentational) engaged throughout this project?

4. What kinds of resources can you draw on among colleagues and friends for help in the actual movie-making and film-editing stages?

5. Think about the individual learning styles and aptitudes of your students. What roles would you suggest individual students take on within the project's framework so as to develop their language abilities *and* bolster their comfort level in using the language?

6. Throughout this project, it is suggested that language be modeled using authentic texts in the target language or teacher discourse. Reflect on the role modeling plays in learners' language development. What underlying theories are associated with a pedagogy built on modeling?

7. Reflect on the impact video can have in language learning. What are some advantages and drawbacks to using videos in the classroom?

IT'S YOUR TURN!

Learning a language takes a long time. And, as we all know, it isn't enough just to cover a particular topic and move on to the next. It's not enough to learn about adjective endings, practice them for a few days, and take a test. It's not enough to memorize a set of vocabulary words related to clothing and move on to the word list related to cooking. Learners need to revisit these again and again, each time gaining more confidence in understanding and use.

The types of extended projects described in this chapter—newspaper, World Cup soccer, gardening, and film festival—reflect the fact that language learning and development take a long time. And that repetition of vocabulary, grammatical forms, and related language functions is a good thing. As the project advances, some of the moving parts stay the same. Learners encounter some of the same vocabulary, some of the same turns of phrase, and can more readily add what is new to what has become familiar.

Do you have a heritage speaker in your class who speaks the target language almost fluently but has relative weaknesses in reading and writing? Do you have a student who has a near-perfect command over the written intricacies of the language, but speaks very haltingly? The complexity of these projects means that there's something for everyone in them. Some jobs rely on creative thinkers. Others demand good organizational skills. Some will be carried out best by gregarious individuals, those who have no trouble talking with people they don't know so well. Others will be best accomplished by detail-oriented writers.

As you set the projects in motion, you may wish to allow students to choose their own jobs, thus enabling them to slip into the kinds of work they're most comfortable with and good at. The heritage speaker may serve as newspaper reporter, and the excellent writer may be newspaper editor. Other times you may wish to shake things up a bit by assigning students to do the kinds of jobs that encourage them to push forward and practice aspects of language they need help on. The excellent writer who is reluctant to speak can work as reporter; the heritage speaker who needs help with literacy skills can work as editor.

Perhaps the best thing about using extended projects (Principle 6) to organize your teaching is that they draw on all the other important guiding principles discussed in this book. Courage (Principle 1) comes from both the relative comfort students will feel as they work consistently with the same kinds of language and from the possible good fit between the project roles and student strengths. Students will be invested (Principle 2) in the project if care is taken to attune the project content to student interests. Linguistic and cultural authenticity (Principle 3) is assured if culturally relevant topics are chosen and attention is given at each step of the way to connect the project to the target culture. Students will be using the target language because they need to (Principle 4), because each student has a different role to play and is reliant on others for success. And, finally, the projects are experiential (Principle 5) in nature, as students initiate ideas and respond to the real-life circumstances that present themselves. The project unfolds not according to a pre-established script, but is created—and experienced—by students along the way.

And, upon completion of each multifaceted project, learners feel an amazing sense of accomplishment—one that can be tied directly to the fact that each learner had a specific individual role to play that was critical to the overall success of the group. The resulting feeling of community provides important momentum as the class gears up to tackle their next project. They now know that they can set and achieve multiple short-term goals in the service of their long-term goals. They know that they can succeed as an interdependent learning community. And what better life lesson is there than this?

Discussion Questions

1. Projects are excellent ways to marry content to language. You can take any interest you personally have—and one that fits well with the interests of your students—and develop a project around it. Identify one such interest. Using our activities as models, figure out which materials you need, think about ways you can generate interest among your students, demarcate individual phases of the project and come up with ways to evaluate progress along the way. Think about any possible interdepartmental cooperation that would enhance the project. Which colleagues in other departments might be a good fit?

2. Select a project (one of ours or one of your own). Identify the different jobs associated with the execution of the project. Which individual strengths and interests go with each job? Think about the students in your class. Who would fit most easily into each role? Which roles would provide your students with personal challenges to address their relative weaknesses?

3. Select a project (one of ours or one of your own). Spend some time thinking about the lifespan of the project. Which aspects of language need to be introduced at the very beginning of the project? Which aspects need to be introduced in later phases? Which aspects retain their importance throughout the execution of the entire project?

4. Projects take a great deal of time and effort. Your students will be justifiably proud of their accomplishments. How can you show off the projects? Think about ways in which parents and friends, even members of your community, can come to appreciate what your students have done. Can you use the projects to showcase your department within the school or possibly in the recruitment of new language students? Are there any long-lasting products resulting from the project that your class could contribute to the school or community?

For Further Reading

Grennon Brooks, J., & Brooks, M. G. (1993). *In search of understanding: The case for constructivist classrooms.* Alexandria, VA: Association for Supervision and Curriculum Development.

Katz, L. G. & Chard, S. C. (2000). *Engaging children's minds: The project approach* (2nd ed.). Norwood, NJ: Ablex.

Moss, D., and Van Duzer, C. (1998). Project-based learning for adult English language learners. ERIC Digest ED427556. Online at www.ericfacility.net/ericdigests/ed427556.html

Skehan, P. (1989). *Individual differences in second-language learning.* New York: Routledge, Chapman and Hall.

Helpful Web Sites

The Internet Public Library, with links to hundreds of online newspapers from around the world, is a wonderful source for authentic materials: http://www.ipl.org/div/news/.

Visit http://www.thecoachingcorner.com/soccer/index.html for information on the game of soccer, including a list of basic rules and player positions.

Find anything and everything you need to know about gardening on the American Community Gardening Association links: http://www.communitygarden.org/links/. Click on "Gardening with Children" and follow the numerous "School Gardens" links for wonderful ideas and illustrations.

Gather ideas about each step in the film-making process by visiting http://www.learners.org/exhibits/cinema. Then check out the Academy Awards Web site at http://www.oscar.com and do a Web search for film festivals held in regions where your target language is spoken.

chapter

8

Bringing the Principles to Life in Your Classroom

By now you've learned about the Concordia Language Villages and have read through some sample activities that represent the Villages' "Best Practices." Rereading the titles of the chapters up to this point reminds us of the fundamentals that underlie this program's approach to language teaching and learning:

- Building a Learning Community
- Giving Learners Courage
- Learner Investment
- Linguistic and Cultural Authenticity
- Creating a Need to Communicate
- Experiencing the Language
- Learning within Extended Projects

Now all that's left to do before you put down this book – and enter back into the busy life you've temporarily put on hold – is to focus for a few minutes on what you can do to bring our principles to life within your own classroom and school.

CREATING A PLAYWORLD

Within the villages, the principles seem to be enlivened and energized by a prevailing mindset that is supportive of play—one that brings time, space, and participants together within a kaleidoscopic playworld. This playworld nourishes a wide range of learning activities that offer learners opportunities to use the target language in many more ways than would be possible in the run-of-the-mill world. Let me explain. In the world of a regular summer camp, campers are campers. They act as campers do, swimming, playing ball, and eating ice cream. They talk as campers do, teasing a friend, getting a Band-Aid, and asking for more cake. In the world of play, campers can become movie stars accepting film awards (Activity 7.4) or waiters taking beverage orders from their customers (Activity 5.2); they can even befriend Bob the Fly (Activity 2.4). In short, the playworld in its many guises allows learners to come together over time with different constellations of people in different places to use the target language to accomplish different kinds of tasks. And these different tasks present learners with the chance to draw on various aspects of their developing language abilities. Learners need to use more formal language as waiters addressing unfamiliar customers than when yelling to their soccer teammates to go for a goal. And these differences in context are vitally important to the development of a well-rounded, communicatively competent second language speaker.

This playworld is based on two different senses of the word *play* as outlined by Broner and Tarone (2001). The first sense follows Lantolf's (1997) discussion of play as exercise or rehearsal of target forms, as is commonly used in the term *role play*. The second sense follows Cook's (1997:227) use of play as enjoyment and relaxation, what Cook calls "exhuberance of the mind"—and what participants in the villages call "fun"! These two senses of play allow us to resolve an apparent paradox in what we've just written about the connection between the guiding principles and the creation of a playworld in which learners use and develop language. How can authentic products and practices coexist with the notion of a playworld? Aren't *real* and *pretend* diametrically opposed to each other?

No, not necessarily. If we assume that the playworld is the dominant conceptual framework within which activities take place, we can see that authentic materials are useful to participants as they try out authentic (real-world) practices and even try on new identities within the relatively safe haven of the playworld. Of course, this isn't a new concept to any of us. We've seen preschoolers try on Dad's jackets and Mom's shoes and even lug around older siblings' school backpacks—and have a blast doing it! The jackets, shoes, and backpacks are all authentic objects in the real world that serve children's basic desires to role-play events and situations in the workplace or in school that are beyond their current scope. But if these role plays were just rehearsal for getting older—and were not inherently fun—they wouldn't engage in them. It is in this sense that we relate the authentic world to the playworld—and how we relate both senses of the term *play* to the creation of this playworld.

Skeptical? With good reason. Even within the villages, learners react differently to the playworld. For many learners, the very existence of a playworld that provides varied opportunities to learn and speak the target language is enough to spark them into playing along. They jump right into their new play identities and take full advantage of the opportunities. For many others, however, the temptation to cling to their real-life identities—and to continue to speak English—is strong. Since these learners are not required to take an oath to speak only the target language, the motivation has to come from elsewhere. Creating opportunities is irrelevant if learners don't take advantage of them.

So what's the solution?

THE CREATIVE TILT

Within the villages, a key to motivating even the most reticent learners to participate in the playworld is the practice of keeping learners slightly off guard. Counselors and instructors begin by establishing clear routines and expectations. Once learners' expectations and routines have become established, the counselors change them slightly, just as in improvisational theater or jazz music. Learners are surprised at this *creative tilt* and wonder what is going on. This slight uncertainty causes them to perk up a bit, to pay a little more attention in an attempt to figure things out. (See Bruner, 1986, for a useful discussion of the relationship between surprise and the gaining of attention.) Two concrete illustrations from life at Waldsee, the German language village, may help to clarify how this works. The first relates to dining hall routines; the second to singing. In both cases, learners are enticed to participate by altering the expected, known routine, standing it on its head.

Dining Hall Routine

Before breakfast and the evening meal each day, learners gather in a circle around the market square in the center of the village. After singing a song and reciting a poem, the village dean (director) asks those gathered if they are hungry (*Habt ihr Hunger?*). Upon hearing a loud *Ja*, the dean directs them to go across the square to the dining hall (*Dann gehen wir zum Gasthof!*). The villagers learn on the very first evening that they should gather outside the right-hand entrance to the *Gasthof* and wait while the counselors enter through the left-hand entrance. While the counselors are finding places at the tables, the villagers sing *Wir haben Hunger, Hunger, Hunger'...* ("We're hungry") and shout together *Können wir bitte essen?* ("Can we please eat?"). When everything is ready in the *Gasthof*, the counselors invite them to come in by answering *Ja* and singing one of several songs, *Kommt das Essen ist bereietet ...* ("Come. The food is ready"), as the learners walk to their tables. Routines continue throughout the time in the *Gasthof*, with meal presentations, announcements regarding upcoming programs and classes, a weather show, and a closing song being interspersed within everyday mealtime conversations.

One evening, Waldsee's dean did the unexpected: He directed the villagers to enter the *Gasthof* immediately by going through the left (counselors') entrance and the counselors to gather in front of the right entrance and wait. A brief moment of confusion ensued and then a new energy surged through the entire group. The learners immediately took on the behaviors and associated language of the counselors, which up until this point they had only witnessed and never practiced. They entered into the *Gasthof* and distributed themselves among the tables. Several took

on the roles of the counselors who stand in front of the right-hand entrance, directing the villagers' singing and questions to the staff. For their part, the counselors ran toward the dining hall and began to sing the villagers' song. When the villagers inside decided it was time to allow the counselors in, they began to sing *Kommt das Essen* at the top of their lungs, a song that they had only *heard* before. The opportunity had presented itself for the learners to use the instructors' language—and the words (and melody) were all in place! More importantly, any boredom associated with routine had been erased and supplanted by newfound motivation and energy to participate in the program.

Songs

Singing is pervasive at Waldsee. Villagers learn 20 or more songs a session by heart, including hiking songs, traditional and present-day folk songs, "oldies," and current top-of-the-charts hits. Each day learners learn songs in an hour-long singing session and then practice these songs at circle times, before and after meals, and at evening campfires. Songs are critical both to language learning and to community building within the village.

The village songs themselves are often subject to the creative tilt, whereby portions of a familiar song's text are changed. Such parodies are frequently modeled by counselors during meal presentations. For example, one "oldie" entitled "Bossanova" contains the line *Schuld war nur der Bossanova* ("Only the Bossanova was guilty"); a meal presentation about Müesli, a breakfast food containing oat flakes, contains the rewritten line *Schuld waren nur die Haferflocken* ("Only the oat flakes were guilty"). Upon hearing the fractured lines, learners' ears perk up; they notice the unexpected differences and wonder what is being said. Instead of listening mindlessly to a song they have already memorized, surprise propels them into the playworld, and they pay attention to the new portions of the text. This technique is also used with a different twist in a favorite rainy day program. Villagers are asked to take songs they have learned and to reshape and perform them in a different musical style. A rock song might be sung as a Gregorian chant; a simple good-night song might be performed as a rap.

The creative tilt is a dominant tool in all the villages and is applied to more than language. Just as language becomes a resource to be reshaped and played with, objects such as clothing, sports equipment, and kitchenware are frequently used for purposes other than those for which they were originally intended, often in combination with language play. Tennis rackets turn into pretend guitars, table tennis paddles represent butterfly wings in a skit, a jester's hat serves as an impromptu puppet, and even a knife and fork can be conversational partners.

When one considers the important role that confounded expectations play in intercultural misunderstandings (see Agar, 1994), it is not surprising that a program that seeks "to prepare young people for responsible citizenship in our global community" would value playing with learners' expectations. Such play gives learners practice in responding with emotional comfort and intellectual acuity and helps them to remain open-minded in situations of uncertainty. This is a critical survival skill for a global citizen.

We all know exciting learning environments such as these don't just happen. Yes, students contribute a lot and frequently do make the difference between a group you look forward to teaching and one you might even dread. But the lion's share of the responsibility for the creation of the environment within the classroom rests on the teacher's shoulders. Certain conditions make teachable moments more likely to surface. Certain frames of mind make identifying and capitalizing on these moments more likely.

FIVE KEY TEACHER ATTRIBUTES

As I think about successful staff members I've come to know over my three decades with Concordia Language Villages, five attributes flash to the front of my mind: *passionate, creative, flexible, energetic,* and *caring.* These seem to me to be the keys to the success Concordia Language Villages enjoys among the parents, staff, and young people who take part in its programs. You've got all these qualities. You're a teacher, after all! Perhaps, amid the hectic multitasking of everyday life, you may just need to be reminded how vitally important these attributes are to the transformative education of young people and to the implementation of any educational program.

The most important among these five characteristics is passion. Teach what you're passionate about and everything else will fall into place. Language is everywhere. No matter what your passions are, they almost certainly involve language, or at least can be talked and written about using language. Sports? Art? Politics? Music? Poetry? Carpentry? Cooking? Take what energizes you and use it to energize your students. Use one of our sample activities as is, or adapt it to whatever fascinates you! Once you've got the idea, it isn't difficult to do.

Let's think for a moment about the sensory path described in Activity 6.1, Experiencing the Language. Students can help design the path, collect the elements, and construct it—all using the target language. Once the path is ready to be used, you have several options. The first is to focus primarily on its usefulness in practicing some aspect of the target language—adjectives used to describe the smells, sights, and sounds of rocks, leaves, bark, moss, and water, for example. Perhaps your students will take off their blindfolds and be motivated to use some of this newfound language in their own poetic compositions. The second option is for you to focus primarily on the path's usefulness in the quest to learn about nature and environmental issues—explored through the target language, of course. Students can think aloud about natural and human influences on the shape and size of rocks and trees. They can wonder what makes moss grow on some trunks and not on others. The third option is to use the path as a springboard to learning about the target culture, perhaps focusing on how environmental groups in the target culture work with industry, government, schools, and citizens to protect nature. Your students can read nature poetry or look at nature paintings from the target culture, comparing and contrasting what they read and see with what they encountered on the path.

Now, you might be thinking that this sounds good, but there simply isn't enough time and money to carry out these ideas. This is where flexibility and creativity enter the picture. Remember when a big refrigerator box could be transformed into a rocket ship and a fish bowl could be a space helmet? Such creative thinking can go a long way to solving financial shortfalls. Ask your students to help you out. This will save time and money and gets your students invested in your projects. Give your students an idea along with some cardboard, paint, and a box of old clothes, and see what inspiration can do! If there's really no time at all to prepare, remember Bob, the Imaginary Fly (Activity 2.4)—imagination is free and demands no prep time at all!

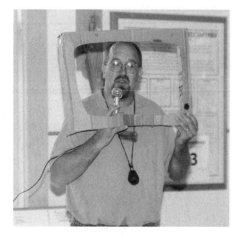

And the remarkable thing about drawing on the creativity and flexibility of you and your students is the energizing effect it has. Rather than draining energy, the inspiration seems to conjure it!

Finally, underneath all your displays of passion, creativity, flexibility, and energy, your students will sense a deep level of caring on your part—caring for them as individuals and caring about the role you play together in their future development. The caring will be so obvious that they won't be able to resist caring right back!

YOU'RE READY!

So, you're ready now to try out some of our ideas. As you've already noticed, some activities are quick and easy to implement (such as Activity 6.3, Tracing Bodies), whereas others require a longer-term commitment (such as Activity 7.4, Film Festival). Some set the tone of your classroom and will work best if put into practice right at the beginning of the school year (such as Activity 2.1, Language Masters) and others may work better near the end (such as Activity 7.2, World Cup Soccer). Some can be done within your own classroom (such as Activity 5.3, Telephoning) and others may be most effective if done collaboratively with other language classes or departments in your school (such as Activity 7.3, Gardening). This book is offered, not as a cookbook of ideas, but as the embodiment of a coherent, caring approach to language learning—one that motivates students to use the target language, to learn more about other cultures, to better understand themselves and relate to others, and to be responsible citizens in our global community.

We encourage you to consider offering a wide range of language play opportunities by setting up different physical spaces within your classroom or school areas to be used at different times. Think about how you can regroup students so that they really *do* need to learn from each other when they join other groups. Changing the types of activities will keep the classroom lively and expose learners to different types of language. Adding several shelves of everyday (possibly culturally authentic) objects and a closet full of secondhand clothes can spark learners' creativity and help to maintain an overall play frame in your classroom. Collaborating with faculty in your school's music, art, or drama departments may open up opportunities for the creation of playworlds outside the confines of their usual classroom space.

To encourage more students to enter into the playworld you've created and to take advantage of the language use opportunities it presents, try tipping the scale away from the routine. Solid expectations can be established first and then used as the basis for creative improvisation. Students' interest will be piqued by surprise. It will be difficult for them to remain uninvolved.

You can give students the courage to jump over their inhibitions into the fray of the playworld by keeping both learner and teacher identities fluid and wide-ranging. As you shift your identity from king to shop owner to artist, you become a different kind of conversational partner for your students. As your students shift their identities from newspaper reporter to athlete to museum curator, they will navigate between worlds that offer language use opportunities that go far beyond those available within the traditional roles of teacher and student.

We hope this book has sparked some ideas or has reminded you of activities you've wanted to do for quite some time. You have all the ingredients for success within you. Now it's time to stop reading and get back to your students. Have fun *doing* foreign language with them. And let us know how things go!

FOR FURTHER READING

Agar, M. (1994). *Language shock: Understanding the culture of conversation.* New York: Morrow.

Broner, M. A., & Tarone, E. E. (2001). Is it fun? Language play in a fifth-grade Spanish immersion classroom. *Modern Language Journal, 85,* 363–379.

Bruner, J. (1986). *Actual minds, possible worlds.* Cambridge, MA: Harvard University Press.

Celce-Murcia, M., & Olshtain, E. (2000). *Discourse and context in language teaching.* New York: Cambridge University Press.

Cook, G. (1997). Language play, language learning. *ELT Journal, 51,* 224–231.

Hamilton, H. E., & Cohen, A. D. (2004). Creating a playworld: Motivating learners to take chances in a second language. In J. M. Frodeson & C. A. Holten (Eds.), *The power of context in language learning and teaching* (pp. 237–247). Festschrift in Honor of Marianne Celce-Murcia. Boston: Heinle & Heinle.

Lantolf, J. (1997). The function of language play in the acquisition of L2 Spanish. In W. R. Glass & A. T. Perez-Leroux (Eds.), *Contemporary perspectives on the acquisition of Spanish* (pp. 3–24). Somerville, MA: Cascadilla Press.

Vygotsky, L. S. (1978). *Mind in society: The development of higher psychological processes.* Cambridge, MA: Harvard University Press.

1

Language Functions and Activities Sorted According to Activity

Activity Number	Activity	Language Function	Context
2.1	Language Masters	Asking for information Attracting someone's attention Expressing opinions Giving commands Giving directions Giving reasons Greeting Narrating Reporting Suggesting Taking leave	In the classroom
2.2	Superstar Obstacle Course	Expressing opinions Reporting Suggesting	In the classroom; independent work outside the classroom
2.3	Student Mentors	Attracting someone's attention Describing procedures Evaluating Expressing opinions Giving directions Greeting Introducing oneself Presenting information Suggesting Taking leave	In teaching training workshops; beyond-the-classroom practice sessions after school
2.4	Bob, the Imaginary Fly	Describing places Expressing opinions Giving reasons Narrating	In the classroom within multiple role-play contexts

(continued)

Only those functions that students practice are listed, not necessarily those that they are exposed to.

3.1	Discovering Student Interests	Evaluating Expressing opinions Suggesting	In the classroom
3.2	Students as Experts	Demonstrating procedures and processes Presenting information Reporting Suggesting	In the classroom
3.3	Creative Bulletin Boards	Presenting information Suggesting	In the classroom
3.4	Students' Rights and Responsibilities	Asking for and giving permission Expressing opinions Giving commands Giving reasons Suggesting	In the classroom
4.1	Space and Time Museum	Comparing and contrasting Describing objects Describing people Presenting information	In a museum
4.2	Living Maps	Comparing and contrasting Describing places Giving directions Giving reasons Presenting information	In the classroom
4.3	Culinary Explorations	Comparing and contrasting Describing objects Describing procedures Evaluating Expressing opinions Giving commands Giving directions Requesting	In a kitchen
4.4	Visiting Experts	Asking for information Expressing opinions Expressing thanks Greeting Introducing oneself Taking leave	In the classroom
5.1	School Tour	Describing places Giving directions (expansion) Narrating (expansion)	Outside the classroom within the school

5.2	Eating Out	Comparing and contrasting Complimenting, complaining, apologizing (expansion) Expressing thanks Greeting Making reservations Opening and closing an interaction Requesting Suggesting Taking leave	In a restaurant
5.3	Telephoning	Asking for information Comparing and contrasting (expansion) Greeting Introducing oneself Opening and closing an interaction Making dates or appointments	On the telephone
5.4	E-Mates	Comparing and contrasting Describing people Expressing opinions Introducing oneself Opening and closing an interaction	At the computer sending e-mails
6.1	Sensory Path	Asking for information Describing objects Giving commands Giving directions Narrating	In the classroom and outdoors
6.2	Dancing	Comparing and contrasting Describing procedures Giving directions (expansion)	On a dance floor
6.3	Tracing Bodies	Describing people Narrating (expansion) Presenting information	In the classroom and on a playground
6.4	Simulations	Asking for information Comparing and contrasting Describing people Describing places Describing processes Presenting information	In a new culture

(continued)

7.1	Newspaper	Asking for information (expansion) Comparing and contrasting Expressing opinions Narrating Reporting	In a newsroom
7.2	World Cup Soccer	Asking for information (expansion) Attracting someone's attention Comparing and contrasting Requesting	In the classroom and on a soccer field
7.3	Gardening	Describing objects Describing processes Giving reasons Reporting	In the classroom and in a garden
7.4	Film Festival	Describing people Evaluating Expressing opinions Giving directions Introducing someone else Narrating	From a movie studio to an awards ceremony

appendix 2

Language Functions and Activities Sorted According to Function

Language Functions	Activity	Page Number
Apologizing	5.2 Eating Out (expansion)	104
Asking for and giving permission	3.4 Students' Rights and Responsibilities	65
Attracting someone's attention	2.1 Language Masters 2.3 Student Mentors 7.2 World Cup Soccer	22 32 156
Comparing and contrasting	4.1 Space and Time Museum 4.2 Living Maps 4.3 Culinary Explorations 5.2 Eating Out 5.3 Telephoning 5.4 E-mates 6.2 Dancing 6.4 Simulations 7.1 Newspaper 7.2 World Cup Soccer	74 79 84 104 111 116 131 138 148 156
Complaining	5.2 Eating Out (expansion)	104
Complimenting	5.2 Eating Out (expansion)	104
Describing people	4.1 Space and Time Museum 5.4 E-Mates 6.3 Tracing Bodies 6.4 Simulations 7.4 Film Festival	74 116 135 138 168
Describing places	2.4 Bob, the Imaginary Fly 4.1 Space and Time Museum 4.2 Living Maps 5.1 School Tour 6.4 Simulations	39 74 79 99 138

(continued)

Only the functions that students practice are listed, not necessarily those that they are exposed to.

Introducing oneself	2.3 Student Mentors	32
	4.4 Visiting Experts	90
	5.3 Telephoning	111
	5.4 E-Mates	116
Introducing someone else	7.4 Film Festival	168
Making reservations or appointments	5.2 Eating Out	104
	5.3 Telephoning	111
Narrating	2.1 Language Masters	22
	2.4 Bob, the Imaginary Fly	39
	5.1 School Tour (expansion)	99
	6.1 Sensory Path	125
	6.3 Tracing Bodies (expansion)	135
	7.1 Newspaper	148
	7.4 Film Festival	168
Opening and closing an interaction	5.2 Eating Out	104
	5.3 Telephoning	111
	5.4 E-Mates	116
Presenting information	2.3 Student Mentors	32
	3.2 Students as Experts	54
	3.3 Creative Bulletin Boards	60
	4.1 Space and Time Museum	74
	4.2 Living Maps	79
	6.3 Tracing Bodies	135
	6.4 Simulations	138
Reporting	2.1 Language Masters	22
	2.2 Superstar Obstacle Course	27
	3.2 Students as Experts	54
	7.1 Newspaper	148
	7.3 Gardening	161
Requesting	4.3 Culinary Explorations	84
	5.2 Eating Out	104
Suggesting	2.1 Language Masters	22
	2.2 Superstar Obstacle Course	27
	2.3 Student Mentors	32
	3.1 Discovering Student Interests	46
	3.2 Students as Experts	54
	3.3 Creative Bulletin Boards	60
	3.4 Students' Rights and Responsibilities	65
	5.2 Eating Out	104
Taking leave	2.1 Language Masters	22
	2.3 Student Mentors	32
	4.4 Visiting Experts	90
	5.2 Eating Out	104

References

Agar, M. (1994). *Language shock: Understanding the culture of conversation*. New York: Morrow.

Asher, J. (1982). *Learning another language through actions: The complete teacher's guidebook* (2nd ed.). Los Gatos, CA: Sky Oaks Productions.

Banks, J. A., and Banks, C. M. (Eds.). (2004). *Multicultural education: Issues and perspectives*. Boston: Allyn and Bacon (see especially chapters by Erikson, "Culture in Society and Educational Practices" and Ovando, "Language Diversity in Education").

Blyth, C. (Ed.) (2003). *The sociolinguistics of foreign-language classrooms: Contributions of the native, the near-native, and the non-native speaker*. Boston: Heinle & Heinle.

Broner, M. A., & Tarone, E. E. (2001). Is it fun? Language play in a fifth-grade Spanish immersion classroom. *Modern Language Journal, 85,* 363–379.

Brown, H. D. (2000). *Principles of language learning and teaching* (4th ed). White Plains, NY: Pearson Education.

Brown, H. D. (2001). *Teaching by principles: An interactive approach to language pedagogy* (2nd ed.). Upper Saddle River, NJ: Prentice Hall Regents.

Bruner, J. (1986). *Actual minds, possible worlds*. Cambridge, MA: Harvard University Press.

Canale, M., & Swaim, M. (1980). Theoretical bases of communicative approaches to second language teaching and testing. *Applied Linguistics, 1,* 1–47.

Celce-Murcia, M. & Olshtain, E. (2000). *Discourse and context in language teaching*. New York: Cambridge University Press.

Chamot, A. U., Barnhardt, S., El-Dinary, P. B., & Robbins, J. (1999). *The learning strategies handbook*. White Plains, NY: Addison Wesley Longman.

Cook, G. (1997). Language play, language learning. *ELT Journal, 51,* 224–231.

Cook, G. (2000). *Language play, language learning*. New York: Oxford University Press.

Dornyei, Z. (2001). *Motivational strategies in the language classroom*. New York: Cambridge University Press.

Ellis, R. (2003). *Task-based language learning and teaching*. New York: Oxford University Press.

Fantini, A. E. (1999). Comparisons: Towards the development of intercultural competence. In J. K. Phillips (Ed.), *Foreign language standards: Linking research, theories, and practices* (pp. 165–218). Lincolnwood, IL: National Textbook Co.

Gardner, H. (1993). *Frames of mind: The theory of multiple intelligences* (10th ed.). New York: Basic Books.

Gardner, H. (1999). *Intelligence reframed: Multiple intelligences for the 21st century*. New York: Basic Books.

Grennon Brooks, J., & Brooks, M. G. (1993). *In search of understanding: The case for constructivist classrooms*. Alexandria, VA: Association for Supervision and Curriculum Development.

Hall, J. K. (2001). *Methods for teaching foreign languages: Creating a community of learners in the classroom*. Upper Saddle River, NJ: Prentice Hall.

Hamilton, H. E. (2004). Repair of teenagers' spoken German in a summer immersion program. In D. Boxer & A. D. Cohen (Eds.), *Studying speaking to inform second language learning* (pp. 88–114). Tonawanda, NY: Multilingual Matters Ltd.

Hamilton, H. E., & Cohen, A. D. (2005). Creating a playworld: Motivating learners to take chances in a second language. In J. M. Frodeson & C. A. Holten (Eds.), *The power of context in language learning and teaching* (pp. 237–247). Festschrift in Honor of Marianne Celce-Murcia. Boston: Heinle & Heinle.

Hebert, E. A. (2001). *The power of portfolios: What children can teach us about learning and assessment*. San Francisco: Jossey-Bass.

Kagan, S. (1989). *Cooperative learning: Resources for teachers*. Riverside: University of California.

Katz, L. G., & Chard, S. C. (2000). *Engaging children's minds: The project approach* (2nd ed.) Norwood, NJ: Ablex.

Klee, C. A., Lynch, A., Tarone, E. (1998). *Research and practice in immersion education: Looking back and looking ahead*. Selected Conference Proceedings. Minneapolis: University of Minnesota.

Kolb, D. A. (1984). *Experiential learning: Experience as the source of learning and development*. Upper Saddle River, NJ: Prentice Hall.

Kramsch, C. (1993). *Context and culture in language teaching*. New York: Oxford University Press.

Krashen, S. & Terrell, T. (1983). *The natural approach: Language acquisition in the classroom*. Hayward, CA: Alemany Press.

Lange, D. L. (1999). Planning for and Using the New National Culture Standards. In J. K. Phillips (Ed.), *Foreign language standards: Linking research, theories, and practices* (pp. 57–135). Lincolnwood, IL: National Textbook Co.

Lantolf, J. (1997). The function of language play in the acquisition of L2 Spanish. In W. R. Glass & A. T. Perez-Leroux (Eds.), *Contemporary perspectives on the acquisition of Spanish* (pp. 3–24). Somerville, MA: Cascadilla Press.

Lefevre, D. N. (2002). *Best new games: 77 games and 7 trust activities for all ages and abilities*. Champaign, IL: Human Kinetics.

Moss, D., and Van Duzer, C. (1998). Project-based learning for adult English language learners. ERIC Digest ED427556. Online at www.ericfacility.net/ericdigests/ed427556.html.

National Standards in Foreign Language Education Project. (1996). *Standards for foreign language learning: Preparing for the 21st century*. Yonkers, NY: American Council on the Teaching of Foreign Languages.

National Standards in Foreign Language Education Project. (1999). *Standards for foreign language learning in the 21st century*. Yonkers, NY: American Council on the Teaching of Foreign Languages (this revised version includes sections devoted to standards for the following languages: Chinese, Classics, French, German, Italian, Japanese, Portguese, Russian, and Spanish).

Nunan, D. (1998). *The learner-centered curriculum: A study in second language*. New York: Cambridge University Press.

Omaggio Hadley, A. (2001). *Teaching language in context* (3rd ed.). Boston: Heinle & Heinle (see especially chapters 5 and 8).

Savignon, S. J. (1997). *Communicative competence: Theory and classroom practice* (2nd ed.). New York: McGraw-Hill.

Skehan, P. (1989). *Individual differences in second-language learning.* New York: Routledge, Chapman and Hall.

Vygotsky, L. S. (1978). *Mind in society: The development of higher psychological processes.* Cambridge, MA: Harvard University Press.

Online Resources

HELPFUL WEB SITES

Chapter 1

To learn more about Concordia Language Villages, visit http://www.concordialanguagevillages.org

To learn more about the Standards for Foreign Language Learning published in 1996 by the American Council on the Teaching of Foreign Languages, go to www.actfl.org. Click on "Proficiency Guidelines" and then select "Standards for Foreign Language Learning: Executive Summary" under publications.

Rubrics: For help in creating your own materials to evaluate your students' progress and performance, visit http://www.rubistar.4teachers.org and http://www.school.discovery.com/schrockguide/assess.html and follow other leads from there.

Student Journals: See Cobine, G. B. (1995). Effective use of student journal writing. ERIC Digest online at http://www.ericfacility.net/ericdigests/ed378587.html

Chapter 2

The Web has endless examples of successful peer tutoring and mentoring programs, such as the Cross-Age and Peer Tutoring program outlined in the ERIC Clearinghouse digest on Reading, English, and Communication Digest #78: http://reading.indiana.edu/ieo/digests/d78.html

Valuable resources are available to language teachers through 14 federally funded Language Resources Centers. Start your exploration through the joint Web site at http://www.ed.gov/help/site/expsearch/language.html

Share ideas for encouraging learners with other language teachers on the FL-TEACH listserv: http://www.cortland.edu/flteach/flteach-res.html. The FL-TEACH Web site also includes a variety of links to language teaching and learning resources.

Chapter 3

Guide learners' research using a WebQuest: http://webquest.sdsu.edu/

A fun language-learning lesson plan for making rules with your students is on the Boggle's World Web site: http://bogglesworld.com/lessons/2002janfeb.htm

Chapter 4

Start getting ideas at the variety of museums that make up the Smithsonian Institution http://www.si.edu/; then check out Web sites for museums in regions where your target language is spoken, such as the Prado, Louvre, or Uffizi.

National Gallery of Art online tours in five languages (many of which can be downloaded as PDF files): http://www.nga.gov/onlinetours/onlinetr.htm

Check out the Global Schoolnet teacher annotated resource page for reference tools such as maps, language translators, measurement, time zone, and currency converters to supplement your lessons: http://www.globalschoolnet.org/resources/index.html

Find the map you're looking for at http://www.worldatlas.com

A magazine site, from any target culture, such as *America's Food and Wine*, http://www.foodandwine.com/, will provide great ideas for food-based lessons.

Would you like to bring target language television programming into your classroom? Contact SCOLA, a nonprofit educational consortium that receives and retransmits television programming from more than 70 countries at http://www.scola.org. SCOLA even offers a program called Insta-Class that prepares and distributes weekly lessons based on 5-minute transcripts of the programming in selected languages.

Yahoo! http://www.yahoo.com

Looking for authentic materials to expose students to the target language? The Web is an excellent source for articles, poems, music, travel guides, advertisements, and more. Check out Yahoo's International sites written entirely in the target language. The Internet makes finding up-to-date materials on target culture current events, famous people, arts, and popular culture easy and, in most cases, free.

Argentina *http://ar.yahoo.com*

Brazil *http://br.yahoo.com*

China *http://cn.yahoo.com/*

Denmark *http://dk.yahoo.com*

France *http://fr.yahoo.com/*

Germany *http://de.yahoo.com/*

Hong Kong *http://hk.yahoo.com*

Italy *http://it.yahoo.com/*

Japan *http://www.yahoo.com.jp*

Mexico *http://mx.yahoo.com*

Norway *http://no.yahoo.com/*

Spain *http://es.yahoo.com/*

Sweden *http://se.yahoo.com/*

Taiwan *http://tw.yahoo.com*

Association of College and Research Libraries provides a collection of literary texts in 17 Western European languages: http://www.lib.virginia.edu/wess/etexts.html

Covering animal vocabulary? Discover Sounds of the World's Animals. Make it a multimedia adventure by visiting Georgetown University's Sounds of the World's Animals Web site: http://www.georgetown.edu/faculty/ballc/animals/

Chapter 5

The wonderful list of guiding questions for speaking activities on The Internet TESL Journal Website can be used for all languages: http://iteslj.org/questions/

E-pals is one of the many commercial organizations that can put learners in touch. Visit http://www.epals.com

The Learning Scenarios Web page from the Languages Other than English Web site is a wonderful instructional resource that provides thematic, integrative units of study for foreign language teachers in Arabic, French, German, Japanese, Latin, Russian, and Spanish: *http://www.sedl.org/loteced/scenarios/welcome.html*

Chapter 6

Check out the Environmental Protection Agency's Environmental Kids Club at http://www.epa.gov/kids/ where you'll find wonderful teacher resources and student activities.

Stuck on how to find a dance you'd like to teach? Start by visiting http://www.humankinetics.com. Check out Christy Lane's *Multicultural Folk Dance Treasure Chest*, volumes 1 and 2, that includes videos and CDs as well as guides with background information and dance instructions. Also search for Web-based dance magazines from your target culture.

To find anatomical drawings and terms for Activity 6.3, start with *Gray's Anatomy* online at http://www.bartleby.com/107/ and then search for similar sites in your target language.

Supplement your simulations using information from the United Nations: http://www.un.org

To read an interview with Howard Gardner on his theory of multiple intelligences, go to http://www.nea.org/neatoday/9903/gardner.html

Chapter 7

The Internet Public Library, with links to hundreds of online newspapers from around the world, is a wonderful source for authentic materials: http://www.ipl.org/div/news/

Visit http://www.thecoachingcorner.com/soccer/index.html for information on the game of soccer, including a list of basic rules and player positions.

Find anything and everything you need to know about gardening on the American Community Gardening Association links: http://www.communitygarden.org/links/. Click on "Gardening with Children" and follow the numerous "School Gardens" links for wonderful ideas and illustrations.

Gather ideas about each step in the film-making process by visiting http://www.learners.org/exhibits/cinema. Then check out the Academy Awards Web site at http://www.oscar.com and do a Web search for film festivals held in regions where your target language is spoken.